WHAT PEOPLE ARE

T0303097

GOING BEYOND T

GOING BEYOND THE JESUS STORY *is an impressive and thought-provoking work. Drawing on a wealth of scholarly material, the book develops its arguments in a way that is both engaging and accessible. It not only connects contemporary religious and theological ideas with recent work in the philosophy of mind and consciousness, but also shows how much there is still to be gained from the mystical and contemplative traditions, as well as from other more esoteric sources. Lockhart's conclusions connect with some of the most innovative current thinking about meaning, mind and self arguing for a view of human existence as neither wholly internalised nor wholly externalised, but as constituted in the 'between' of mind and world in a way that encompasses both.*
Jeff Malpas, Professor of Philosophy and ARC Professorial Fellow, University of Tasmania, Distinguished Visiting Professor, LaTrobe University

This is an invitation to an exciting journey of exploration of one's self and its very core . . . [Douglas Lockhart] invites you to examine Christianity . . . as an experience of awakening and self-understanding. At this time of rampant religious fundamentalisms, this journey is as refreshing as it is irresistible – even for religious skeptics and scientific rationalists.
Professor Jan Pakulski, School of Sociology and Social Work, University of Tasmania, Australia.

I've finally got round to reading [Douglas Lockhart's] marvellous book. The body, sensation, and above all awareness of presence are, for me, the cornerstone of anything I might call "spirituality", [and the] energy of present, conscious awareness comes crackling off the page.
Dr. Peter Batty, (Historian) University of Southampton

In this remarkably clear and original study . . . Douglas Lockhart develops a persuasive case for rescuing Christianity's "lost" religious heritage through a transformation of its form and a powerful re-evaluation of its fundamental categories.

[This] leads Lockhart to the creation of a revolutionary philosophical and anthropological outlook which has not yet been assimilated by academic philosophy of mind and religion.

Nuanced and convincingly supported, this work foregrounds a complex spectrum of impulses from contemporary consciousness studies to gnosis and mysticism.

Yet Lockhart's patient elucidations are written in a wonderfully limpid style. They arguably rank at the same time among the chief monuments of contemporary humanism scholarship as they deploy a modern, unorthodox and highly thought provoking new take on faith, freedom, self-appropriation and the human soul.

Marcelo R. Stamm, PD Dr. phil. habil. Senior Research Fellow, Director Creativity Research Project AIRC Australian Innovation Research Centre Adjunct Professor, Munich University, LMU München Senior Research Fellow, Venice International University VIU

Thank you very much for sending me a copy of Going Beyond the Jesus Story *by Douglas Lockhart. I found it thought provoking. Please do give my... congratulations to Douglas Lockhart. I am sure that Douglas realizes that the fundamentalists in any religion are not so easily moved by... arguments or evidence. Still, one needs to do the right thing. I am glad he has written what he has.*

Ravi Ravindra, Emeritus Professor of Comparative Religion & Physics, Dalhousie University, Halafax, Canada.

A welcome change from the current stream of anti-religious works a la Dawkins. Dump religion by all means, but don't dump the experiences from which religion grew in the first place.

Kim McCaul, (Anthropologist) University of Adelaide, Australia.

Developing themes explored in his earlier books, Douglas Lockhart argues that instead of immersing ourselves in constrictive dogma we should be focusing our attention on spiritual awakening. True salvation... is to be found in the depths of our being. Highly recommended.

Dr. Nevill Drury, author of *Stealing Fire from Heaven* and *Wisdom Seekers*.

Douglas Lockhart offers us a beautifully written, wide-ranging, and thoroughly absorbing exploration of the deeper reaches of contemplative thought and practice. Here you will find an inspired and inspiring guide to the nondoctrinal core of contemplative experience; of what it means fully to be present in the present.

Professor Warwick Fox, School of Philosophy, University of Central Lancashire, UK.

Going Beyond the Jesus Story

An Examination of Christian Beliefs, Mystical Experience & the Ongoing Development of Conscious Awareness

Going Beyond the Jesus Story

An Examination of Christian Beliefs, Mystical Experience & the Ongoing Development of Conscious Awareness

Douglas Lockhart

BOOKS

Winchester, UK
Washington, USA

First published by O-Books, 2011
O-Books is an imprint of John Hunt Publishing Ltd., Laurel House, Station Approach,
Alresford, Hants, SO24 9JH, UK
office1@o-books.net
www.o-books.com

For distributor details and how to order please visit the 'Ordering' section on our website.

Text copyright: Douglas Lockhart 2010

ISBN: 978 1 84694 465 9

All rights reserved. Except for brief quotations in critical articles or reviews, no part of this book may be reproduced in any manner without prior written permission from the publishers.

The rights of Douglas Lockhart as author have been asserted in accordance with the Copyright, Designs and Patents Act 1988.

A CIP catalogue record for this book is available from the British Library.

Design: Tom Davies

Printed in the UK by CPI Antony Rowe
Printed in the USA by Offset Paperback Mfrs, Inc

We operate a distinctive and ethical publishing philosophy in all areas of our business, from our global network of authors to production and worldwide distribution.

CONTENTS

Acknowledgements

I owe a special debt of thanks to my partner Robin Mosley for her endless patience, support and helpful observations as this book progressed, and Robert Cox for his skilful editing when all was complete. Also Jacob Needleman, whose book *Lost Christianity* inspired me to pen my own thoughts on Christianity's obscured premise; Bernadette Roberts for her extraordinary courage and clarity when writing of the contemplative state; Jeff Malpas for his incisive intellectual support and encouragement as I wrestled with this book's contents, and Jan Pakulski for his many insightful comments. Also many thanks to scholars of the Westar Institute in the USA for their rigor in dealing with New Testament problems; and, similarly, the many scholars who have contributed their challenging books and papers to the *Journal of Consciousness Studies* for peer evaluation and review. And last, but not least, my thanks to the late Father Sylvan, Jacob Needleman's mysterious mentor, whose grasp of psychological priorities greatly assisted me in the development of my central theme. Whatever their input, however, those mentioned cannot in any way be held responsible for what follows, that is my responsibility alone.

D.G.L.

Introduction

The greatest derangement of the mind is to believe in something because one wishes it to be true.
Louis Pasteur

I can remember believing all sorts of things about Jesus when I was young. I believed that he was God, yet at the same time independent of God. That in conjunction with the Holy Spirit he was part of a divine threesome, yet somehow God in his own right when praying to the Father aspect of that threesome. I believed he could walk on water, still storms with an upraised hand, conjure bread and fish out of thin air and, when pushed, change water into wine.

Content with the stories of how he had healed the sick and raised the dead, I trundled on through adolescence oblivious to the fact that the miraculous events in Jesus' life flatly contradicted everything I was learning at school. What I was learning at school belonged to a different realm of mental activity. Enthralled by the idea of this wonderful man wandering around Palestine working miracles on a regular basis, I accepted *all* of the New Testament's stories about Jesus without question.

I found this easy to do because the adults in my life either reinforced the New Testament's claims about Jesus, or never saw fit to question them. Jesus was untouchable. He was all good, all knowing, all wise, all loving, and he had sacrificed himself on the cross of Calvary for my sins. This had been his mission while on Earth, his farsighted plan hatched by himself before the world had come into existence. As God he had conceived of the idea that he, in the form of Jesus, would be born as a babe in Bethlehem and die on a crude Roman cross crying: "My God, my God, why hast thou forsaken me?" In fact the whole of human history and religious experience prior to that event had been no more than a limbering up exercise, a preparation for that moment in time when God himself would break into history as a human being.

On the cross Jesus experienced a loss of his God identity yet managed, at the same time, to rescue humanity from the torments of a hell reserved for those who rejected Christianity's claim that it held the definitive revelation. A place of punishment existed for those who rejected or ignored the Church's interpretation of the Gospels and Paul's letters, and it made sense to accept the proclamation that God had sacrificed himself to himself on behalf of all human beings alive then and now. What a mystery it all was. How could we ever hope to understand or appreciate why God had thought up such an extraordinary scheme?

And that was that. Nothing else was required beyond going along with this scheme. Yes, you should thank God, or Jesus, at regular intervals for his gift of salvation, but apart from prayer and praise and living a good life, the show was over. We were off the hook. There was no more to the spiritual life than that. When God looked at a believer, what he saw was his own saving act while extended into the world as Jesus. All we had to do was believe that this was so, tell other people, live a moral life and our spiritual destiny was secure.

And to make sure everyone stayed on the Christian path, Jesus/God had risen from the dead, ascended physically into the sky and returned from heaven as the "Holy Spirit" to influence the minds of all future believers. All in all a remarkable story which, if accepted without question, had the power to change lives.

Now there is no doubt whatsoever that those who invest belief in the Jesus story reap substantial rewards in this life. There is immense satisfaction in believing that when you die you are going to live in the presence of God/Jesus for all eternity, and that you have been saved from everlasting punishment in hell. For that is where unbelievers go; they go down to hell; whereas believers go up to heaven. And when you think about it, this is a quite sensible scenario, for the good have to be separated from the bad, don't they?

Strange as it seems to me now, I used to believe in hell, and it seemed perfectly natural to do so. As a youngster I believed in hell and the devil, and saw no need to doubt or question such an arrangement. And I believed that God wanted it that way, that he unwillingly, but inevitably, was forced to turn his back on unbelievers and leave them to experience unimaginable horror for having rejected the Jesus story. The Jesus story was divinely revealed truth; to reject it was to reject God's revelation to the whole of humanity.

I must have been around eighteen when it began to dawn on me that there were a lot of people in the world for whom the Jesus story could never be anything other than a story like any other story. Moslems, Jews and Hindus had their own stories, and although just as miraculous in content as the Gospels, the idea of Jesus being God, and therefore worthy of worship on a universal scale, was not part of their faith tradition. And the old idea that they should be persuaded to change their minds was no longer tenable – missionary work was now viewed as anti-cultural, a remnant of the bad old days of colonialism. We believed what we believed because of geography and upbringing, because our culture was saturated with a particular set of religious ideas, not because these ideas were indisputably true.

In light of what is now known about our world, and the universe, the approach of many Christians today is to say that Jesus could not have walked on water or stilled storms. The world has never been God's play thing, they will tell you. It is a law-governed domain in which even God can't interfere in a willy-nilly fashion. With the help of medicine and a little psychology the sick can certainly be healed, but Jesus' talents had never at any time extended to bringing the truly dead back to life. As a man of flesh and blood, he had been bound by the same fundamental laws as everyone else. A Jesus raising the dead or sailing majestically off into the heavens was acceptable as poetry, or as metaphor, but if taken as factual, such stories disabled the Bible's "poetic truth."

Fundamentalist and evangelical believers in the Jesus story are understandably nervous about "poetic truth" – it just doesn't have the same ring as *revealed truth.* A poetized Jesus is a Jesus reduced to human standards. When applied to the New Testament, poetry and metaphor absorb its shimmering energy and make Jesus into no more than a divinely inspired man. No, God obviously expects us to believe in the highly improbable Jesus story as it has come down to us, and it is the act of abandoning ourselves to such improbable religious ideas that makes the whole thing work. At least that's the theory. God's plan of salvation is, as St. Paul suggests, a foolishness to the unbeliever, and we have to believe in this foolishness to pass the test of faith.

When it comes to Christians trained in science or philosophy, however, only a handful seem capable of sustaining any level of belief in a Jesus who walked on water, or in a God who ignores his own laws. Carefully qualified statements are suddenly rife. The events of the New Testament are sifted and subjected to historical, psychological or alternative theological analysis, the Jesus story made to undergo radical scrutiny and reinterpretation.

In light of what is now known about the early history of the primitive Church, and of Christianity as it grew and developed in Rome, never mind the extraordinary advances made in human knowledge since Jesus walked the streets of Jerusalem, reasonably aware people are under obligation to rethink past conceptions of the Jesus story. To believe that every jot and tittle of that story should be taken literally not only jeopardizes their capacity to grow and mature as people, it also endangers the lives of others in terms of the conflicts it so easily generates. The idea of "Christian soldiers marching as to war" takes on a whole new, deadly significance.

Knowing what we now know about our solar system, the nature of the universe, gravity, and much else besides, it stands to reason that Jesus did not, could not, and even if he had been God would not have ascended into the sky as the New Testament record states. As a man of flesh and blood, Jesus was bound by the same fundamental laws of nature as everyone else. Such ideas belong to a time long since gone, an age when human beings believed all kinds of extraordinary things. To qualify as spiritual, should we really be expected to lay aside our education, our commonsense and our experience of the world and submit our minds to what is no more than pious exaggeration? In saying this I'm not suggesting an abandonment of Christianity. I'm suggesting, in conjunction with many another, a rescuing of our religious heritage and a renewal of its form.

I'm also suggesting that Christianity's faith tradition, when it is of the literalist variety, is doing a disservice to Jesus' message when it sells us the stock-in-trade Jesus story. Jesus was not schizophrenically alluding to himself when he talked about, or to, his Father in Heaven, he was pointing beyond himself. The idea that faith is composed of beliefs *about* Jesus, or God, or the Church, is a misinterpretation of what faith is in its essence – an opening up, not a closing down, of the self. Faith is not about circumscribed 'beliefs', it is about 'trust'. Not trust in a God who interferes in human history, a God who takes sides, a God willing to torment a particular group of human beings for all eternity, but in our intuition of something inexplicable in the depths of human nature.

This God has no face, no body, and no plan in mind. In fact this God does not have a mind. This God transcends the human in all aspects. He has no eyes, no nose, no mouth, no tongue, no larynx and, subsequently, no voice. And he isn't a he. In fact this God does not actually exist in any sense that we can understand. Perhaps this is why the God of the conscious mind, the constructed God of belief is described as a jealous God, a God who loves and hates. He is just us in our intellectual and emotional infancy inflated to enormous proportions.

In terms of faith renewal, it is interesting to note that Christian contemplatives often challenge theology's circumscribed conception of deity and invite a different evaluation of spiritual truth. Literalist definitions are out, ambiguity is in. Certainty of belief is out, the dark night of the soul is in. Struggling to comprehend the spiritual life, the contemplative descends into the darkness of the self and is confronted with the possibility that Christianity's essence is quite different from what he or she has supposed it to be. The God of surface consciousness evaporates and is replaced by an altogether different experience of spiritual reality, a reality that challenges pet assumptions.

But such a possibility cannot be realized if we believe that spiritually everything that has to be done has already been done by Jesus on our behalf. If this is the end of the matter for us, then there is no need to approach the challenging darkness of our inner life, or the challenging obscurity of a world as yet only partly understood, no need to penetrate beneath the surface of manmade doctrines or face up to the fact that belief in the Church's interpretation of the Jesus story has, throughout the centuries, caused the death of millions of human beings. To slavishly believe in that story is to ignore the fact that our faith tradition has, to say the very least, been found wanting, and that belief in a "menu of beliefs" about Jesus is, in terms of method, spiritually deficient.

In this context we may believe that Jesus/God is speaking to us directly through the Holy Spirit. This idea hides a multitude of sins; it is a form of wishful thinking. The mind plays tricks on itself, and the idea that divinity in some shape or form is whispering inside our heads has to be seen for what it is – a potentially dangerous delusion. Yet it is a claim made by many Christians, a claim used by them to bolster the notion of a special one-to-one relationship with Jesus/God that annuls doubt, renders questioning obsolete and furnishes them with the equivalent of a cosmic telephone. Convinced that their beliefs about

Jesus are beyond contradiction, they do not notice the dangers inherent in their situation.

This is not to gainsay the still small voice of Elijah's experience; it is to highlight the improbability of that voice turning into a radio broadcast. To me, the still small voice is that which arises during great sorrow or suffering, or in times of great challenge, or in a deeply observant or creative moment. It is a presence at the heart of life, it is deeply compassionate, and it is available to everyone.

This "presence" is what the Christian contemplative understands as the presence of God, and it is intricately related to our own felt presence. Lost most of the time in thought or deed, we only occasionally become aware of ourselves (and others) as a living presence, and as a result seldom touch upon what underpins or supports the self we assume ourselves to be. In this sense, to become aware of the self is to go beyond the self. It is to discover that the fleeting and ever-so-delicate sense of self which occasionally arises within us is more than a mere waking up to where we are, or to who we are, but also an intimation of what we are in the depths of our natures.

Let me say again that I am not trying to demote the Christian vision; I am trying to restate and reinstate what lies at Christianity's core – the discovery that the human and the divine are closely related. The God/Jesus nexus points to the possibility of a relationship with our own depths that can, as St. Paul was well aware, inform and transform the conscious mind. But not in some miraculous, magical fashion through a blood sacrifice. The divine is not an elderly super-being stationed in a dimension beyond our ken, or a god-man stranded in history. It is something deeply transformative at the heart of our common humanity.

Douglas Lockhart
Tasmania
May, 2010

PART ONE: BETWIXT SELF AND NO-SELF

1: The Veil of Illusion

I am learning to see. I do not know why it is, but everything penetrates more deeply within me and no longer stops at the place, where until now, it always used to finish. I possess an inner self of which I was ignorant. Everything now passes in thither. What happens there I know not.
Rainer Maria Rilke
The Notebooks of Malte Laurids Brigge

Intro: 1.0

Existence is a puzzle. If we're religious in the Christian sense, then that puzzle falls into a neat, manageable set of beliefs and observances. If non-religious, then into a pattern where we accept the vicissitudes of life and invest meaning in ourselves and in our fellow human beings. If a believer in some aspect of New Age philosophy, then we sail along as part of a mysterious "larger meaning" carrying multiple explanations and choices, and if an aimless *I don't give a damn about anything* type of person, then we simply struggle through as best we can. These categories, rough as they are, describe the majority of people living in the world's different cultures, and in that similarity lies our common humanity, our common search for truth, and our equally common disregard for truth.

The ultimate question facing all of us, of course, is this: Is there any such thing as a final, all-revealing truth, or is truth always bitty and piecemeal? Will science's "Theory of Everything" reveal a final truth that encapsulates and explains religion, or is it that religious experience holds within it the answer science refuses to accept? Or is there a halfway house in such matters? Might it be that science and religion will one day acknowledge each other's strengths and form a pact that allows the best of each to surface? Or will Richard Dawkins and

Christopher Hitchens have their way at the expense of Paul Davies and other winners of the Templeton Prize? These are some of the questions facing us as we move erratically into the 21st century, and we should perhaps attempt to answer them speedily if we want to survive as a species.

The question of truth can of course be put another way: is there a God, or are we humans alone in our quest for meaning? This question divides us as surely as gender does, and past attempts by theologians, philosophers and scientists to answer it have delivered up a mountain of material few of us will ever have the time, the patience, or even the inclination, to wade through. Yet the question remains, and the fact that it is probably a non-question, a question that no one can ultimately answer because one would almost have to be God to supply a satisfactory answer, does not deter us from trying to sneak up on this question by some other route. There are tantalizing clues scattered in unexpected places, and researchers both religious and secular sometimes feel themselves to be on the verge of a breakthrough.

One such group of researchers is beavering away on behalf of the Westar Institute, an organization in the US dedicated to the task of spreading religious literacy in the world. Composed of around two hundred internationally respected Biblical scholars, philosophers and historians of religion, Westar's Fellows are known as the Jesus Seminar, and they have in their time galvanized religious opinion with some startling observations and pronouncements. Some co-religionists denounce them as heretics, others laud them for unflinchingly taking on the difficult questions and accepting the often difficult-to-accept answers they come up with. With such well-known figures as Don Cupitt, Bishop Shelby Spong, Lloyd Geering, Karen Armstrong and Karen King in their midst, this is a formidable troupe of scholars who have put their reputations on the line for the sake of religious truths that are both credible and useful in the modern world.

But there are also hundreds, if not thousands, of secular scholars equally intent on pursuing answers to the really hard questions arising in religion, science and philosophy. These scholars are involved in research projects to do with mind, body, emotion, perception, experience and the nature of the self, and regularly share their theories and discoveries in learned papers for the benefit of the whole academic community. As with Westar scholars, they are not afraid of a fight; they will and do attack one another's ideas in their search for the underlying truths of a reality that is proving itself daily to be even more complex than previously supposed. Self, other and world are not the straightforward targets of investigation they had at intervals hoped. They are curiously intertwined, one with the other, and are resisting attempts to be teased apart.

Strange as it may seem, some research projects in the secular area are concerned with definitions of God, mysticism, the soul, cosmic consciousness, meditation, death, morality, out-of-body experience, lucid dreaming, the paranormal and a whole gamut of other fascinating subjects of a religious or semi-religious nature. Hardly anything is left out. These researchers are not, on the whole, prejudiced against religion; they consider its claims in the light of what is known about reality, and demand, rightly, that a language and methodology be created whereby such claims can be coherently verified and tested. Some say that that is simply not possible, that religious experience does not lend itself to the harsh light of scientific or philosophical scrutiny. But what if science and philosophy prove themselves capable of empathy? What if some scientists and philosophers are also advanced meditators/contemplators capable of tracking their experiences, or the experiences of others, into the depths of consciousness? What if some philosophers, psychologists and physicists have encountered realms of experience difficult to explain by the usual yardstick of their own professions? What then? And if, as I've discovered, the term "spiritual" is often just a way of naming and controlling what we do not really understand, then what are the possibilities if religious scholars link up with their so-called secular brethren in the quest for an understanding of existence that fully acknowledges its astonishing depths?

The philosopher Don Cupitt is a case in point. Now retired from his post as Dean of Immanuel College, Cambridge, he manages to integrate religion, science and philosophy in a manner that challenges pet assumptions and enlightens not a little. And there are many others. The ongoing debate between science, religion and the humanities is, for instance, richly portrayed in the *Journal of Consciousness Studies*, a source I've consulted regularly while writing this book, and in other technical journals of similar status. Taking on the important questions religion forces to the surface, these on-the-whole secular researchers give of their best in an attempt to unravel who we are, what we are, and why we are as we are, three questions religion has long considered its special province. But that, as we shall see, is no longer the case: the doors of perception have been thrown open, and we have little alternative but to step through whichever door happens to confronts us.

In the sleeve notes for *The Sea of Faith,* Don Cupitt's 1984 book dealing with the decline of supernatural religion, Matthew Arnold's metaphor of religious decline as the "melancholy, long, withdrawing roar" of the Sea of Faith is used by the publisher to perfectly capture Cupitt's notion that Christianity's dogmatic beliefs are worn out and in need of replacement. But with what? With "a spiritual path, an ethic, and a way of giving meaning to life," according to the same sleeve note. Religion is a human construction, so it should be practiced without dogma in alignment with "the twentieth century's bleak view of man's place in the universe." We are alone and must muster our own resources in the face of a universe that may, as Einstein posited, be unfriendly to our needs.

But Cupitt is not all doom and gloom; he suspects there may also be gains in the sense of "unexpected continuities."[1] But what exactly are "unexpected continuities", and how might they help? Well, in Cupitt's terms the answer lies in our collective "sense of loss," a sense of loss that is only temporary; the "leap of faith" required of us now is that of embracing ambiguity and uncertainty in the sure knowledge that we will eventually answer the questions we currently cannot answer. Continuity of meaning will return if we can find the courage to hang in there. What was "given up will come back, though transformed and seen from a new viewpoint."[2]

For Cupitt, critical thinking should reject dogma; it should question and undermine fixed ideas. René Descartes' confidence should be our confidence. A comprehensive critique of tradition has freed us from supernaturalisms and the headaches of theologians are well-deserved. But as Cupitt is quick to point out, theologians are attempting to straighten out the whole mess; they are busy fighting off the advances of philosophers and scientists while at the same time doing battle with the faithful over changes they know in their heart of hearts cannot any longer be avoided.[3]

Going Beyond Paradigm Shift 1.1

According to the historian Morris Berman, "cyclical recurrence of heresy implies the possibility of a different future."[4] New futures in the sense of heretical breaks, ruptures and realignments with the past are necessary and unavoidable. They are, however, "rarely anticipated by those living at the time"; they surprise us in exactly the way the twentieth and twenty-first centuries' heretical agenda has surprised churchmen.[5] Witness their concern over what they consider New Age heresies, or their astonishment over pronouncements made by scholars whose publications have progressively stripped the Gospel Jesus of his divinity. It is as if the very idea of Jesus being no more than a human being fulfilling a role in Jewish society has come out of nowhere, whereas in reality it has been gathering momentum for at least a hundred and fifty years. As with climate change and the possibility of a tipping point in weather patterns, so with ideas about Jesus and Christianity's deeper meanings. We are fast approaching a point of no return, a point of dramatic, irreversible change where our pet notions about Christianity and its founder will undergo a metamorphosis. But it isn't the ideas in themselves that are frightening churchmen. It is their shared sense that the tipping point has finally been reached, that the game of theological hide-and-seek is all but over. Cupitt puts it thus:

> When we have fully accepted these ideas and have freed ourselves from nostalgia for a cosmic Father Christmas, then our faith can at last become fully human, existential, voluntary, pure, and free from superstition. To reach this goal is Christianity's destiny, now approaching.[6]

But alas, such changes to the way in which we perceive reality may not deliver us from the habit of re-entrenching ourselves in other limited and limiting paradigms. Escape from misconceptions about reality will certainly take place, and that will be valuable, but when all is said and done we will, as has happened numerous times in our history, find ourselves returning to the selfsame questions in new guise. We will have shrugged off much that was holding us back from the clarity we crave, but that very clarity will again prove insufficient as we head deeper into our new future. We may very well find, as Morris Berman suggests in his seminal book *Coming to Our Senses,* that we have swapped "Descartes' clock for Von Neumann's computer" and failed to notice the similarity.[7]

Churchmen will nod their heads sagely at such thinking, but it applies as much to them as it does to any other professional group, and with a twist. Moves towards modernity in church doctrine will be viewed by conservative churchmen as destructive of Christianity's inner core, but that may not be the case. An updated theology that uses real history in place of tradition will certainly cancel out most, if not all, of Christianity's supernatural idiosyncrasies, but will it satisfy, as Cupitt undoubtedly thinks it will, our deep longing for, well, whatever it is we seem to have a deep longing for? Berman captures this point succinctly when he says, "far more important than finding a new paradigm is coming face to face with the immense yearning that underlies the need for paradigm itself." Paradigm shifts in history are vital staging posts in our growth and development as human beings, but they can also be "gap-filling" devices that allow us to continue much as before. If really serious about change, then what we have to explore is not so much what is *in* a paradigm, but what we fear most, "the empty space or silence that exists between concepts and paradigms."[8] The controversial Catholic contemplative Bernadette Roberts puts it this way:

> The ideal... is to begin our investigation with no prior assumptions, paradigms or belief systems regarding self and to allow the experiencing self to ultimately reveal its own eternal or non-eternal status, reveal its own origin and end. This way we avoid premature closure which only keeps the subject moving in an endless, pointless, self-perpetuating circle." [9]

Cupitt's notion that all we require is a paradigm shift to offset, in religious terms, our "sense of loss" with regard to faith, may not be sufficient in itself to bring about that intrinsic change in perspective we require to survive as a species. He himself is aware of this deficiency when he says: "All theories are merely man-made and provisional. Sooner or later the time will come when they will be found wanting."[10] But Cupitt's hope is, I think, that this ongoing process of reasoned replacement will eventually deliver the goods, a process he links to religious wakening in the sense of "an inner path of renunciation and progressive purging of illusions."[11] It is critical thinking that will release us from our stupidity, and that is to do "in a modern way the kind of demolition job that was done by the prophets and teachers of old."[12]

Given the dangers we face in terms of climate and rampant religiosity, a new arrangement of symbols and signs attractive to our 21st century mentalities may not be enough to save us in the end. Yes, our technical abilities will advance beyond our wildest dreams, as will our capacity to answer some of the most obdurate questions of our time, but our tendency to drift out of control even as we gasp at our own brilliance will also undoubtedly gather momentum, and that will distort and disable our most ambitious utopian hopes and desires for the future. The intrinsic change in perspective required for our survival as a species may not reside in swapping one set of ideas for another, but in confronting what it is in our makeup that endlessly hinders us in our search for truth and collective sanity. We are so clever, yet at the same time so dumb it is a wonder we've even made it this far.

Self-realization and Presence 1.2

But Don Cupitt is perhaps not all that far behind Berman concerning the long-term relativity of ideas. He tells us that religion's earlier forms were "collectivist", whereas its newer forms are "more concerned with self-realization."[13] Self-realization requires the "painted veil of illusion" to drop away, and that in turn requires from us a concerted effort to become more aware than we previously have been. But what does becoming "more aware" mean in real terms? Is it simply a matter of spotting anomalies in our reasoning, or in the reasoning of another, or of having a greater grasp of the sociology and psychology of our culture? Or is it to undergo change in the depths of our being to such an extent that we can, as Carl Jung suggested decades ago, step out of the historical process altogether? I doubt that anything as radical as that was in Cupitt's mind when he wrote these words, but there's no doubting Berman's take on this point when he tells us that it is only "real presence, real bodily engagement with the world" that will free us from our inbuilt intellectual limitations.[14] This strikes me as being well beyond "paradigm shift"; it is to articulate a premise that at first glance does not seem to make much sense, and at second glance causes us to feel decidedly uneasy. The human body as an instrument of change in its own right? What could such a directive possibly mean?

At the conclusion of *Jesus the Heretic,* my first book dealing with the origins and development of Christianity, I drew attention to Jacob Needleman, an American philosopher who helped clarify for me the heavily obscured spiritual premise of Christianity.[15] Having identified perceptual processes not generally associated with the Christian message, Needleman spoke of an energy within the self that required the development of "attention" or, as he so carefully rendered it, *the force of attention.* Carrying his readers far beyond Christianity's virtue-bound theories of the spiritual life, he offered a radically different interpretation of Christianity's basic premise. At its most fundamental level, Christianity was not about "salvation", "redemption" or "transcendence", he said, it was about reconnecting us with our "somatic depths", and through that enlivening experience with the creative energies of Being. As I had already happened upon a similarly oriented scheme of thinking in the writings of the Harley Street surgeon Kenneth Walker, I was immediately intrigued.[16]

As with Needleman, Walker homed in on "attention" and "awareness", suggested that human beings were not properly conscious even when apparently fully conscious, and with a little help from the psychologist William James triggered off in me the disconcerting realization that I too did not seem to be fully conscious most of the time. As this was the same basic conclusion come to by Needleman in relation to what he perceived as "advanced monastic thinking", I did a double take, for through a study of Christian heresy I had already reached the conclusion that there was much more to Christianity than most Christians realized. Reading this philosopher's text with care (I had learned early on that it is one thing to agree with someone, but quite another to agree with them for same set of reasons), I found that we were in fact on the same track: our mutual premise stemmed from the experiential work associated with the relatively unknown Armenian thinker George Ivanovitch Gurdjieff. Knowledge of Gurdjieff had arrived for Needleman via the writings of a certain Father Sylvan (an amazing story in itself, and one we will return to later), and for me via Kenneth Walker, whose'50s book carried the name "Gurdjieff" in its title. The enigmatic Mr. Gurdjieff, it seemed, was our mutual key, Christianity the lock into which this intricately cut key fitted.

As I completed my research for this my third book dealing with Christianity's dilemmas, I literally stumbled over Morris Berman's 1990 Bantam edition of *Coming to Our Senses* on the floor of a local bookshop, and as I flicked through its pages I knew I had been favored by the gods yet again. I should say immediately that I do not think for one second that this encounter was somehow arranged by Fate; it was simply a book that had fallen from a shelf and I just happened to be the person to pick it up. But certainly fortunate, there's no doubting that; for as I discovered on reading this well-written, well-argued text, Berman had traversed much the same territory as myself, and his conclusion was all but identical to the one I was busy formulating.

According to Berman, we had come to deny, or ignore, the importance of our physicality. Our bodies had become no more than biological mechanisms to be prodded at and manipulated by medicos. It was as simple as that; or as profound as that if you appreciated what had been going on century by century. Our physical experience of the world, embedded as it was in the larger culture, had been usurped. We had taken on the position of artificial intelligence advocates and accepted Douglas Hofstadter's opinion that dreams were no more than "confused brain patterns". We had accepted "cybernetic holism" and "systems-theory analysis" as the defining paradigm for the 21st century, and were in danger of succumbing to a new totalitarianism.[17] And even more importantly, we had all but ceased to sense our bodies as an important source of information. The somatic level of experience, the still small voice of our physical existence had been dumbed down, its visceral voice all but silenced.

What surprised me about Berman's study was his mention of G.I. Gurdjieff *and* Jacob Needleman. Gurdjieff was referred to in the rather odd context of having "possibly" instructed Himmler's Jew-hating prodigy, Gregor Schwartz-Bostunitsch (formerly known as Grigorij Bostunic) in occult practices, whereas Needleman was hailed as the writer of *Lost Christianity,* a book dealing with the "bitter and recurrent struggle of heresy vs. orthodoxy." Later, however, Berman also linked Gurdjieff to Needleman, and this led him to speak of "presence" in the context of our physical engagement with the world."[18] As "presence" or "presencing" had been the underlying theme of Walker's book, and Walker's whole approach to the mind/body problem was based, like Needleman's, on Gurdjieff's ideas, I knew we were heading into difficult territory. Knowledge of Gurdjieff's philosophical system had arrived for Morris Berman via Jacob Needleman, for Needleman via Father Sylvan, and for me via Kenneth Walker. Gurdjieff was therefore our mutual touchstone, his observations what had driven all four of us to explore what it meant to be a fully conscious human being

The Enigmatic Mr. Gurdjieff 1.3

G.I. Gurdjieff was, however, a man with an unusual history and a perplexing reputation. Born into the Greek quarter of Alexandropol, in Russian Armenia, in or around 1866,[19] he had gone on to become a major influence in the lives of many prominent individuals. Viewed as a charlatan by others, or just plain crazy, he nevertheless left an indelible mark on many of the most able minds of his time. In the sleeve note to a biographical study of Gurdjieff, James Moore describes him as a "potent myth (offering) sundry ill-assorted Gurdjieffs: heroic man of action; new Pythagoras, seeming charlatan; poet of surreal situations; white magician; black magician."[20] Louis Pauwels follows suit in his not always flattering portrait of Gurdjieff by asking colorfully: "Was Gurdjieff the satanist who designed the inverted swastika for Hitler" or "a secret intelligence agent of the Tsar?" Then, more soberly, "Or was he... painfully releasing the fabulous gifts locked up in our bodies?"[21] Such questions have been asked for decades of those favoring Gurdjieff, and I suspect there is little hope in ever fully squaring this enigmatic character with the many apocryphal stories surrounding him.

As the West is culturally "Christian" in its orientation, so it is with Christianity and its doctrines that we have to deal when attempting to unravel our complex relationship to self, other and world. Cupitt, Needleman and Berman agree on this point. We are the product of a long and tortuous history during which Christianity, for good or ill, has helped shape our individual and collective psyche. Our fundamental ideas about the spiritual life stem from this close and sometimes disturbing relationship, and ignoring that relationship will not make it go away. And to further muddy the waters, heresy lies alongside Christianity as an important partner in the evolution of human thought, but not quite in the way many might think. Heresy, Berman tells us, "is an attempt to restore body cognition to the center of human consciousness."[22] This is what Berman thinks the heretical movements in the history of the West were all about. The principal argument in heresy vs. orthodoxy was not about "doctrine", he tells us, it was about "experience". The very fact that this central issue got translated into debates about doctrine is proof positive that the heretics seldom got to speak for themselves. The winners wrote the history books.

To my mind, Berman's explanation regarding heresy is probably the most insightful I've ever come across. In his final analysis, heresy is not about "ideas" or "beliefs," it is about the "cognitive, perceptual history of the West." The so-called heretics rejected the dominant culture's cerebral formulas for what they were, "formulistic," and in turn directed attention *back to the body as the seat of experience.*[23]

This centuries-long avoidance of everything to do with the deep end of somatic experience has, in due course, had a disastrous effect on our view of physical experience. Caught up in the rarefied atmosphere of our intellectual processes (secular and religious), we have neglected, condemned or demonized the body as a potential threat to civilized life. Rene Descartes' declaration, "I think, therefore I am," has become the mantra of our commonsense approach, "self" no more than an offshoot of language and thought lodged firmly in our heads. Through Christianity's imagined manipulations of the body by sentient evil (the Devil), the physical has become God's antagonist, the conduit through which the conscious self can be subverted by evil forces. The human body is the Devil's chosen domain of action; it houses "intermediate substances and transitional zones" [24] where heretics and witches can ply their craft of psychic deceit.

Self-presence 1.4

In Needleman's terms, the lost aspect of Christianity is our ability to sense ourselves as a presence, to consciously hold sense of self in place while engaged in everyday tasks. As a result of

Christianity's evolution, however, this deep sensitivity towards the self as "presence" has been swapped for a set of rote beliefs about Jesus and God. And so we have a one-dimensional response to life and living, whereas it ought to be two-dimensional in the sense of *fully occupying the space in which we move and have our being.*[25] What we're looking for, indeed hunting for, is not some great spiritual force outside of ourselves, some grand spiritual revelation to once and for all time silence our questioning minds, but a sense of our own intrinsic worth, a sense of being fully awake and aware. We are ourselves the missing element in our own existence puzzle; we have evaporated into thinking and doing and got lost among religious fears and philosophical wranglings.

This is Needleman's extraordinary insight: in spiritual terms we are not seeking the presence of God as such, but rather the ability to remember, or re-*member*, our own psychophysical presence moment by moment. That is the missing factor in our lives, in our prayers, in our contemplative or meditative moments, in our relationships and in much of our scholarship. We have lost sense of our psychophysical wholeness to such an extent that we have become strangers to ourselves and a danger to everyone around us. Not to mention the planet.

But we are of course still influenced by our bodies, and by the bodies of others. We still "know" one another at the primeval level of smell, taste and touch, by the way we move, or by tone of voice. We are still connected to our bodies, to the deep visceral experience of the body-self, but have become overly cautious in what we allow of this realm to surface. There is a deep-seated fear in us of the somatic level; the "subjective" level of mind and being is our enemy. Our bodies are an embarrassment; they remind us of the "gap" across which we have to communicate, not to mention the firmly entrenched "split" in our own body/mind relationship. And so we hold visceral reality at bay. God forbid that that reality – the reality of our separate bodily presence – should break into any given moment and disrupt our mental processes. This is of course a well-grounded fear, for unbeknownst to the conscious self there exists within us the sublimated body of the child, a core understanding of our undifferentiated level of being that we can't quite get to grips with. But it's there, and it does not go away.

But looping the self back into the self via "self-presence" is a bit like trying to see the back of one's head without a strategically placed mirror – it puts a creative strain on the sensory system. Meeting psychological resistance, our tendency is to become "submerged" in thinking and doing, to choose the easier route and sink thankfully into streams and dreams of almost continuous conscious engagement. So great is the effort required to initiate self-presence that our surfacings are no more than momentary flashes. These glimpses of the somatic self as a "presence" are infrequent, infinitesimal in duration, counter-intuitive and seldom of any intensity. The German philosopher Martin Heidegger captures our problem in his 1945-1946 letter on "Humanism". In relation to our sense of "Being" he says: "Being is the nearest to man. But this nearness remains furthest from him."[26] We do, however, sometimes break through when listening to great music, or poetry, or when grief-stricken, or when in physical pain. We are not altogether cut off from ourselves.

Being "present" to ourselves is not an easy thing to accomplish; it is downright difficult to sense ourselves as a presence as we go about our daily lives. We continually forget to physically re-*member* ourselves as a presence. We get caught up in doing and thinking and self-presence disappears into a miasma of jumbled thoughts and internalized arguments. As Guy Claxton points out in his intimate history of the unconscious, *The Wayward Mind,* we are undoubtedly conscious as we mumble our way across streets or drive our cars on what we term "automatic pilot", but something is missing, and that "something" is our sense of ourselves *as* a self.[27] For Needleman, Walker and Berman, real spiritual experience is not about mystical ecstasy and wondrous visions, it is about openness to ordinary, everyday experience in the sense of being aware of our own psychophysical existence as we "think" and "do" our way through a day, hour or minute. And for Berman this means learning, or relearning, how to navigate the difficult territory of somatic experience and energy, a subject we will return to. Wittgenstein appears to have been of much the same opinion; his concern was to free the analytical mind from its frantic involvement with thoughts and reunite it with its estranged physical roots. Claxton homes in on this point and suggests that philosophers and schizophrenics "may be paralyzed by the compulsive explorations of disembodied possibility." Why? Because they have lost their "common sense" and are apt to neglect intuition, feeling and sense of embodiment.[28]

To help clarify these issues, Berman refers us to the Jungian psychologist Erich Neumann's argument that individual consciousness passes through the same stages as that of the human race, and that mythology is the map of that evolution. The first myths were creation myths: the Earth was in a submerged state and was brought forth from a watery chaos. The human ego (read "hero" in Berman's terms) became enmeshed in the archetypal territory of "journeys" and "conquests" where it did battle with unconscious forces and, if lucky, emerged victorious. The ancient myths were therefore about "emergence", the emergence of the "self" from the "not-self" (the so-called unconscious), and this process of emerging into ever greater awareness was/is far from complete. Morris Berman notes that the American psychologist Lawrence Kohlberg posits six stages of moral reasoning ranging from "Piaget's 'moral realism' to a growing awareness of the role of the intentions of others to an emphasis on abstract principles of human rights and justice," and that Kohlberg and others hold these stages to be developmental and not merely cultural – individuals in every culture studied went through the same developmental stages.[29]

The Fluctuating Self 1.5

There are, however, ongoing problems with this view; there are still technical things to sort out concerning self and its place in consciousness. We may have successfully emerged from the unconscious, but the idea of further emergence, never mind what actually does the emerging, is still under debate. According to Kenneth Walker, John Hughlings Jackson (founder of the British School of Neurology) and the much maligned philosopher Friedrich Nietzsche, the notion that "self" was the *continuous form of personal awareness* we assumed it to be was a misnomer. Noting anomalies, Jackson argued that consciousness was neither a fixed quantity nor quality, but something that underwent change moment by moment. Nietzsche was of the same opinion. Consciousness was not of fixed magnitude; it was "intermittent" in nature. Getting down to specifics, Nietzsche observed that because we believe ourselves to already possess consciousness, we give ourselves very little trouble to acquire it. We may not be quite as conscious as we think we are.

This was also Gurdjieff's observation: in his scheme we are all but oblivious to the fact that our conscious life is conducted mainly at an unconscious level. So taken up are we with mental and physical activity that there is seldom any attention left over for an experiential consciousness of the self by the self. Being embedded in "thinking" and "doing", we disappear into a submerged conscious state, and enter a state of "conscious sleep", a state from which we only occasionally emerge or awaken.

What struck me as important about Nietzsche's observation was the idea that we do little to "acquire" greater consciousness; we just assume ourselves to possess it in full and continue on merrily. It does not occur to us that something is amiss, that we spend a great deal of time in a mumbling, cut-off state of consciousness within which our empathic natures have difficulty in operating. We have, as it were, stepped into a crack in time and space where only the object of attention rules, a subjective domain where the self-aware subject of consciousness resembles drifting smoke.

In this sense "self" is not of fixed duration, an opinion backed now by much recent research. There is, we are told by numerous professionals, no fixed form of self at the center of conscious awareness. Consciousness goes through continuous fluctuations, and as such cannot sustain a permanent "I" structure, only a fleeting or intermittent one. Continuity of self is therefore an illusion, a chimera, a concept without substance in psychological reality. There is an "I-structure", but it is composed of a "procession of I-moments" cleverly synthesized into what appears to be a singularity. Identity we certainly have, but it is no more than a backgrounding haze conjured out of past memories. Everything is in a state of flux, a state of coming and going, a state of existing and not existing. Or, as the philosopher David Hume put it, mind or self is believed to be a unity only because of the "felt smoothness of the transition which imagination effects between point and point." Our idea of having a continuous self is pure supposition.

Picking up on this idea in a more positive and helpful manner, the Jungian psychologist Erich Neumann observed that the logical statement of identity – "I am I" – is in fact a tremendous achievement because it is an act "whereby an ego is posited and the personality identified with that ego – however fallacious that identification may later prove to be".[30] Out of this process comes a "self-orienting" consciousness, and it is our capacity for self-orientation that makes all the difference. But note Neumann's qualification: *however fallacious that identification may later prove to be.*

Here then is much the same observation as that made by Nietzsche, Jackson, Hume, and countless others, whereas in Neumann's terms the disconcerting discovery that our idea of being a self may be an illusion is turned from a negative into a positive. The illusion of having a self, of being an individual entity, of having a personality constellated around an "I-structure", becomes an achievement of which we need not be ashamed. The appearance in consciousness of a "self-orienting principle" was an evolutionary event of major psychological importance, an event without which we would lack the internal focus to exist and function as self-aware biological systems. The psychoanalyst David Black concurs: "Where there is no subject, nothing is of any importance."[31] The Catholic contemplative Bernadette Roberts follows suit:

> self or consciousness is not an entity or a being; it is not an individual person, a soul or a spirit temporarily dwelling in the body; nor is it divine, eternal or immortal. Self or consciousness is, however, the experience of all of the above – entity, being, soul, spirit and so on. Self or consciousness is a specific, unique experience or set of experiences. Take away self, and all its experiences go with it.[32]

If Berman and Needleman and Walker are correct in their conclusion, the appearance of "presencing individuals" in our societies may herald the next significant development in our evolution as a species. Our bodies may seem to be no more than vehicles within which our minds travel like passengers, but they may be much more than that. They may in fact be the means by which we can free ourselves from the natural limitations of our struggling intellects.

2: The Energy of Attention

The Vision of Christ that thou dost see
Is my Visions Greatest Enemy . . .
Thine is the Friend of all Mankind,
Mine speaks in parables to the Blind
William Blake
The Everlasting Gospel

Intro: 2.0

Something that has fascinated me for years, many years, is how complicated religious matters are. Why is that the case, I wonder? Why are religious experiences so... how can I say it without causing offence, *oddball?* Why, for instance, is meditative experience in India so radically different from, say, the English contemplative tradition? Why are the results so different? And why, oh why, does the Virgin Mary keep turning up for Catholics but not for Protestants of equal faith and sincerity? We have to assume, surely, that many Protestant Christians are of equal faith to their Catholic counterparts, and no less deserving in the eyes of God in relation to observances dutifully kept and prayers routinely offered. Particularly for and by the sick. Which is to ask why Lourdes is Catholic and a Pentecostalist laying on of hands is Protestant? Is it all just a matter of culture, of which part of the world we were born into, which family setting we happen to have, indeed, which side of the street the stork chose to visit? Or is something much deeper going on, something intrinsic to our being human that we have yet to identify?

But what of God's role is in all of this? It stands to reason, if you are religious, that it is God who decides these things. If the Virgin Mary turns up or does not turn up in your faith tradition, then it must mean something, mustn't it? And as that is surely the case, then why doesn't the Christian God keep, for the sake of all Christians of good faith, a level playing field in relation to the two principal Christian traditions? He is after all GOD; he can do whatever he wants. So why allow Mary to appear to one and not the other? Is it favoritism? Is he saying in a not-so-subtle way that one of these groups has the "truth" and the other has not, and that all other religious traditions are mistaken? Is it as blatantly simple and straightforward as that, or is something else going on?

Then there's the route you to take to contact whichever version of God you worship. Why are these routes so diverse? Why is it that in the Indian sense of religious practice it is necessary to learn, as yogins do, complicated breathing techniques and attempt to bend the body into extraordinary shapes? Or if you are a Catholic, or Anglican monk, recite fixed prayers, scrub your way to God on an empty stomach and avoid the Eastern notion that direct union with God is possible? Or if you are an evangelical or fundamentalist Protestant Christian, sidestep all this mystical stuff and believe that everything, absolutely everything, depends on articulating the formula that Jesus is your personal savior? What is this all about? Is only one of those belief-sets the correct set, or is some vital ingredient missing in our overall comprehension of what it means to be religious?

I should say immediately that the above questions are not an exercise in flippancy; they are an attempt to focus attention on the more important question of what religion might be in its heart of hearts. Is it only about who has the "truth" and who has not? Is there really some grand religious truth or design that we all have to bow to, or is the very idea of such a grandiose truth a mask for an ingrained ignorance we are unwilling, or unable, to shed? Is religion's innate tendency towards claims of superior insight reflective of some Grand Truth, or have we simply exported our cultural and tribal inadequacies into the heavens? Whatever our religious persuasion, these are just some of the questions we have to ask ourselves, for they reveal cracks and fissures and the odd chasm or two in our disparate notions of religious truth that cannot any longer be avoided. Why? Because religion, whatever its variety, has become a bit of a headache for the world's developed and fledgling democracies. Problems arise when we take our particular religious persuasion to be undiluted truth, when the only truth worth bothering with, perhaps, is our need for truth.

The Framing of Questions 2.1

This is particularly so in the sense that those who adhere strongly to a religious tradition are generally unwilling to question that tradition's claims and promises with any rigor. Alert to how mythology and wishful thinking operate in other religions, they find it all but impossible to identify the same underlying mythological themes in their own tradition. They have the "truth", everyone else has either lies or a distorted version of their truth. This fact is so obvious, so blatant that they blink in real surprise when it is suggested that they are in the same boat as everyone else. Suggest "conceptual blindness" and hackles will rise.

Our ability to evaluate ideas and experiences depends on our ability to question ideas and experiences. We have to be able to conceive and frame questions before they can be asked, and, luckily for us, that capacity seems to be innate. We have a built-in curiosity that drives us to question just about everything, and in answering most questions we develop and mature as human beings. This does not mean that we come to understand everything we question; some questions are too difficult to immediately break open into answers. They instead lie around in our systems as "needs", to use the psychologist William James's terminology, and in that role they add a dimension of "not knowing" to our knowing that tempers our tendency to always expect neat answers. Not everything is "certain" in life, some things remain forever hidden. It is perhaps this very fact that makes us seek truth in religious form, for through religious truth our deepest "not knowings" can be turned into manageable semblances of "knowing", our insecurity back into what appears to be factually based certainty.

So what to do? Religion has obviously a part to play in life, so the question is: to what extent should we rely on its idiosyncratic formulations of reality? Do these formulations in some sense make sense even when they seem to make no sense at all? Is that their sensed attraction? Or are they no more than a form of mental subterfuge, an excuse to escape the task of sorting out our deepest needs? Or, there again, is there perhaps an inner core of reasoning to religious truths that resonates with our own inner core, a core identified in the Christian tradition as the "soul", an indefinable "something" that links us to realms of experience and knowledge not available to our factually driven minds. Is it perhaps that that stops us from questioning what in so many instances demands the asking of questions?

Another reason for the suspicion that questioning religious ideas and values might lead to their undoing is that questions, even apparently innocent ones, have a bad habit of generating other questions of more serious import. Question some innocuous aspect of faith, and before you know it the whole edifice is under threat. For it stands to reason that reason will demand further and further adjustments to our cherished beliefs, and that these adjustments will, in the end, deal a fatal blow to our faith. But is that really the case? Does using "reason" automatically lead to a diminution of trust in what we once trusted? Is reason the natural enemy of faith? In the limited sense of reason being no more than an extension of raw "logic", the answer is yes, it is dangerous, but in the more expansive sense of reason being a tool *in the service of our experience of being alive,* it is not true. There are two different kinds of questioning at work here, and we should be aware of their weaknesses and their strengths.

Writing with his usual flair in the sphere of language, poetics and history, George Steiner captures this more advanced interpretation of questioning when he says: "To question truly is to enter into harmonic concordance with that which is being questioned."[1] The idea that we should be "initiator and sole master" in the mechanistic sense should be swapped for a laying open of the self to what is being questioned. Here is the heart of the matter, the heart of what Morris Berman was getting at when he suggested that we lacked "real presence, real bodily engagement with the world." We have to become, in Steiner's terms, "the vulnerable locus, the permeable space of its (the question's) disclosure." For him that has in turn its parallel in "the risk of nakedness in the dialectic of prayer."[2] Suddenly, unexpectedly, questioning turns into something else, an opening up of the self to the self through the asking of authentic questions.

The question of "authentic" and "unauthentic questions" is of course a difficult one; being faced with the further question of whether our questions are worthwhile can try our patience. Steiner comes to our rescue with a handy yardstick. There are, he says, two discernibly different types of questions that can be asked, the "questionable" (we are asked to note the pejorative inflection) where facts constitute terminal, settled and therefore inert answers, and "worthy of being asked questions" in the sense of questions that are *inexhaustible.* The meaning of human existence is such a question; it cannot be answered in the same fashion as, say, "How far is the Earth from the Sun?" In this sense the question and the questioner can be "dignified" by the mode of questioning chosen. Knowing how far the Earth is from the Sun is a useful fact; confronting the question of meaning in relation to human existence is altogether different in caliber.

This is to say that questioning is an activity vital to our growth and development as human beings; without it we atrophy for want of depth and substance. Greater depth is always possible; there is no such thing as a spiritual bottoming out in the sense of having accomplished everything in one hit. If a Christian, then the meaning of "Christ" should be pursued into the depths of our being, not merely held up in the mind like a sports trophy. Enter Father Sylvan, Jacob Needleman's mentor with this directive: "Not until you reach the heart should you permit yourself to speak the ancient language. Until then, even Christ must be chased out of your mind. You have made Him into a monster through your emotions and conditioning." And then an equally remarkable statement: "I have suffered because of my clinging to the old language. But one day I began to see that the seed of love is the desire to know, to understand."[3] Father Sylvan's directives will disconcert many Christians, but for my money he has his finger firmly on the pulse of what it means to be Christian.

So who is Father Sylvan? What are his credentials? To what order did he belong? As it turns out, these are difficult questions to answer. In the introduction to his book *Lost Christianity*, Jacob Needleman tells us that he first came across Father Sylvan (a Westerner with a strong, unidentifiable accent) while attending a conference in the Middle East. Seated in the audience, at the rear, this priest had asked some pointed questions of the panel, and later turned up in the same airport queue as Needleman. Due to a delay, they had repaired to the airport dining room for coffee and passed the time chatting. A second delay of three hours had, however, changed "chat" into a discussion that left Needleman the philosopher "full to overflowing with more ideas and information about the Christian tradition than (he) could possibly manage." So extraordinary was Father Sylvan's thinking that he later found himself "revising almost everything (he) had ever thought about Christianity."

This was a life-changing moment for Jacob Needleman; he was not the same man afterwards. His book *Lost Christianity* spells out why; he had stumbled into the presence of a Christian monk whose "interpretation of Scripture, morality, mysticism, metaphysics, the soul, the place of the Church... was, to say the least, extremely unorthodox." So much so that Needleman had difficulty relating what he heard to the kind of Christianity he was familiar with. And not once did he demand proof for what was being said, or argue back, or even ask the man's name, for there was, Needleman recalls, a quality in the man's presence that made all such inquiry redundant. So imagine his surprise when about a year later a tattered manuscript written by Father Sylvan arrived on his desk, a manuscript within which his unique interpretation of Christianity was further enlarged upon. Father Sylvan was dead, but his researches were about to turn Needleman's life upside down and inside out.

What we make of this meeting with Father Sylvan is our own affair, but as I read *Lost Christianity* I began to appreciate Needleman's excitement, for with every sentence a whole new vision of Christianity's core purpose began to surface, and it was one I in part recognized from other sources, one of those sources being G.I. Gurdjieff. Whoever Father Sylvan was, he was in himself a formidable example of Gurdjieff's term "real presence", and it was this that had stopped Needleman in his tracks.

Knowing and Not Knowing 2.2

As noted earlier, our "not knowing" is as important as our "knowing"; it tempers our need for overly neat and tidy answers. All knowing is embedded in our not knowing. To not know something is to know that we do not know it, and that is the springboard of our future knowing. Conversely, all knowing is a form of not knowing, for there is always more to know. And so we come to the question of knowing or not knowing God, and to what that might mean. But first we have to understand something about our past and present conception of God. In classical terms, God had no objective existence in time or space, and as such was beyond definition. The ancient fathers did not waste their time contemplating what God was; they admitted straight up that they did not know and listed instead what he was not. And yet God was/is the guarded subject of Christian contemplation. Why guarded? Because to contemplate God directly is to face not only the "unknown", but also the "unknowable", and as a result be emptied of everything we "think" we know.[4] Dangerous stuff. And so Jesus was by necessity theologically sandwiched between us and God to safeguard our sanity, and from this a secondary problem arose that we're still in the throes of dealing with: Jesus as cultic figure.

The nature of this secondary problem is that Jesus does not inspire contemplative emptying; he inspires instead "emotional identification" and the "filling up" process that goes along with that. This is what Father Sylvan is getting at when he says that we have made Christ into a monster through our emotions and our conditioning and has to be chase him out of our minds. We've reduced him to a utilitarian formula and replaced the springboard of our creative "not knowing" with a "knowing" that must by its very nature collapse into historical and psychological absurdity. Why? Because the idea of sandwiching Jesus between ourselves and God, clever as it is in theological terms, produces a state of dependence on an *affectively charged* idea that can, in some instances, permanently undermine our ability to sensibly question our own religious framework.

Tackling this problem, Father Sylvan refers to "men of Salvation" who have "drawn the energy of attention away from the body (and) walk the earth like explosive devices ready to be set off at random."[5] Now there's an image to conjure with, and it was penned decades before 9/11! But there's more, and it's devastating. In Sylvan's terminology, to draw "the energy of attention away from the body" is to "abort the soul a thousand times a day." The soul does not exist in finished form, he tells us, it is an energy that has to be activated and accumulated. What

Christianity has lost is its teaching on how this energy can be extracted from ordinary experience – it has been turned into the rambling demands of belief and moral rectitude. Powerful experiences such as the threat of death or deep disappointment can and do drive us into a "present tenseness" that we find unsettling, but the same energy is available to us from ordinary events, happenings and interactions if we know how to go about it. We can decide, if we know how, to *fully occupy the space in which we exist,* but fail to do so because we haven't the foggiest idea what that means in practical terms.

We have become creatures of the surface with little experience of our own unfathomable depths. We surf the energy stream of our emotions and hope (or pray?) that our decisions, fed as they are by ideas influenced by the same unpredictable energy stream, will keep us on track both intellectually and morally. But it hasn't worked; we are as unpredictable and as dangerous as we've ever been.

Jacob Needleman develops Father Sylvan's meaning in relation to our misuse of emotional energy to include the possibility of our "serving as a channel for the force that can alter the whole of the self."[6] Now that is quite a claim, and he isn't using "force" in a *Star Wars* sense. He is suggesting not an external, independent force that can affect change in our lives (God, or Jesus as God), but a force or energy fundamental to our own psychophysical makeup capable of short-circuiting us out of our emotionally driven naivety. As "intrinsic change" is the crux of regular Christianity's failed hope for the world, the crux of psychological, philosophical and psychiatric explorations into the human psyche, and the crux of the evangelical/fundamentalist vision, then this highly unusual view of our creative (spiritual?) capacities is worth considering. Change in the sense of an updating of ideas, or in the more dramatic sense of paradigm shift, will undoubtedly play an important role in our immediate future, but as Morris Berman suspects, and I concur, it will take much more than that if we humans are to survive our own dark brilliance.

Soul-Making 2.3

But lets get back to Father Sylvan's definition of "soul" as *an energy that is constantly aborted,* for within that clearly stated definition lies the clue as to how the whole crumbling spiritual edifice of Christianity can be rebuilt. And as the bitter arguments and in-fighting between liberal, conservative and evangelical camps plainly show, it is crumbling. To believe otherwise is to ignore the looming threat of schism in the Anglican communion, the equally serious challenges to Rome's authority from within its priestly ranks, or be so immersed in the evangelical/fundamentalist dream that questioning ceases altogether. Enter Father Sylvan with a definition of "soul" that rocks the barque of Christ, a definition that resets the whole complex mechanism of Christianity and offers it the chance to rediscover its own lost soul. And how is this to be done? Through the "activation of attention" and the "accumulation of energy", a two-pronged experimental process that requires our full, conscious participation, and not just a blind acceptance of pre-packaged beliefs. That's pretty specific, I think. It tells us that we have to do something to kick-start the process of "soul making", and that we must then persist with this process or the energy of which soul is composed will be lost.

Before tackling what this means in practical terms, we must first take a detour via the surprisingly modern writings of the 2nd century Church Father Irenaeus, the philosopher John Hick whose present-day challenge to conservative Christian thought calls for a "soul-making" theology based on the Irenaean tradition, and the critical writings of R. Douglas Geivett, a fellow philosopher to whom Hick's thinking is untenable for the very reason that it raises the specter of soul-making as an alternative to salvation through Christ. But there's a problem here, for although Hick seems to be advocating what Father Sylvan advocates, he is in fact serving up a soul-making process based solely on what we learn as we live out our lives daily, and that, in spite of it having to do with how we react to everyday events and happenings, is far short of what Father Sylvan has in mind when speaking of the potentially transformative "energy" that all situations, events and encounters secretly harbor.

It was around 130 CE that Irenaeus began to frame systematic expositions of Church thinking in the East. One such exposition shows him to have been ultra- modern in how he approached the Adam and Eve story. With a few strokes of his pen he tells us that if the serpent had truly tempted Eve, then God was Himself the author of sin. And blaming the serpent's ability to speak was equally unacceptable, for if that had been the case then demons would never have ceased using it in their deception of humankind. This and other rational criticisms of the Fall story reveal a mind fully aware of the story's allegorical sense. The existence of Adam and Eve, the first human beings, is treated as a literal event, but not so the language of the text. Irenaeus reads between the lines. He is so clear and rational in his approach that in his 1924 Bampton Lectures, Norman Williams is forced to admit that his Adam belongs, "in respect to his moral status, to the category of *hominidae* or "sub-men" rather than to that of *homo sapiens."* Williams adds for good measure:

> If this primitive... conception of man's primeval state had never been overlaid by the rabbinical imagination as to Adam's supernatural perfection and splendor, later Christianity might have been spared even the appearance of a conflict with Darwinism.

The point of mentioning all of this is that the idea of salvation through Christ's death on the cross rests on how the Adam and Eve story is viewed. Accept it as a cosmic drama that spread evil throughout humanity and you set up the situation where the "men of Salvation" can rule the spiritual roost until the end of time. That, in essence, is what traditional Christianity is all about; it is about saving us from the generic stain of our First Parents' sin (their disobeying God's command to not eat of the Tree of Good and Evil) plus our own lifetime of accumulated misdemeanors. So there is no doubting what Father Sylvan is getting at when he talks of these "men of Salvation" in such derogatory terms; he is saying loud and clear that it is time to ditch St Augustine's dour interpretation of sin's origin and replace it with a "soul-making" conception of human life based, not on the quality of our actions, but on the quality of the perceptions that set these actions in motion. But much more than that even, for he is not advocating Hick's boot strap morality plus Christ, but what may have lain behind Irenaeus's rejection of the Fall story: soul as an accumulation of psychic energy that can be squandered like the Prodigal Son's "substance" in a far country.

We don't know for certain what inspired Irenaeus to interpret the Adam and Eve story in the way he did, but as a principal player in the framing of Christian thought in the second century, we can legitimately suspect that his radically different interpretation of that event resulted in other theological curiosities that in the West have undergone a process of adjustment. And it isn't as if Irenaeus was the only Church Father to think of the Fall as a lapse due to weakness and immaturity alone.[7] Clement of Alexandria, Methodius and St. Gregory of Nazianzus were of much the same opinion, and in conjunction with Tertullian, Chrysostom, Origen, Basil and Cyril he is known to have argued that the Virgin Mary was not only conceived in sin, but that she had also committed sin. Irenaeus may be held up today as a staunch supporter of orthodoxy, but his own writings are more than a little worrying when compared with the Church's later evaluation of Christ and his mission.

So where does this leave us? Well, it shows that Father

Sylvan's conception of what it means to be a "soul-maker" is quite different from that of John Hick, and that although this philosopher of religion comes close to this unusual idea, he in the end loses his way and finds himself in deep theological waters where Geivett's language games equal his own at every turn. It becomes a matter of words, and then more words, and the heart of what "soul-making" may have meant to Irenaeus turns into no more than an exercise in moral rectitude with the added fantasy of Christ's vicarious sacrifice spliced into it.

In his intriguing novel *The Shoes of the Fisherman,* Morris West captures the essence of this problem when he says:

> It cost so much to be a full human being that there are very few who have the enlightenment or the courage to pay the price... One has to abandon altogether the search for security and reach out to the risk of living with both arms. One has to embrace the whole world like a lover, and yet demand no easy return of love. One has to accept pain as a condition of existence. One has to court doubt and darkness as the cost of knowing.

Compare such a stance with those who believe that everything is tied up with a theological bow. How can we abandon the search for security and reach out to the risk of living if we believe that the Christian God has already worked out a set formula for our spiritual existence? How can we embrace the whole world like a lover if we believe that world to harbor a contagion of evil that is passed on generation by generation? How can we accept pain as a condition of existence if we are convinced pain is sent from God to test us? How can we court doubt and darkness if we believe that knowing with certainty is the name of the game? And if we happen to be a contemplative, or have leanings in that direction, how can we develop a genuine spirituality if we are carrying a suitcase of theology in each hand?

Enter the philosopher Jacob Needleman with the observation that "it is not the experience of God that is drawing Christians to contemplative practices, but the experience of existing as such."[8] That throws us in at the deep end of questioning and returns us to Father Sylvan's claim that we *abort our soul a thousand times each day.* It's not just another wrinkle of theology that's missing, or another word battle between Hick and Geivett that we have to digest; it's a matter of finding out what "to exist as such" means in terms of our day-to-day existence.

3: Waking Up

"Immersed in the ideas of this first chapter, I am rarely conscious even of where I am."
Eric Schwitzgebel
Is Experience Limited to What's in Attention?
Journal of Consciousness Studies

Intro: 3.0

There are, I'm pleased to say, people in the world of science, psychology and philosophy seriously considering some of the questions embedded in Father Sylvan's thinking, and these questions are edging us ever closer to an unexpected, and in many quarters unwanted, truce with Christianity. But not the Christianity of the churches, or of evangelical or fundamentalist citadels, but to a form of Christianity that the philosopher Jacob Needleman terms "lost" in that it has progressively given way to power politics and emotional identification with Jesus as God. As deeply satisfying as this experience may be (there's no doubting its capacity to enthrall) it falls dramatically short of what is required of us as we face the uncertainties of a future where different forms of religious extremism threaten the very fabric of our individual lives.

Enter Eric Schwitzgebel, associate professor of philosophy at the University of California whose research interests include "our poor knowledge of our own conscious experience, the nature of belief, and the role of reflection in moral psychology." Using a simple "beeper" experiment with his students, Schwitzgebel pursues the "promise and the problems of sampling conscious experience" in a paper titled *Do You Have Constant Tactile Experience of Your Feet in Your Shoes? Or Is Experience Limited to What's in Attention?*[1] In asking this question, Schwitzgebel cuts to the core of the problem I've attempted to outline in relation to the writings of Morris Berman, Jacob Needleman and Father Sylvan, for his question reveals that the quality of our conscious awareness moment by moment may reflect things about us that we never suspected to be the case.

For instance, when not attending to your feet in your shoes, or the hum of traffic in the background, do such experiences drop out of consciousness? When observed in thinking about some unpleasant interaction, do we arrive at the parking lot and "wake up" with no explicit memory of having driven there? Is it possible to have no conscious experience of the road as we drive to work, or is it a case of intermittent conscious experience? Is consciousness nothing more than "experience" by another name? Could it be that behavioral responses as we drive while thinking about something else are merely automatic adjustments similar to those we exhibit when leaning against a hard object? Are we then in some intrinsic sense both conscious and unconscious simultaneously? Are we "blind", "deaf" or "dumb" to some stimuli while being attentive to, and aware of, others? These are just some of the questions raised by Schwitzgebel, and they are good questions, for they drive us into ourselves in an unexpected manner.

In what sounds like a tone of resignation, Schwitzgebel informs us that he has largely devoted his career to criticizing introspection as a means to answer such questions, but that he has had to lump for a "more empirically controlled means of addressing this question introspectively." This is the only way the different theories concerning consciousness can, in his opinion, be resolved. And so he gives his students beepers to wear during their normal daily routine, and these beepers "go off at long intervals when participants are likely to be immersed in other things." The beauty of such an experiment is the element of surprise. The participant is "objectively" primed for the experiment, but reacts "subjectively" when the beeper goes off. This means that he/she reacts "authentically" because of the element of surprise. Yet Schwitzgebel has qualms about his experiment; he knows it isn't perfect. There's a chance of salvaging something that legitimately "casts at least some initial light on the phenomena and starts to expose the theoretical and empirical possibilities," but there is also the chance of the student's mentally interfering with the experience even as it is taking place.

There follows a hugely complex array of data, and the often surprised reactions of students who expected one result, only to get another. Most students reported becoming absorbed in their own activities to such an extent that they completely forgot about the beeper until it went off. Submerged in conscious activity, they were surprised to remember that they had forgotten all about the experiment they were engaged in.

In his final analysis, Schwitzgebel is hopeful, but careful in his summation of what is going on here. If a participant got it right in the first few seconds after the beep, then it was unlikely they would misreport later – everything depended on that tiny window of opportunity. Information of a reliable nature was available, but it depended on those involved "waking up" to the fact that they had, for an instant, "woken up". Schwitzgebel reads this "instant" as potentially objective rather than subjective because of the manner in which it has arisen. He explains himself thus:

> A beeper is appealing because it has a sharp onset, targeting a single, specific moment of experience, and because participants can be told in advance what to reflect on in the targeted experience. No seconds-consuming verbal query is necessary. One can combine the advantages of surprise and preparedness.[2]

An important point to recognize here is that falling into conscious engagement is never ever recognized as having happened in the instant that it happens, but that *having been asleep,* or "engaged", is always a potentially rewarding state of mind in that it affords us the possibility of glimpsing ourselves objectively when we do wake up. This simple but telling fact is not elaborated on in Schwitzgebel's paper; he is concerned with other factors, but for our purposes it is an all-important ingredient. Our tendency to topple back into conscious engagement is to miss out on what might be termed *the arising of a moment of existential freedom.* In the tiny gap between not being aware of tactile sensations, and becoming aware of them, we are not only confronted with previously unregistered physical phenomena, we are also presented with the opportunity to expand that experience into an appreciation of ourselves as a living presence. This is such a subtle point it can be easily missed, and just as easily dismissed as illusory, but it does in fact harbor a powerful realization: we are seldom fully sentient, and only become so *as we awaken* to the fact of our being almost continuously submerged in thinking and doing. In religious terms, this awakening could be described as a form of "resurrection", a *coming back to (our) life* through our senses.

Lucid Dreaming 3.1

Keeping all of this in mind as best we can, we must now turn to the research of Celia Green into what is termed "lucid dreaming", a condition described as "lucid" not because such dreams have unusual visual clarity, but because the dreamer is "aware, at the time, that he/she is dreaming."[3] As Director of the *Institute of Psychophysical Research* in Oxford, Green raised an eyebrow or two in the '60s with her ground-breaking work on individuals who claimed the ability to "consciously reflect" while dreaming, a claim flatly contradicting everything we think and know about sleep and dream. And guess what? She refers in the final chapters of this seminal work to the writings of the Russian philosopher P.D. Ouspensky, and Ouspensky just happens to have been a lifelong student of G.I. Gurdjieff, the inspiration behind Father Sylvan, Jacob Needleman and, to some extent, Morris Berman. Gurdjieff isn't mentioned in Green's text, but he's there by proxy.

Awake while sleep? Surely not. Sleep is sleep, being awake is the opposite of being asleep. Generally, yes, but not always. There are, it seems, dream states within which the sleeper is simultaneously conscious although caught up in the machinations of some dream reality. That this can happen is well attested to, not only in Green's research but in the research of others, and what interests me is the rather obvious correspondence between "waking up" out of "conscious engagement" as described by Eric Schwitzgebel, and that of "waking up" within the dream state itself, a parallel experience in that it is an alternative reality within which we become consciously submerged. There is, to say the least, a tantalizing similarity between these states, and it may well be that they're connected in some way.

Ouspensky's contribution to this subject was his claim that he could enter the lucid dream state without going through the normal transition of entering the sleep state. He had in other words mastered the art of holding his conscious awareness in place as his body fell asleep. Celia Green remarks that this capacity is different from that reported by other lucid dream travelers (different indeed), and throughout her book refers again and again to Ouspensky's often highly original observations. In Ouspensky's view, for instance, dreams were no more than the result of physical sensations, or memories formed while awake, or due to image association within the dream itself. He rejected psychoanalytical methods of dream interpretation, and believed that we generated our dreams out of dream images. That is, images are generated out of images through subtle acts of conscious association and instantly woven into a tapestry of elaborate and coherent plots. So speedily do we do this that the instants of change in our dreams seemed to be of their own making, whereas they are more probably constructed out of subtle clues subliminally registered. This is, as we will see later, a contentious point, and it may be that Ouspensky was a little hasty in some of his judgments.

In alignment with this unusual material, an interview with Professor Charles Tart of the University of California is of particular interest. Conducted by the journalist Jayne Gackenbach, this well-known researcher in transpersonal psychology is asked how he came to write a book dealing with the phenomenon of lucid dreaming, a book called *Waking Up*. After some introductory remarks about reality being perceived by some spiritual traditions as similar to that of the dream state, Tart's researches are revealed to be based on the work of both P.D. Ouspensky and G.I. Gurdjieff, and with this connection made, Gackenbach homes in on a technique developed by Gurdjieff to help his students wake up out of submerged conscious engagement.

> **Gackenbach**: As I understand the Ouspensky-Gurdjieff material… there's essentially an asking of a critical question, a self-reflectiveness, an attempt, purposely, to reflect on what you're saying and doing as much as possible through the day.
> **Tart**: It's not usually expressed as a question, but if you did, it would be asking yourself something like, "What am I doing right now, what am I perceiving right now, what's my state right now? You could do it that way, but it's usually not done in such a verbal formation.
> **Gackenbach**: How is it usually done?
> **Tart**: It's an immediate shift of attention to being conscious of the normally unconscious. Once you do it, you realize that our ordinary state is that we're "lost". We don't know what's going on much of the time. We're just as passive in ordinary life as we are in dreams. Events happen and our mental processes react. Buttons get pushed, to use that wonderful old '60s

language, and our conditioned responses occur. A set of mental scenarios begin. Normally you're just running on automatic with these things all the time. Becoming self-reflective, you consciously see yourself doing these. As you pay enhanced attention more and more, you begin to get an option to be present to your experience more continuously, and to both have more control and be more open to new experiences.

In a phrase, this is self-awareness without a beeper. It is a conscious act, a waking up to the fact that we function mostly at an unconscious level when engaged in daily affairs. One thing leads to another in an endless stream of events and happenings where our only input is to react out of habit, habits formed out of the endless series of events and happenings that constitute our lives. Automatic pilot indeed, and dangerous in that acts of fully conscious discrimination are mostly missing. And there is also the possibility of observing oneself from an unhelpful perspective.

Tart: There are a number of ways to observe yourself. Some ways are biased or have built-in preferences. For example, lots of people observe themselves from their superego. Your superego has a listing of what is good and bad. It watches you and gives you a shot of anxiety when it thinks you are doing something bad. That's not what I'm talking about. In the first place, superego witnessing is automated. In the second place it's not yours, it was conditioned into you by outside forces – society, your parents and so forth.
Gackenbach: So the "effort" aspect is not there?
Tart: There is an effort, but it is a small effort. It's not much... The effort is to remember to do it, because what you discover is that you are constantly swept away by phenomena.[4]

There is, in essence, no difference here between the experiment set up by Eric Schwitzgebel and that of the waking-up technique proposed by Charles Tart. And there is, as suggested earlier, a parallel between waking up consciously inside a dream structure, and that of waking up inside the cascading phenomena of our daily lives. There is a sense in which life *is* a dream, not in the sense of life being no more than a dream, but in the sense of our living it *in a state not dissimilar to that of dream.* For Tart this is the meaning of "samsara" or "maya" in the Eastern tradition. It isn't that the world is unreal; it's that *we* are mostly unreal. Submerged in thought and deed we are at the mercy of every passing event whether good or bad. There's simply no one at home most of the time.

An adjunct of this is the fact that we physically wake up from sleep and go about our daily business. So there are in fact three levels to this phenomenon, not two, and this commonly experienced level of "waking up" in the morning, or after a nap, is, similarly, *a coming to our senses* immediately usurped by conscious engagement in thinking and doing. Three distinct levels of waking up are available to us, and each constitutes an escape from a submerged state of consciousness. The first is from out of ordinary sleep itself, the second, if we are lucky, or particularly skilled like Ouspensky, is within the dream state itself, and the third is from the so-called "awake state" that we equate with full sentience.

The most obvious "waking up" is from sleep; the difference between being asleep and being awake is stark. But so also is coming consciously awake during a dream; to wake up inside a dream is to be confronted with a distinct sense of one's normally awake self while engaged with the often bizarre scenarios dreams afford. That, too, can be a bit of a shock. But so also is realizing that it is possible to wake up while apparently fully awake. Who would have thought *that* possible? Our normal awake consciousness may not be as normal as it seems; it may harbor another superior level of awareness.

The Inner and the Outer 3.2

Another conundrum of consciousness detected by the philosopher Jacob Needleman is the assumption that "thinking" and "emotion" constitute our "inner life." He flatly rejects this idea, and says in response: "The inner and outer world have been misunderstood, and this misunderstanding has had disastrous consequences both for Christianity and modern culture."[5] How? Why? Because the world of "thoughts" and "emotions" constitute not our inner world, but the outer world in the sense that they are predominantly about the outer world. Our thinking is mostly about external things, our emotions reactions to external things, our dreams composed of external images. We have, in a sense, turned ourselves outside in and failed to detect not only this anomaly, but compounded the problem by mistakenly equating "feeling" with "emotion" and slamming shut the door to our senses.

This is to say slightly more than Needleman indicates, but it is no lie to suggest that we have difficulty relating to our body's deeper sensations, and that this is the underlying reason for our distrust of introspective behavior. Our emotions are, as we know only too well, unreliable as guides in terms of how we perceive reality, the thinking that attends emotional evaluations similarly tainted and untrustworthy. But we have perhaps gone too far in our search for clinical distance, our attempt to be emotionally neutral as we deal with reality. Something got lost as we became more and more scientific in attitude, and that something is our ability to sensitively evaluate reality from the standpoint of the body's deeper sensations, not merely from the ramparts of our isolated and lonely intellects.

Feeling and Emotion 3.3

To bring this about it is necessary for us to wake up as intelligent, well-informed human beings and experientially tease "feeling" and "emotion" apart. In dictionary terms, this is not difficult to do. Emotion is defined in the *Concise Oxford Dictionary* as agitation of mind, feeling, an excited mental state; whereas feelings are extended to include sense of touch, physical sensation, emotion (often hope, fear, etc), sympathies, readiness to feel, tenderness to others, suffering, and, lastly, *conviction not based solely on reason.* (Author's italics) Not until the very end of this definition do we stumble into a clear negative, the notion that feeling is untrustworthy in relation to reasoned propositions. All other parts of the definition lend themselves to positive outcomes in relation to the body and our relationships with others. Emotion, on the other hand, stands condemned immediately as unreliable because an overly agitated and excited mind tends towards irrationality.

That emotions contain feelings, and feelings, emotion, are not in dispute. What is in dispute is the assumption that emotion allied to feeling automatically disallows the demands of reason. It is clearly the case that feelings are "evaluative" at base, whereas emotions are "reactive" at base. Yes, there is an emotional element in feeling evaluations, but not in the sense of haywire constructs. One may, for instance, be excited by an idea arrived at after effort, but that does not mean one is somehow out of mental control. Emotion in the service of evaluative feeling is a positive, not a negative. Reactive emotions are quite different; they tend towards a disruption of reason because they are sudden, and often explosive. In this sense our subjectivity has two poles, one negative, one positive, the quality of our introspection being governed by which pole happens to be operative.

In his introductory essay to *Man and His Symbols,* Carl Jung differentiates between "feeling" and "thinking" in much the same manner as I've differentiated "feeling" from "emotion". Jung refers to feeling as "a judgment of value", and in this sense it is not an emotion. Why? Because a judgment of value is not involuntary, it is not "reactive" in the sense that emotions are – it is an ordering function much the same as ordered thinking.[6]

So what happens when we "wake up" to the fact that our inner lives are composed almost entirely of external images, people, arguments, ambitions, hopes and desires? What happens when we realize that our emotions are mostly reactions to external stimuli and little else? I can answer only for myself: It's one helluva shock. You immediately begin to re-evaluate what having an "inner life" means, and that leads one into considering what the word "spiritual" might really mean, and that carries one quickly towards the realization that Christianity's grocery list of *beliefs about* Jesus, God and much else, is sadly lacking in *interiority*. The inner life of the body, us *as* body, is, as a result, hardly ever listened to because its voice has become indistinct; it is in most cases a mere whisper, a distant murmur drowned out by emotional outbursts and all too often sterile intellectual wrangling. [7] Enter Father Sylvan with this bit of advice:

> Christianity is lost. How to search for it? When you have lost something, you must look for it exactly where you have lost it. Study, observe, watch; where, exactly, do you lose being and consciousness? In what do you lose yourself? You will not discover this by speaking the old language or by cultivating the old attitudes of religious piety or "morality". You will not find Christ by going to Christ, but only through seeing, clearly and with precision, how you crucify Him. Only then will *you* appear.[8]

The question is, who or what is this you?

4: Beyond the Comfort Zone

Not even God Himself can help a man
who has no attention.
Father Sylvan
Lost Christianity by Jacob Needleman[1]

Intro: 4.0

To go beyond the Jesus story is to go beyond the present meaning of that story; it is to wake up out of that story in the same way that one wakes up from a dream. It is altogether unlikely that Jesus perceived himself as Israel's God come to Earth to save fallen humanity, or that he was offering, at the same time, a new code for behavior designed to outshine the Jewish Torah. It is much more likely that he saw himself as a teacher attempting to discipline the minds of his disciples through an exaggerated moral process that mirrored their low levels of awareness. On examination, this was not a teaching meant for the whole of humanity, it was a mental discipline communicated to a group of students who often found it difficult to understand what he was getting at.

This is to suggest that there is another Jesus story to be told, a story quite different from the one we are used to, and that this other story carries within it much more than the message of "instant salvation" we have come to associate with Jesus. The comfort and sense of security derived from this story cannot be denied, of course, it is ubiquitous among the faithful, but a faith that promises salvation for all eternity on the basis of *beliefs about* a man who lived two thousand years ago should where possible be updated in the light of modern scholarship and the spiritual practices of those who have put their faith to the test. If a believer in the Jesus story out of habit and little else, that comfort zone is curtailed to times of personal and collective crises. If an unbeliever for reason of having examined that story and found it wanting, then Christianity's offering is generally viewed as beneficial in terms of its rituals, but regarded as otherwise deceitful. If, however, Father Sylvan is correct in his suggestion that "questioning" is a necessary spiritual exercise in its own right, then believers ought to be applying a greater degree of thoughtful pressure to the Jesus story.

It is now widely accepted among New Testament scholars that the Jesus story has been pulled out of its Jewish context and made into something it was never intended to be, but it may in fact go much further than that. It may be that even in its revived Jewish context the Jesus story carries much more than a sectarian vision rejected by Judaism and translated, step by step, via St. Paul into an alternative faith with Jesus as its centerfold. It may be that we have altogether lost the meaning of that story and been left with an empty husk. For it can be argued, and argued cogently, that the later Church transformed this sectarian Jew's deepest insights into a set of moral demands ordinary people find all but impossible to keep, and that in doing so they not only displaced and distorted Jesus' teachings, they also set in motion a cult of the personality that pushed this Jewish rabbi's intentions into reverse. As King Midas was cursed with the capacity to turn everything he touched into gold, so Jesus' teachings were turned into a series of sad literalisms. With everything this Jesus did and said constellated around the notion that he was in some incomprehensible sense Israel's God come to Earth in the form of a human being, an alternative faith to Judaism was offered by the Church that hardened into the Christianity we are all familiar with today. A cult in which "possession" by this divine Jesus became a prerequisite for a successful spiritual life became the norm, Jesus' "presence" in your life (God's unimaginable presence stepped-down to a manageable level) became the deciding factor in whether you were headed for hell or heaven.

The Core Message 4.1

The approach to Christianity being offered in this book is obviously quite different from that of the above; it is an approach based on the view that the Jesus story has been so misused down the centuries that its core message has been lost sight of. In the author's opinion, this core message annuls the need to believe "this" or "that" *about* Jesus; it points rather to a dimension of experience so dramatic that it cancels out belief *and* unbelief in relation to this remarkable man. But first a few things have to be straightened out, and head of the queue is the fact that the Jesus story is a story like any other story except that it has taken on the quality of a myth, a sacred dimension that transcends the basic story itself. As our culture is nominally Christian in outlook, we go through childhood and adolescence with this myth embedded in our minds as a species of fact, and emerge as adults for whom this story is (1) a matter of faith and belief that should not be questioned, or (2) a story accepted out of habit and not much else, or (3) rejected as a result of critical examination. These are the three basic approaches to the Jesus story, but there is also a fourth, and this fourth approach challenges us to rethink everything we think we know about Jesus, his life and his intentions. This is not merely to fall back into critical mode and debunk the Jesus story; it is to sensitively question our way into the heart of this story's meaning in the hope of uncovering what has been inadvertently obscured.

For instance, in the 6th century *Codex Cantabrigiensis,* a rewriting of the New Testament story of Jesus' interaction with the man caught working on the Sabbath (this codex is thought to contain much earlier materials), an extended version of Jesus' original statement – man is not made for the Sabbath, but the Sabbath for man – has Jesus say:

> O man, if thou knowest what thou doest, thou art blessed, but if thou knowest not what thou doest, thou art accursed and a transgressor of the law.

It should be immediately obvious that the words "if thou knowest what thou doest" do not refer to this man recognizing that he is breaking the law, but to the possibility of his choosing to exist on another level of awareness. Breaking the law is mentioned not as a something in its own right, but as a result of something else: the level of awareness possessed. Jesus is saying that if you do not have a distinct and present-minded awareness during an act, any act, then it is automatically accursed because you are not properly conscious. Without this intrinsic level of awareness, this present-mindedness, this authentic seeing of reality beyond automatic responses, every act is in a fallen state. The Jesus of this codex is telling this man that if he doesn't have the requisite level of awareness then he is bound by the law, but if he is awake and aware and properly conscious then instead of being bound he is free, not to break the law whenever he feels like it, but to make real decisions about the law and much else besides. It is automated reactions that are the problem, not the niceties associated with strict observance.

In *The Nazarene Gospel Restored,* Robert Graves and Joshua Podro are onto something similar when they suggest that Jesus "insisted on the need for gratitude to one's enemies when their hostility pointed to faults in oneself."[2] This helps confirm the above interpretation of Jesus' moral intentions by way of its inner complexity. To counsel that if your enemy sues you for your shirt, you should let him have your coat as well, or that if he strikes you on the right cheek, you should proffer the left, is to counsel a mode of perfection simply unattainable in ordinary life. Such injunctions make no sense except in a subtle teaching situation. It is to intentionally suffer through an attempt to do what is clearly nonsensical. It is to set in motion a moment of conscious clarity, a bare-bones confrontation with one's innate emotional tendency to react out of impulse. It is to wake up and stay awake *by means of* the irritation that arises when one is misunderstood, when one is falsely accused, or when one is confronted by an embarrassing truth about oneself. It is to be thankful in the throes of an inner anger that is caught in the "act of arising" and held in the glare of an *inner attention* that is never fooled. It is to *know,* in the sense of the *Codex Cantabrigiensis,* what one is doing as one is doing it. It is to hear Jesus' words "Father, forgive them for they know what they do" and realize that he may have meant something quite different from what we previously thought.

Impossible Possibilities 4.2

Christianity presumes itself to be in possession of a great spiritual truth that can help us overcome our all too human nature, and in an odd kind of way it does possess such a secret. It has, however, scrambled that secret beyond recognition and constantly falls short of its own high ideals. Why? Because it is unconscious Christianity – it is Christianity fast asleep inside its little hot-house of belief. Why aren't we being taken seriously? Why are we the butt of so many jokes, so many attacks, so many investigations? Why can't we agree among ourselves? All of which suggests that the plan Christianity has in its possession is being read upside down and back to front, that like the plan for a very intricate machine that has been torn up and scattered to the four winds, Christianity's plan is in equal disarray and is in need of accurate reassembly.

Perfect goodness. Perfect compassion. Perfect love. Three impossible possibilities taunting us in our trance-like condition, the condition within which we collectively assume that we are fully conscious, fully responsible and fully alive. Love your neighbor as yourself, etc, etc. An avalanche of moral demands that we mostly ignore. The whole business of morals such a hit-

or-miss nightmare that we give up on the perfection stakes and grasp for something a little more realistic – a basic tolerance of other people's stupidity, and our own. And all the while the nagging voice of our social and religious conditioning signals that we're not even making it on this most basic of levels.

Waking up to all of this takes an act of will, a "seeing" rooted in a sense of one's own existence that goes far beyond any idea of self we may be carrying in our minds. Slowly, painfully, we begin to surface from the dream of submerged doing and thinking, and each surfacing teaches us a little bit more about the self we did not know ourselves to be. This means that some of our decisions are real decisions, some of our statements are real statements, some of our affective experiences are the result of evaluative feeling and not just raw emotion. Our tendency, however, is to drain our energy away in mental and physical activity, replenish it through sleep and eating and endlessly repeat the process. So what we need is a resurrection of the self to the self, a resurrection through the senses so that we can unhook ourselves from conscious distraction and learn, slowly and methodically, the difference between having, and not having a will.

As with Schwitzgebel's students when their beepers went off, a self sensitized to its own existence rises from the dead at regular intervals; it is alive to the fact that its tendency in each moment is to go with the distractive flow and lose all sense of its own existence. In a word, to be constantly engaged and submerged in conscious activity is to be at the mercy of our reactive emotions. We are forever being taken by surprise. Awakened abruptly from the sleep of engagement we react to situations out of social or religious conditioning, and in doing so limit our ability to fully appreciate what is going on around us.

Meister Eckhart, the great German mystic, helps clarify what this means in relation to a self that is free of automatic responses. He puts it this way:

> The Holy Scriptures shout that man should be free from self, for being free from self, you are self-controlled, and as you are self-controlled you are self-possessed, and as you are self-possessed you possess God and all creation.[3]

This is not Eckhart stuffily confirming that moral behavior leads to self-control and thence to possession of God, but to the fact that real morality is dependent on possession of self; that is, on our being freed from the limited, reactive self whose life is one of constant distraction. To lose this limited self is to "wake up"; it is to transcend the self that sleeps and acquire real will. A new self forms and occupies the old self's location, and this new self heralds the capacity to make *real decisions.* And so Eckhart can say what seems to be utterly contradictory, namely, that losing self equals self-control. For to the extent that we lose our old morally rigid self (are truly present to ourselves moment by moment), then this annuls the ingrained habit of our being consciously usurped by world, thought and deed. In as far as this is accomplished, we are potentially in possession of God and all creation. Why? Because we have swapped our consciously engaged mind for a state of mind in which we properly exist, and this is for Eckhart, as it is for the writer of the *Codex Cantabrigiensis,* a potentially blessed state.

The Pelagian Heresy 4.3

The 4th century Celtic theologian Pelagius Britto argued that the human will was free and a God-given right. In taking this stance he was anathema to people like St. Augustine who believed the opposite. In Pelagian terms we were born free of sin, and as such were capable of maturing into beings with the ability to discriminate between virtue and vice. Augustine did not agree. Our fleshly appetites, he believed, were so oppressive, so overwhelming, that their tyranny could not be shaken off. Only Christ's redemptive power could rescue us from ourselves – we were basically helpless. In alignment with this dour notion the Church's catchphrase since the end of the 4th century has been that we are all helpless, that we cannot effect real change in our lives without God's grace. Accept the Pelagian argument and you not only contradict St. Augustine, you make a nonsense of God's plan of salvation, not to mention the Church's present notion as to why it exists at all. Choose the Pelagian path and you return Christianity to a morality governed by the rigidities of law and not much else.

The Church's rejection of the Pelagian proposal probably sounds fair given the brainwashing we've been subjected to over the last fifteen hundred years, but it is hinged on St. Augustine's distorted view of human nature, and that view fails to recognize the capacities and abilities our deeper nature harbors. We are without doubt defective beings when it comes to governing the wayward appetites of our emotionally reactive natures, but we are not completely helpless. Something vital is missing in the Church's overview of the human, and that something is that we each have the inbuilt ability to wake up out of our emotionally driven state and witness our own folly. This happens quite frequently, in fact, but we choose to ignore such nudgings because the path of least resistance is the easier one to take. A flickering moment of real consciousness before we again dive into the pool of conscious engagement and disappear to self, other and world.

Father Sylvan clearly understood the necessity of "self-possession" in the Eckhartian sense. He tells us that we have to "separate our sense of self from all thoughts and logical reasoning in order to reach the relative void from which *the certainty-that-has-no-name may speak.*" [4] In saying this he is quite obviously not referring to certainty of "belief" or "doctrine"; he is referring to a core realization that arises gradually within the awake self, the realization that reality is a little more complex than our intellects suspected, that waking up to our state of conscious sleep is in fact

Christianity's lost dimension, the secret it carries in its heart of hearts. Whether Christian, Jew, Moslem, Hindu or Buddhist, this is what needs to be operative if we are to experience even a moment of spiritual freedom. It is the quality of our awareness that is important, not the beliefs we cart around in our heads.

On the intellectual level, having an examined faith is a prerequisite if we are to go beyond the limited and limiting aspects of the Jesus story, but in the end it is the quality of our awareness that matters, not the sharpness of our intellectual observations. Such observations may well be accurate, even true, but if they lack the core dimension of our humanity (self as a "presence" to self), then they may well backfire on us. It's once again hit-or-miss. We are, in other words, in constant moral danger as we go about our daily business. Father Sylvan sums up our position with characteristic force:

> Ego is the systematic affirmation of emotional reaction. This system is fuelled by the energy of attention. Therefore as long as a man has no control over his attention his possibilities remain imprisoned in the ego no matter what ideas he espouses and no matter what effort he expends.[5]

The challenge is not whether we can mortify the flesh or believe the unbelievable; it is whether we can find sufficient energy within ourselves to wake up to what "waking up" actually means. Socrates' injunction to know the self (it actually belongs to Solon) takes on new meaning in relation to this discovery. Waking up has little to do with information gathering; it has to do with *gathering ourselves in until we fully occupy the space in which we exist.* Jacob Needleman puts it this way: "All the right thinking in the world will not change my essential nature, my intimate self, my very being."[6] His conclusion is that we each have to fully comprehend the seductive property of our thoughts if we are to survive as a species.

The Balancing of Attention 4.4

The central issue facing all of us is the activation of an entirely new faculty of attention, a sensing of our core existence that carries us ever closer to the boundary of being. Such a condition of psyche cannot be brought about through "inner engagement" with objects of attention; it can be enticed to appear only when our system of attention is *simultaneously directed towards the inner and the outer.* A balancing tension within psyche and body has to be set up, and out of this creative tension comes our first rudimentary experiences of being awake.

Before going into what this experience entails, it's necessary that we return to Needleman's definition of "inner" and "outer" experience. He flatly rejects the idea that "thinking" and "emotion" constitute our inner life. It is, he believes, a misunderstanding that has had disastrous consequences for both Christianity and modern culture. We have overlooked the fact that our so-called inner world is predominantly composed of outer world phenomena and landed ourselves in a muddle. Even our emotional responses are "outer", for they hinge mostly on outer world interactions. What we are really engaged in is the *interiorization of outer experience,* a domination of the inner by the outer that causes us to lose all sense of what and who we are. We are, in a word, lost to ourselves, not in the sense of being lost to sin and evil, or as a lost sheep that has to be herded back into some religious fold, but lost to ourselves as living beings. We've gone missing. We're not at home. We are *vacant.* And our constantly being vacant allows even the little energy of attention we manage to accumulate to wither like a leaf on the bough. And all thanks to St. Augustine who, in his wisdom, sounded what Morris Berman describes as the death knell for the voice of interiority. Roman Catholic Cardinal Jean Daniélou, professor of primitive Christianity at the Institut Catholique is with St. Augustine. In his view, "The saved are those who believe, regardless of their level of interior life."[7] I am indebted to

Professor Needleman for this quote.

Other philosophers have written about the incomplete self and its problems, but Needleman pushes further than most and identifies this chattering self as an enemy. He means by this that the tendency of human beings to trust what is only a part of themselves is to continue in a self-perpetuating mistake. And so he advocates a spiritual psychology in place of a theology of belief, and asks what it is we ourselves can contribute to the situation. The answer given is complex, for how can a self that is incomplete contribute anything of worth? This has of course been the Church's contention for centuries: we are simply too sinful and must, in the end, rely on Jesus' saving power, and on the Church's assessment of spiritual reality. This assessment is that we are powerless in the face of evil, an inherited evil in the sense of a deep and abiding flaw passed on to us from our First Parents (Adam and Eve), and an evil sometimes referred to as *sentient* (the Devil and all his hordes). Needleman's assessment is that we are caught in the psychological dilemma of not knowing how to disentangle ourselves from mental and emotional processes that are debilitating. We each have the capacity to wake up out of the little self's conscious dream, but it's a matter of comprehending what that means in experiential terms.

As an experience, waking up can be described technically as *being while we do.* We are either consciously submerged to the extent that we cease to have self-presence, or we rally our wits and hold our living presence in place as we go about our daily lives. This, as we quickly discover, is no easy task; it takes energy and skill to accomplish this act, and it is an act that forever fails even as it seems to succeed. Backwards and forwards we go between being engaged *with* self-presence and being engaged *without* self-presence. Continually toppling into submerged engagement with self, other or world, we begin to realize that the difficulty isn't in waking up, it is in staying awake. So natural has the state of being consciously submerged and engaged with reality become that we keep forgetting to remember to stay awake. Awake. Asleep. Awake. Asleep. Awake. Asleep. A disappearing act that goes on second by second without our generally being aware of it. Yes, we are awake to ourselves as a presence at intervals, but our understanding of what is going on is such that we don't recognize the difference between the two states. It takes conscious recognition of our submerged state to trigger us out of this state, and it takes an "act of will", an act of existential courage to sustain that state for anything more than a fraction of a second. We are at the mercy of hard-wired perceptual systems that have taken millions of years to evolve, and have arrived at the erroneous opinion that these systems are all we need to survive. Survival equals success, and we will use anything, and do anything to meet the requirements of this dominating drive.

But there's more to us than a mere drive for survival; we aren't that simple an organism. We have other levels to our nature, and these levels interweave with our conscious minds. The Jungian analyst Erich Neumann describes these levels as "phases of the ego", and through an analysis of these phases sketches in for us the ego's containment in, and eventual escape from, the unconscious. These phases are birth, puberty, middle age, old age and death,[8] and Father Sylvan confirms this approach when he says, "When you speak of transformations, remember that you are speaking of a process that obeys the same laws as the growth of the physical body."[9] But our escape from the unconscious is only partial, for the ego-personality that evolves is a divided system, a system of conscious and unconscious attributes, the tension between which constitutes its creative and transformative dynamic. The emergence and transformation of the ego is stamped from beginning to end with interactions and confrontations at the unconscious level. Whether conscious of this level or not, we sense or glimpse something of this level's capacity to express itself when we inadvertently dip towards it in grief, or due to pain. Or we may simply be overpowered by it if our style of life, or thought, causes us to ignore its promptings. Whatever the case, each phase has its transition point, and this point is generally experienced as a crisis with creative potential.

In analytical psychology a person's life from birth to death, from unconsciousness to what Neumann calls "the integration of the final phase", is marked by phases or archetypal zones. These zones, phases or sectors punctuate the life stream at intervals, and are responsible for the ego's growth toward, and interaction with, *the ground of being.* Neumann captures the essence of this interaction when he tells us that the ground of being "fills the psychological inwardness of the anthropos (man)."[10] We are not merely empty creatures governed by "drives"; we are creatures constantly interacting with the deepest levels of the self, and as such are in contact with capacities and abilities that rise up in us when least expected.

What has to be realized is that these interactions are actually "encounters", encounters with the "formless center of being", and that the form they take in consciousness depends on the kind of people we are. They are *our* encounter, and because of this they are experiences touched by the quality of our thinking and the texture of our daily lives. Jesus can call this encounter with formlessness "father"; we may not find the experience quite so comforting. And who is to say how many encounters Jesus had with his "father" before he became comfortable with formlessness? Formlessness is by its very nature ambiguous, and ambiguity is the sworn enemy of religious certainty. In this context the development of the ego becomes important, for it is the ego that undergoes the experience and is changed or transformed. Everything depends on the stage reached by the ego, the zones traversed, the phases completed.

Erich Neumann's grasp of what it means for a human being to be encountered by the archetypal level, by the formless ground of being, is deeply challenging. Describing such an encounter as a shattering of the ego's ordered world, he speaks of the ego being "encompassed", and of it undergoing a change in personality. This change can be orderly in spite of its disruptive effects, chaotic and apparently directionless, religious, delusional, artistic, or simply the experience of falling in love.[11] In this sense everything is potentially archetypal, for every event or happening carries a hidden charge capable of triggering within us a sense of the deeper mystery we are each involved in. Reality, like a work of fiction, carries us towards uncertain conclusions. In the Gospel of Thomas, the writer has his version of Jesus say something that highlights this potential relationship we can have with our own depths.

> If you bring forth what is within you, what you bring forth will save you. If you do not bring forth what is within you, what you do not bring forth will destroy you.

This statement from a so-called apocryphal Gospel (a Gospel not accepted by today's Christianity as legitimate Scripture) carries us far beyond the dictates of the conscious mind. This Jesus is not advocating salvation through vicarious sacrifice; he is directing our attention to our much-ignored gut feelings

To "wake up" in the sense of Eric Schwitzgebel's beeper experiment is to catch sight of ourselves as we emerge from the dream of conscious engagement. To "wake up" to what that means in itself is to become aware in a much more dynamic manner; it is to realize that our usual form of awareness is "mono-directional" in the sense of forever pointing in only one direction: inward or outward. Only occasionally is there a sense of balance between the two, and these are generally our most insightful moments. Why? Because a deep-structure form of communication has been set up between conscious and unconscious levels, and the tension generated frees us from the limitations of conscious construction and fabrication. Our dilemma, however, is that this doesn't happen very often. We are either "all wrapped up in ourselves", or "estranged from ourselves". It's an either/or situation that flickers from the "inside" to the "outside" depending on circumstances, and as the inner is composed mostly of thoughts about the outer, we are mostly estranged from the inner even as we seem to be engaged with it. It's a Catch-22 situation ultra difficult to detect and deal with, and it is that very fact that makes it the greatest challenge of all.

The Esotericism of Energy 4.5

In the parable of the Prodigal Son, the returning profligate is described as having *wasted his substance* in a far country. Father Sylvan interprets this as a reference to squandered energy, and links it to our being so wrapped up in thoughts and sensations that our soul (self as "presence" backed by the energy of "attention") can be described as *being* in exile.[12] This is a unique interpretation of a parable thought to be about God's forgiveness, but it does not strain the story to interpret it in this fashion. Sylvan also speaks of "the accumulation of the force of inner attention,"[13] and in doing so suggests that we have the capacity to act as *accumulators of energy.* Jacob Needleman links this energy to "deep self-questioning" (the kind of questioning proposed by George Steiner at 2.2), and describes the result in terms of the soul coming into existence and "gather(ing) itself into an independent entity."[14] Father Sylvan refers to such "gatherings" as *the esotericism of energy.*[15] Here, then, is the center of the cyclone, the heart of the matter in relation to our becoming more aware. The hidden teaching of Christianity is about an accumulation of energy from out of which grows a new kind of human being, and not just in a psychological sense. Psychological adjustment in Neumann's terms will take place, but the greater adjustment will be our relationship to Being as an experience.

Strange as this may sound, it is an idea not foreign to Christian thinking; it is in fact part of St. Paul's doctrine concerning resurrection. With reference to the physical body after death, Paul declares that it will be *raised a spiritual body.* Alluding to this statement in *The Illusion of Immortality,* Corliss Lamont quotes Canon B. H. Streeter on what Paul may have meant by such a claim. Lamont is not impressed by Streeter's reasoning, but the Canon's words are intriguing. "We may suppose," he says, preparing to extend Paul's argument somewhat, "that during our life on earth we are, although we know it not, building up an unseen celestial body which is a sort of counterpart of our earthly body but more exactly adapted to the expression of the character which our thoughts and conduct are all the while developing." This inadvertently supports Sylvan's and Needleman's idea of an independent spiritual entity forming from the energy that has been accumulated, but it immediately falls back into the trap of making this entity's development dependent on moral factors alone. All you have to do is believe in Jesus, live a moral life and your celestial body will form.

Father Sylvan and Jacob Needleman would be unlikely to disagree that a strong sense of morality is a necessary part of the spiritual life, but given what we have already gleaned from their thoughts on soul and energy, they would, I think, consider such qualities of secondary importance to that of an intrinsically awake self. And Meister Eckhart is on their side. It isn't moral behavior that delivers up a spiritual life, he tells us, it is "possession of self" (the cultivation of self-presence) that liberates us from our morally inadequate selves. If we want to "wake up" in real terms, we have to firstly wake up to the fact that we are asleep on our feet. Then, and only then, will the energies necessary for soul-making begin to accumulate.

5: Depth

There is an opening downward within each moment, an unconscious reverberation, like the thin thread of the dream that we awaken with in our hands each morning leading back and down into the images of the dark.
James Hillman
The Dream and the Underworld

Intro: 5.0

In his paper "The Ominous Numinous", the research psychologist J.A. Cheyne draws our attention to what he terms "a more sinister and primordial other... at the most fundamental biological roots of our being."[1] Yes, it sounds scary, and it is scary, for Cheyne's contention is that the presence of this psychic "other" is so radically different from the ordinary self that it can dominate consciousness. We can experience a psychic tap on the shoulder that sends a shudder right down to the core of our being; and it isn't just our imaginations playing tricks. There is "a primordial core consciousness", and it has a nasty habit of surprising us as we walk down a dark street, or pass through a shadowy wood, or as we *descend* into sleep and dream.

Experiences of a "sensed presence" resulting in visual, auditory and tactile hallucinations are known to erupt during "sleep paralysis," an awake condition of physical immobility during which only the eyes can be opened or closed. Estimates suggest that 30% of young adults report such experiences, and that out of this frightening condition "grow elaborate and complex... accounts of incubus attacks, demonic possession, old hag attacks and, more recently, alien abductions."[2] Although experienced while awake, such encounters are classified as "dreams" due to what is termed "the superpositioning of dream imagery and affect on waking consciousness," a condition believed to originate in the limbic system. This, in turn, is associated with a "vigilance system" that activates in relation to possible danger. This is a complex business that can't be gone into fully here. Suffice it to say that it holds clues as to the nature of the sinister experiences we sometimes have during sleep and dream.

One approach is to label such experiences transcendent and supernatural, another is to interpret them as purely natural, that is, as evolutionary and related to our primordial past. The second explanation sounds right to our modern ears, but in what sense are such experiences evolutionary? A strong sense of "evil" accompanies experiences of sleep paralysis (between 78% and 98%), and that is an anomaly that can't be ignored. Feelings of threat and fear are one thing, but a "sensed malevolence" in connection with a strong "presence" is quite another. One respondent described the experience as "fear for his soul," another as "an intense feeling of indescribable evil," and such descriptions are common. So has the Church been right all along about sentient evil (the Devil and his hordes waiting in some dark domain to attack us), or are churchmen today simply bamboozling us and themselves due to the state of deep psychological conflict they are in over the question of evil? They have after all been proffering the notion of evil as an independent force or energy for centuries, and this notion, deeply embedded as it is in our culture, hangs around at the back of our minds like an empty cobweb. Yes, the web is empty, but the very existence of the web suggests it could be otherwise.

The Creative Unconscious 5.1

Something not generally known is that we are all adept at imaginatively constructing scenarios out of thoughts, memories or external sounds as we slip into sleep at night, and slip out of sleep in the morning. A radio alarm's sudden introduction of a news item or the sound of music is often built into our semi-awake condition as a dream that makes perfect sense until we actually emerge from sleep. What made sense one moment is recognized the next as a subtle creation of our own half-awake mind, a clever incorporation of external events into our inner psychic space through mental trickery. Even when half asleep, we are busy making sense of the world through interpretation and translation. So P.D. Ouspensky's observation that through subtle acts of association while asleep we generate elaborate and coherent plots out of dream images, physical sensations and memories is basically accurate, and the fact that some researchers have gone as far as to suggest that through internal dialogue when awake (creation of the mental scenarios that generally background our bouts of automated behavior) we actually create the illusion of self-continuity spoken of by Hume and others shows plainly how complex our interactions with self, other and world are at base.

During sleep paralysis, or nightmare, we creatively fill in the blanks in an attempt to explain what we feel or sense, and what we feel or sense may well have arisen for reasons completely different from the ones we imagine. This is the state of "vigilance" brought on by darkness, and at its deepest level it is connected to our primordial past, our biologically ancient sensibility of being alert to the threat of predators. Beings of the Twenty-first century beings we may be, but we are carrying deep within ourselves an instinctive capacity for survival that the onset of darkness triggers into action, a capacity laced with primitive interpretations of reality where ancient fears bubble to the surface. But notice the overlap: it isn't just a matter of "creatively making something up"; it is also a matter of these deep-seated fears splicing themselves into nocturnal events that may or may not be threatening.

But dreams of horror aren't just about our prehistoric ancestors' fear of the dark and their alertness to the often hidden presence of predators; they are also about cultural baggage, consciously and unconsciously imbibed ideas concerning unsavory entities that exist on some other plane of existence. These too splice into the overall psychic picture, elements of nightmare being constructed out of Church teachings where ideas about sentient evil continue to be fed into the society by evangelical and fundamentalist Christian groups. On the larger scale of Western culture, such ideas are absorbed through the bombardment of commercialized horror films and books that the Church, privy as it is to modern knowledge, coyly ignores for reasons best known to itself, and the result is psychological and spiritual confusion on a mass scale. Enter the Jungian-oriented psychologist James Hillman with this observation:

> Christianism, in a two-sided masterstroke, both did away with the underworld and horrified it as the perpetual alternative to the Christian path. Christianism or underworld: one had to choose, and who would choose the horror?[3]

I have in earlier writings drawn attention to James Hillman's penetrating ideas, and will recap on some of them here.[4] In *The Dream and the Underworld,* a text that explores the connection between psychology and mythology, Hillman explains this connection thus: "Mythology is a psychology of antiquity. Psychology is a mythology of modernity."[5] The ancient world did not have a psychology in our sense of that word, he tells us, but it did have a system of myths that showed the relationship between humans and forces and images of a "more than human" capacity. We in the modern world are in the same boat, only in reverse: we have our fields, instincts, drives and complexes to help us deal with inner forces and images, but no mythology to speak of.

Drawing our attention to Eugen Bleuler's early 20th century invention of the term "depth psychology", Hillman speaks of our shift from "the activity of taking things apart to the vision of seeing them in depth,"[6] a change in perspective that carries us back to the ancient definition of the human soul as bathun – *depth.* We owe this definition to the Greek philosopher Heraclitus, who believed the soul to be a hidden, invisible dimension of the human, a dimension without limitation that had to be descended into. And not just the soul, as it turns out. In this scheme everything that existed had its own soul, its own "darkness" or "depth", and could be fathomed only through an "entering" that revealed its hidden nature. The truth of a thing was not *in* its depths, but in the fact that it *was* "depth", a concept we will return to.

The ancient Greek god of "depths" was Hades. No temples or altars were raised to him, no artistic form created to represent him. There was no trace of him in the upper daylight world, and he had no descendants. Hillman notes that he was also referred to as "Pluto" (wealth), or as "Trophonios" (nourishing), and speculates that these names or disguises were a subtle reference to the hidden wealth and nourishment enjoyed by those who made this challenging descent. There is an interiority or depth that cancels out as "a hidden presence – even an invisible fullness."[7]

Another important factor in the myth of Hades is the underworld's lack of time. Time is an upperworld concept and has no role to play in the House of Hades. There is no time element, but there is "limitless depth", and this interior realm of the self, this "underground" (*ge*) should not be confused with the cold, dark realm of the "underworld" (*Chthon*).[8] The "underground" (instinctual body or earthly soil) is fertile; the "underworld" (what is below the earth and of the dead) is infertile. Well, not quite. The polytheistic mind often merged these terms, as in *ge-Chthon,* and in doing so added a *ge* perspective to *Chthon.* And to further complicate matters there was *zoe,* a vitality belonging to *all* underworld phenomena. Here then is the mythological realm of the psyche, the realm modern psychology has translated into a series of levels, fields, instincts, drives and complexes, a "fantasy of structural levels"[9] gleaned by Sigmund Freud from his study of mythology.

So what's my point? Haven't we rightly replaced mythology with psychology? What is the benefit of retracing our steps into this murky area of the ancient imagination? What is to be gained from translating what we now know about the human psyche back into these archaic levels and terms? Well, firstly, it could be said that we have been hoodwinked if we think present-day psychology's grasp of the human psyche is in any way complete, and, secondly, the influence of Christianity on the psychology of religion has been such that our greatest fear is of our own psychic depths. Modern humans we may be, but our collective attitude toward the mind and its deeper, darker aspects in our Christianized cultures is one of educated horror. We have developed an "occult" view of the mind's depths, and through fictions such as *The Exorcist* and the novels of Stephen King have come to view the deep end of psychophysical experience as spiritually dangerous. The Swiss psychologist Carl Jung turns this view on its head when he says:

> In reality we can never legitimately cut loose from our archetypal foundations unless we are prepared to pay the price of a neurosis, any more than we can rid ourselves of our body and its organs without committing suicide.[10]

Hillman castigates Christianity for its role in changing the underworld into a place of horror. He tells us that the Church, in a two-sided masterstroke, both did away with the underworld and horrified it as an alternative to the Christian path. The taboos against psyche were in place, and they would be endlessly refined until even the slightest indication of underworld experience would be interpreted as evidence of satanic activity.

But is this altogether fair? Is Christianity solely to blame for how psyche came to be viewed? Given what we now know about our primordial past, and about the nature of dream, is it any wonder that early Christianity interpreted things the way it did? Yes, we can get spooked on a dark street, or by a film or book with an occult theme, but in this day and age wouldn't that more properly be interpreted as the result of our ability to suspend disbelief than to church teaching. We choose to be afraid. We're actually free of all that silly stuff. We've outgrown the idea of the demonic with its dread presences and spooky happenings. Spirits and demons have been eradicated from our world view due to the rise of sound intellectual discipline and common sense. Really? Are you absolutely sure about that? Morris Berman has his doubts.

> It became 'irrational' to have irrational fears. Hybrid monsters and fabulous beasts seemed to vanish under the glaring light of the new science. In reality, they only scurried away, found a place to hide in the recesses of the mind. The language of psychoanalysis and depth psychology... now starts to make much more sense. Fear expressed is very different from fear repressed.[11]

Carl Jung concurs. We are often moved by forces from a deep source that is not conscious, and is not under our control. Such forces were once referred to as demons or gods, and they are as active today as they were in our distant past. The old theology certainly got routed with the rise of the scientific revolution, but it was by no means eradicated. The legacy of science over the last few hundred years has been that of a distancing effect between our conscious mind and our so-called unconscious mind. So entrenched has this distancing effect become that *any* intimation of a subjective nature is treated as potentially unreliable. Hence Eric Schwitzgebel's inordinate care when setting up his beeper experiment. The material gathered had to come from within that tiny few seconds after the beeper went off; any later and it would have been considered untrustworthy.

But what exactly is it that's untrustworthy in such moments? What exactly is a subjective response? Is it our interiority that lies? Does our heart lie when it misses a beat, or our liver lie when it's on its last legs? Would it not be more accurate to say that it is our conscious ineptness in relaying what is going on in our interior depths that constitutes the problem? If it takes a lapse of only a few seconds for our conscious minds to scramble the evaluative feelings presented by our bodies, then that suggests we should to be paying much closer attention to why that is the case. It is not our interiority that's lying; it's we who are inadvertently misrepresenting what our interiority is trying to say because of distraction and/or conscious prejudice.

As a result of science's search for clarity and exactness, and the backgrounding influence of a Christianity that rides without conscience on the coat tails of our primordial natures, we have developed a sinister view of our own depths, a fear of interiority that drives us to accept often limited intellectual arrangements of thought alongside beliefs about Jesus that annul any desire to explore our inner natures. We are, in other words, continually avoiding ourselves; or, more accurately, *voiding* ourselves. The experience of ourselves as depth has gotten lost among theoretical constructions and theological imaginings. In science's scheme soul has been abolished; in Christianity's scheme soul is a psychic object dished out by God at birth and taken away at death to enjoy either the rewards of heaven or the torments of a now ambiguous hell.

Hell is of course in the cellar, Latin *cella* (subterranean storeroom), and that requires a descent into Hell (Hades) if we die without accepting the Christ formula. In Christian terms it is then too late to make amends, and in depth terms it is equally too late to be of psychological benefit. The "opening downward" referred to by Hillman in the quote prefacing this chapter has been successfully closed off, the *thin thread of the dream we awaken with in our hands each morning* exchanged for a view that robs us of even the inclination to pursue our deeper feelings to source. Soul has been exchanged for spirit, a pneumatic spirit that rises to meet Christ in the air," (1 Thess. 4:17) and the reason for this is that in Christian tradition Christ has already descended into hell and forced Thanatos (death) to hide behind his own door. Christianity's consciously directed mission has been successful: polytheism (the old mythology of the soul) has been wiped out, our interior darkness flooded with an upperworld light (theology), its sacred purpose scrambled beyond recognition, or destroyed. Progressive ensoulment through descent has been exchanged for a seductive magical formula: Christ as dying savior. In contrast to this, Bernadette Roberts signals that we should be traveling in the opposite direction. "The tendency," she says, "is to be afraid of interior darkness, have wrong views or interpretations of it. Instead of going down into their own emptiness, people try to fill it in with the pleasures of this world. They run from darkness, nothing and emptiness..."[12] Even more to the point is a statement made by Roberts in relation to Jesus' own consciousness:

> God does not know himself as God nor know he is God. Thus neither in his humanity nor divinity did Christ know he was God. That we claim Christ knew he was God attests only to our ignorance regarding self or consciousness and our limited understanding of Christ, human and divine.[13]

The Body's Question 5.2

It is in and through the physical body that we wake up to the fact that our primordial selves are still alive and kicking, but it is also the medium through which soul as depth *(bathun)* can be intercepted. Hence Christianity's taboo against any form of descent into the self that removes Christian markers such as Jesus as God, or God as Jesus. Prayers for the sick, or for the world in general, are acceptable, but any journey inward that lacks this theological overlay is considered dangerous and to be avoided. Why? Because our inner depths have been equated with the Underworld and the mythology that goes along with it, and that disallows it as a spiritually nourishing source. This is of course to avoid the very process that *makes* soul; it is to avoid the experience of being ushered into *our own presence as if into the presence of a stranger.* On one level, that accurately sums up our condition: we are strangers to ourselves and desperately require an introduction. On another level it intimates what Christianity has come to fear most: the presence of something in our depths that is *more* than the conscious self. This something has no name and no history; it is a *hidden presence, an invisible fullness* that blossoms out of our attempts to comprehend real interiority. And it is not a presence in the sense of an entity; it is the *depth of our depths* registering in a manner beyond normal articulation. It is, in other words, the body's question, not ours in any conscious sense, and it is a question we have to learn to live with rather than answer.

Christianity Without Incarnation 5.3

Before going any more deeply into this issue, we have to get something problematical out of the way: the idea that Jesus as the Christ is the only legitimate route we have when approaching *the truth of being.* In true Father Sylvan style, the late Robert Funk, co-founder of the Westar Institute and the infamous Jesus Seminar, sums up this problem with the pugnacity he was famous for:

> It is a good thing that the true historical Jesus should overthrow the Christ of Christian orthodoxy, the Christ of the Creeds. The creedal Christ... is an idol that invites shattering.[14]

Worship of the man Jesus *as if* he were somehow Israel's God come down to Earth in person has to been seen through for what it is: a mistaken theological construction. Jesus needs to be liberated from this kind of projectionism and reinstated in his proper historical context. Only by doing this can we learn to face the creative darkness of our own depths without distortion and distraction. Facing those depths without this Jesus is the spiritual challenge of our age, just as interpreting the Eucharist as not involving an actual transformation of the bread and wine into the blood and flesh of Jesus in some psychic sense was the challenge facing Christians during the Reformation.[15] Our theologically driven notions about Jesus need to be reconsidered and adjusted in the light of the available historical evidence, for as a result of those notions we have become bogged down in absurd literalisms and have come to believe that God manipulates history and much else for his own ends. Or we play theological games with the material in an attempt to hold the whole crumbling edifice together. Such stretchings of the imagination are unworthy of serious consideration. In this sense Christianity has completely lost track of its original premise and taken to believing in what amounts to fairy tales.

In his essay "Christianity Without Incarnation", Maurice Wiles explores the possibility of a Christianity in which Jesus' divine status is abolished. The sensitivity with which Wiles approaches this thorny question is not surprising, for at the time of writing he was Regius Professor of Divinity and Canon of Christ Church, Oxford, as well as chairman of the Church of England's Doctrine Commission. And yet he can argue for the abandonment of the Church's metaphysical claim that Jesus was the Second Person in a Holy Trinity. Believing there to be a strong case against such a view, Wiles considers the complex weave of ideas associated with incarnation and in conclusion points out that "the precise way in which Jesus is understood... has been a constantly changing phenomenon in the history of the Church."[16]

But he cannot predict in advance how this change in attitude towards Jesus will come about, for abandonment of the divinity model will entail more than logical deduction, more than the correction of historical distortion and theological exuberance; it will also mean engaging the Church in a dynamic discourse around this issue.

Wiles' account of how the doctrine of the Incarnation came about in the first place starts with the observation that it is not something directly presented in Scripture. He tells us that it is "a construction built on the variegated evidence to be found there."[17] The New Testament writers were interpreters, not reporters. Jesus is variously described as eschatological (end-time) prophet, Son of Man, Son of God, Lord, Logos and Messiah. He is seen by some as the pre-existent wisdom of God spoken of in the wisdom literature of the Jews, and by others in the more personal sense of God's pre-existent Son come down to Earth. But all four gospels (even John's) stop short of saying that he was actually God. It was one thing to personalize the wisdom literature, to poeticize its meaning, it was quite another to transform this strictly Jewish conception of the pre-existent wisdom of God into a human being.

The Jews never intended their notion of Sophia (wisdom) to be interpreted in such a literal fashion, and later Christian insistence that Sophia be amalgamated with the idea of Jesus as Logos (the Word of God) is a travesty of their sublime vision. As a concept, Sophia was feminine; Logos was masculine. It could certainly be claimed that Sophia had descended on Jesus at his baptism, but it could not be claimed that Jesus *was* Sophia dropping in physically from the transcendent realm in the form of a flesh-and-blood man. Such a claim is nonsensical. Yet such a claim was eventually made for Jesus, and diverse opinions arose because of it that worried the evolving Church from the end of the 1st century until the end of the 4th. Jesus was this and Jesus was that. Jesus had two wills, not one. Jesus had only one, untainted divine will. Jesus as the Christ was distinct from Jesus the man. Jesus the man was limited to normal human development, but as the Christ he was the recipient of knowledge directly communicated to him from God. Jesus was *all* God. Jesus was *all* man at the same time as he was *all* God.

All in all a mess of pottage that eventually led the Council of Nicea to demand creedal standardization. For by then no one either knew, or could remember, or perhaps even cared, what it was Paul or the original Apostles had believed about Jesus. And anyway, hadn't these Apostles lost track of what they were about and turned into heretics after the death of Jesus' brother James? It was all a bit of a puzzle, and it needed to be sorted out once and for all.

In her essay "A Cloud of Witnesses", Frances Young makes the point that titles such as Messiah, Son of Man, Son of God, Lord and Logos were all in existence *before* Christianity appeared on the scene. They were standard titles used among the many Jewish groups, and they were not always properly understood by later Christian exegetes. Some titles carried a different emphasis, some projected different Christological structures, some were influenced by differing linguistic and cultural environments.[18] Gaining additional importance in a Greek environment, some became a standard way of referring to Jesus, but it was a standard of usage amputated from its Jewish-sectarian roots. Jesus message had been about the imminent arrival of the Kingdom of God. The Church's message, based loosely on Paul's epistles and on the fact that God's kingdom had not arrived, was that Jesus was himself the central issue. Paul's evocation of the mystic Christ progressively hardened into a difficult to refute ecclesiastical literalism, and this literalism swept away all previous conceptions of Jesus as a normal human being. But what had actually made Jesus special was not that he was God, but that he had wholly surrendered himself to his conception of God. He had surrendered not to Judaism, or to Jewish sectarianism, but purely and simply to God alone. And that without an intermediary like himself to offset the pressure of confronting God as *formless void.* For doing so he was deemed heretical by just about everyone, rejected, tortured and crucified, and if alive today would probably incur the wrath of many for exactly the same reasons.

When dealing with the thorny question of Jesus' supposed divinity, Frances Young completes her observations in a reference note by pointing out that the fullness of God experienced by Jesus was the result of choice, will, purpose and election, rather than essential derivative nature.[19] He was a man like any other man, and as such extraordinary for that very reason. Our hope, therefore, is not in his supposed divinity, but in his humanity, in the fact that he could laugh and weep, thirst and be hungry, and still manage to plumb his own depths in such a startling manner. That is the connecting point between him and us. It was out of this all-too-human nature that he stepped into the fullness of an awareness that eclipsed the awareness of his time. And so Frances Young is forced to say that the reduction of all of God to the level of human incarnation is beyond our conceptual capacity.[20] It may be comforting to have a faith complete with a doctrine of atonement and the idea that God has dealt with evil, but that, she suggests, is the language of poetry. Ultimately, all language about God is analogical; it is "the expression of the unknown and inexpressible in terms of the known."[21]

And so we come to the additional problem of how to engage the Church in a dynamic discourse around this central issue. How is it to be done when so few Churchmen are willing to engage in such a discourse? Is there a bridging argument of some kind that would allow this to happen? Luckily for all concerned, there is, and it has appeared in a most unlikely place, in the writings of Bernadette Roberts, a Carmelite nun who eventually married and had children, and who now claims to have broken through into a sustained experience of no longer having an affective self.[22] This is an extraordinary claim, for it locks firmly into the challenge laid down by Father Sylvan with regard to our search for truth, a search that overlooks the fact that the emotions of our constantly submerged conscious self constitute our greatest spiritual hurdle. Surprised at every turn as we surface from our thought-filled reveries, we react out of a self whose emotions are ready to spark off at the slightest provocation. Here then is the issue around which our dynamic discourse can take place, and it is a discourse where Meister Eckhart's suggestion that we should be "free from self" in order to attain self-control takes on further meaning.

6: The Deep End

Until the rug (my 'self') had been pulled out from under me, I never realized how utterly dependent I was upon getting around under my own steam – steam of the mind and emotions, that is, not physical steam. It seems we possess an endless array of subtle energies we don't know we have until they are gone – although later, I was to see clearly how these energies are, in fact, the self's defenses against its own annihilation.[1]

Bernadette Roberts

The Experience of No-Self

Intro: 6.0

The Jungian psychologist Erich Neumann observes that mysticism tends to dissolve the traditional forms of religion and worship, and the writings of Bernadette Roberts confirm this point. In fact I would go so far as to say that her writings on the stages of spiritual awakening stand out as the most revolutionary contribution made by a contemporary Christian to this discussion since Meister Eckhart's time. Christian mystics of the past (Eckhart excepted) could be said to have only partly described their transcendent experiences in comparison with this contemplative's record. It may even be that she has experienced states of consciousness far in advance of those described in the traditional literature, for the states or stages laid down by Roberts eclipse the language of traditional mysticism and carry us, step by step, towards an appreciation of what to be spiritually awake means in terms not heard before in a Christian context. But it is a challenging journey at every turn, for to wake up inside the Christian paradigm in the way Roberts has is to run the risk of being thrown out. The path of theology so well traveled by Christian contemplatives gives way, in Roberts' case, to "an unhinging of every idea or belief we cling to regarding the structure of the world, the self, and God; an unhinging for which there are no substitutes, no life-preservers and no changing in midstream."[2]

Bernadette Roberts' core claim is that she now lives in a condition of mind in which no trace of subjective feelings arises; she is utterly without emotional responses. Now that is quite a claim; it challenges the folksy notion that mystics spend most of their time in an ecstatic state, a state of bliss. As she also claims to have transcended what she calls the 'reflexive self' (the reactive conscious mind), we have a double whammy, for that suggests no reflective or associative thought processes going on either. On hearing such claims, some critics have considered Roberts to be suffering from a pathology, but not friend and confidant Father Thomas Keating. For reasons we will explore later, this priest accepts Roberts' claims at face value, and thinks them indicative of a personal transformation beyond that of classical Christian expression, a stage that clarifies several important points in relation to writings by Christians mystics in the past.

Already acquainted with mystical experience by the age of fifteen, Bernadette Roberts eventually left the cloister, married, and had four children. But it is an experience had fifteen years later that concerns us, for it was then that she broke through into what she describes as an experience of having no self, an experience in which the self as a subjective experience ceased to exist. The libraries, bookstores and people she consulted helped hardly at all, there being no similar account on record culminating in "a complete falling away of the affective life."[3]

Before going into this in practical terms, we should perhaps listen to her on the subject of Jesus, the Church, and the Christian religion in general, for her insights suggest that she has gone well beyond the Jesus story as it has come down to us, a "going beyond" that lifts the whole story onto a new plane of understanding. And all from an experiential base no less, an interaction with interior processes known to underpin Christian mystical experience, but little understood outside of the theological language that has attempted to explain them.

The Jesus Problem 6.1

In the context of waking up spiritually, Roberts' evaluation of Jesus is of particular interest. She says, "I have often thought of Christ as one who fell outside his Jewish frame of reference when he saw the truth in it and went about setting the record straight."[4] The truth was to be found in Judaism, but an embroidery of religious thinking had obscured its shape and meaning. Jesus had "fulfilled the Scriptures (done it all), realized the truth, and set out to open the eyes of those still within this frame of reference."[5] These words not only throw new light on the meaning of the term "fulfilled the Scripture", they also reveal Bernadette Roberts' courage in rattling the literalist cage with regard to how Jesus perceived himself. In Roberts' view this was not Jesus setting himself up as a *fulfillment* of Scripture, it was writer's code for someone who had gone through all of the necessary states and stages prefacing *loss of the affective self.* He had fulfilled the Scriptures in the sense of seeing the process of transformation through right to the end – the end of everything we understand as human. And her interpretation of Jesus' death on the cross is of the same ilk, for it rejigs the Christian paradigm and redefines Redemption as a *giving up of the self.* This is not salvation for the soul through Christ's death on the cross, and neither is it a giving up of the self in the sense of dedicating the self to God; it is to literally lose the limited, self-seeking self altogether.

The basic question being asked by Roberts is this: Did Jesus give up his self so that the rest of us could have eternal life, or did he do something quite different? Did he, perhaps, give up his self to "show us the lengths to which we must go in order to see?"[6] Now that is not standard teaching; it is a quite different interpretation from the one generally offered. And the introduction of the term "see" adds a further dimension to its already challenging implications. It is in fact a reshaping of the language of orthodoxy: Redemption does not hinge on Jesus as Savior; it is conditional in relation to a person's spiritual growth and maturity. Not just any old maturity, spiritual maturity. We are being asked to go beyond our traditional ideas about Jesus and God and "see" in a new way. This seeing does not have to entail spectacular visions or a grand finale of love and bliss. Such experiences constitute the lower end of the contemplative's interaction with reality, and may have nothing whatsoever to do with God at all.[7]

According to Roberts, a good example of this kind of seeing can be detected in Jesus' statement that he had nowhere to lay his head. She suggests that this means Jesus could no longer focus his attention on anything, that he had reached the stage in his contemplative life where there was "nothing to which his mind could be either perceptually or conceptually attached."[8] This is an extraordinary explanation for what seems like a statement of simple fact – Jesus was without a place to live. But we should not reject her interpretation out of hand; whether it actually applies to Jesus hardly matters, for it reveals what Bernadette Roberts means by "seeing", and what she means is that Jesus was no longer attached to submerged forms of conscious thinking. He had, as the Gospels attest, freed himself from that kind of mental engagement.

Integration and Disintegration 6.2

Speaking of the affective, emotionally based self and its integration, Roberts tells us that integration of the self eventually gives way to a disintegration of the self; that is, we can't arrive at the condition of having no-self unless we first achieve a whole self.[9] But this whole self and its creation are only half of the story, the half we seem to be in charge of. The other half is not under our control; for on accomplishing a relative integration of the self and its parts, we inadvertently set in motion an opening out into a higher system that begins to dismantle the affective self. Having access to only incomplete contemplative testimony, theologians are at a loss to fully understand or follow the twists and turns of this situation. And in relation to experiences of ecstasy and bliss associated with mystical states, Roberts informs us that the disintegration of the self should not be equated with a falling back into an infantile state,[10] a state described clinically by Erich Neumann as *uroboros incest.* The disintegration of the self "is a forward, not a backward, movement," she says categorically, and as such heralds a wholeness that is beyond the reach of our emotions.

Optimum stability or integration of the affective system governing our emotions is therefore necessary for the process of expansion beyond the affective system to take place. And presuming, as Roberts does, that the fulcrum between self and no-self is housed in our perceptions, then a true integration of the self necessitates, a *perceptual balancing act between self and world.* She goes on to describe this balancing act as "maximum access to the still point – which is a point not of this system but discoverable through it."[11] "Unity" is not the keyword; the keyword is "disunity". There is a dualistic gap in our perception of self and world that, if we are to successfully shed affective limitation, has to be plumbed. Our feelings and our emotions are at once the problem and the answer, the spanning of the gap between "subject" (ourselves) and "object" (the world) a perceptual balancing act that allows "seeing" to erupt.[12] Oddly enough, Roberts refers to this kind of seeing as "a seeing which *is* the resurrection itself,"[13] and that again pushes the Jesus story well beyond anything presently understood.

The path of mystical theology so well traveled by Christian contemplatives did not, Roberts found, contain the fundamental elements she needed to explain her condition. It contained only "the usual descriptions of love and bliss, lights and energies,

God within and the true self,"[14] not what this explorer of the spiritual domain required to offset her very understandable fears as sense of self disappeared. And to complicate matters further, as the experience of having no sense of self became a permanent condition, out of this condition formed a growing dismay at the Church's theologically constructed belief system about Jesus. For these beliefs, once held so dear by Roberts, and in so many ways instrumental in her transformation, did not properly reflect the realizations she had come to by way of that transformation. Being caught up in words, in definitions, in theological explanations and constructions that obscured more than they revealed, we ran the risk of swapping "the river of truth" for an approach path to that river. The approach path might well reach the river, but it could easily become an impediment by way of ideas dogmatized beyond their intrinsic worth. And so, on reaching the river, and entering it, it was our responsibility to help straighten out some of the path's unnecessary convolutions.

The problem with the mystical record was that the accounts it contained were not "sufficiently personal or detailed to fill the gap between theory and practice,"[15] a problem lamented by professionals in other disciplines. To journey beyond the self was to journey beyond theological frames of reference and encounter areas of theological sensitivity that, as in the past, one tried to avoid. With the Spanish Inquisition breathing down his neck, St. John of the Cross had been unable to tell the full story of his contemplative life, and the outspoken Meister Eckhart had found himself censured by his Church for trying to do just that. Faith had to shift to "seeing" for this kind of thing to be understood; the whole point of religion was to point to something beyond religion.

This ex-nun is forthright in her summation of the overall problem facing the Church. She says the real tragedy of the cross was not that people did not understand Christ's suffering, but that they did not understand him at all.[16] The Jewish elite had not understood him, his disciples had not understood him, the Church founded in his name had not understood him, and in the final analysis we too did not understand him. Our capacity to think of him in either historical or contemplative terms had been overlaid with interpretations based on notions that were, to say the least, inadequate. We looked at him, but did not see him, listened to him, but did not hear him. All we saw and heard was the Christ of childhood, the Christ of theology, the Christ of the Church's imagination, the Christ of blind faith. The man of flesh and blood was no more; his search for God, his finding God and his losing God had been transformed into a magnificent, but deadly tale to pacify our fears. Or, as Roberts puts it, "Someone had to stretch the human limits to find out if there was any truth beyond the self, any life beyond this one, or any God beyond belief."[17]

Bernadette Roberts believes Jesus died on the cross discovering the answers to these questions. A contemplative by nature, she believes this man of intelligence and passion eventually went beyond self and passion, beyond God in the sense that his attachment to the religiously constructed idea of God faded into nothing. Making the claim that she has no God in the same sense as Jesus had no God, that they are companions in "a great mistake,"[18] Roberts then talks of the tragedy of those who have believed in him without ever coming to an understanding of what his life and death meant.[19] And so she equates "seeing" with "resurrection", and in doing so aligns herself with the equally radical views of Father Sylvan. Christ had expected a resurrection, she says, but it did not take place. Instead of resurrection and glory he had experienced nothingness.

The Affective Network 6.3

The main problem for Bernadette Roberts is the Church's acceptance of emotion as ultimately necessary for the appreciation of truth. Though separate from the cognitive processes, the affective life so infiltrates the cognitive life that the two seem to be inseparable. But they are in fact two separate systems that have become muddled. It is at this point that Roberts' observations get really interesting, for she asserts that the sense of subjective, emotional energy associated with self-consciousness actually constitutes the self: we do not *have* an affective life, we *are* an affective life. Our idea of having a self, although backed by a feeling of separateness and interiority confirming individuality, is in fact no more than the effect of the *entire affective network of the body* registered cognitively.[20] Sandwiched between our interiority (the subjective) and the world at large (the objective), we claim the sensation of physical energy as our own, assume that emotion is an expression of the self, and live accordingly. And we're proud of our affective lives. We're only human, we say, meaning that some outburst of emotion marks us out as different from, say, a robot. For who would want to be a robot and not be able to *feel* alive?

But what if we are mistaken about the nature of the self? What if our affective systems veil rather than reveal what we are? What if experiencing life in such a possessive manner is in fact at the low end, not the high end, of the awareness scale? What then? And how do we go about this transformation of the affective self when our feeling-energies are constantly headed in the opposite direction? These are just some of the questions that arise from a reading of Roberts' text, and they force us to reconsider some of our pet notions about what it means to be a human being. Her observations afford us a glimpse of something that may lie beyond the scope of the evolutionary process as it is presently understood, and her writings challenge us to explore this "something" as best we can.

Swapping "Belief" for "Seeing" 6.4

In the larger scheme of things self as an affectively governed system may only be temporary.[21] So it can be said that it is self we have to overcome, not sin; our endless shortcomings are due to the mixing of affective and cognitive perceptions underlying our sense of self. Caught in the trap of having a self governed by negative and positive emotions, indeed composed of these very emotions, we seek forgiveness when we should in fact be attempting to "put an end to the very need to be forgiven."[22] An enormous task, one might think, but not so; there is a way out of the dilemma and it has to do with swapping "belief" for "seeing."

But there's work to be done. Contemplatives scan the continuum of being looking for the still point, and on finding it they focus their gaze on it and allow it to pull them into ever greater stillness, a stillness that eventually turns into a *standstill.* This is how Roberts describes the process, and she adds: "In this way, the still point acts as the greatest inhibitor of the affective continuum... it gradually immobilizes all movement along the continuum."[23] And she delivers a warning to those who, because of devotional proclivity, ruin the experience of stillness and possible standstill because of emotion. Referring to this as "affective overflow," she suggests concentrating on the still point alone, and that, I imagine, means ignoring affective identification with Jesus.

The language she uses is of interest here, for her choice of words reveals not just a methodology but a system of comprehension that helps further refine the methodology described. For instance, she refers to the still point as an "unlocalized spot" within ourselves where we have the chance to run into God. And then she cracks the cosmic code by saying that this unlocalized spot is at the *center of the affective continuum.* So in effect our affective system is not only that which underpins our sense of being a self, it is also that through which we can transcend self. That is what having no-self means in raw terms; it means going beyond the limitations of both our seesawing emotions and our reactive minds. *Feeling* our way to the heart of our affective system through deep-end evaluative feeling, we encounter a stillness of such intensity that it causes the affective system to collapse in on itself.

Reflexive Mind 6.5

The sheer volume of detail on the transcendent state makes Bernadette Roberts' books impressive: she does not hold back on what she knows, and she knows a lot. Well aware that she is on a slippery slope as far as orthodox Catholicism is concerned, she does not resort to camouflaging her material; she chooses instead to speak with the authority one would expect from someone who has gone beyond the limitations of the affective life. In *The Experience of No-Self,* and in *The Path to No-Self,* she describes her experience of ego-transcendence and explains with facility that it doesn't matter whether our reactions are positive or negative, for in the world of reflexive (reactive) mind the one can so easily become the other that their apparent exclusiveness is often no more than an illusion.

Describing reflexive mind as at best "a temporary mechanism for developing a certain type of intelligence, an intelligence we must eventually learn to live without,"[24] Roberts focuses in on an important question: If the affective life falls away completely, what happens to positive emotions like charity, sympathy, compassion and love? The answer she supplies is that for those who make the journey beyond emotion and feeling the need to practice virtue vanishes – virtue remains, but it is a natural state of being arising out of emotional neutrality. This suggests that our normal, affective-governed state of consciousness is not as "normal" as we think it is. A necessary stage in our evolutionary growth it may be, but it is in fact a quite dangerous stage of growth where love and hate, compassion and cruelty are only a few pulse beats away from one another.

Having been informed that the falling away of the affective system invariably signaled a psychotic condition, Roberts points out that it is the affective system that actually causes psychological illness, and that it is this same system that underpins all human suffering. Contrary to what might be expected, the experience of having no-self, and therefore no affective system, is not an inhuman or insensitive state, but rather a highly sensitive and responsive state due to the fact that the cognitive faculty is intact and beyond emotional bias. Unhitched from the affective system, the cognitive system functions in a new way; that is, it remains continuously awake in and to the present moment, so stripping compassion of self-interest and love of ego-clutching. The affective self, on the other hand, linked as it is to a feeling of personal being, cannot escape from its drives, motivations, values and goals. And as these components of the self automatically give rise to memories, desires and expectations, and these in turn fan out into perception and thought, our feelings of contentment, peace, boredom, tiredness or loneliness are virtually unavoidable.[25] Swayed by what is happening around us, and in us, we succumb to the slightest change in our emotionally charged natures.

Meister Eckhart 6.6

What remains when the affective nature is stilled raises serious moral and philosophical questions. Bernadette Roberts enlists the help of Meister Eckhart, the 13th century German mystic as "one who has made the journey and crossed over,"[27] This is an important fix in terms of the quality of her contemplative life, for it challenges both the novice and the expert to reconsider what Eckhart was at pains to say in relation to the self. Noting that the Spanish mystics brought their contemplative experiences into line with the mystical speculations of Thomas Aquinas, Roberts reminds us that this famous German was, by contrast, considered outspoken to the point of censure. Speaking of man's essential oneness with God, Eckhart incurred the wrath of the inquisitors. And all because, in essence, this mystic of mystics believed he had penetrated the truth of being and moved beyond speculative theology. Eloquent where the great churchman Thomas Aquinas was silent, Eckhart revealed what some theologians considered to be theologically improper, that each of us is essentially, and not just accidentally, capable of union with God.[26]

In essence, this is Eckhart's answer to the question: Was Jesus literally God or not? If essentially one with God as a result of his contemplative explorations into God, then Jesus was God in that he eventually shed his nature in favor of God's nature. "I and the father are one," as a statement, inadvertently set the course of theological exposition in the wrong direction, but it was never meant to mislead. And so the mystery of "incarnation" surfaced, and the question of Jesus' identity hardened into the view that he had always been God. Yes, union with God was possible in terms of the affective life brought to the correct contemplative pitch through dark nights of the soul, bliss and ecstasy; but union in terms of identity for ordinary people was considered a spiritual impertinence. Roberts breaks with this tradition and says, "These are two different experiences: union before the breakthrough, identity after the breakthrough."[27]

Meister Eckhart was pulled up on a heresy charge for preaching all of what he knew to the people, so allowing them to intuit that dogma could be transcended. But he was a wily old fox, for not only did he transcend the limitations of theology, he also made himself impregnable to the accusation of error. Intellectually overpowering those who thought him suspect, he opened their eyes to the fact that even language has a transcendent dimension. And so, in one of his fragments he says that God is love because he is above love and affection,[28] and in another that pious practice is never so perfect that it cannot become an obstacle to spirituality.[29] This is another way of saying that God has no affective center, and as such is identical to the self of a human being within whom the affective center has ceased to operate.

Loss of the Infantile God 6.7

Theology is an attempt to make sense of God and his wishes; it is an attempt to fathom the divine mind. Content to accept the theoretical framework built around God by theologians, most Christians remain oblivious to the fact that such constructs are often based on a distorted reading of historical events. Theology has of course existed side by side with profound religious experience for many centuries, and often resides in the same person as a determining impetus towards having such experiences; but theology should not be thought of as ultimately capable of explaining or encompassing such experiences. As a mode of interpretation allied to preconceived doctrines, theology is expressive of a grand network of religious ideas wedded to history and culture, but it remains forever outside of its capacity to fully explain mystical illumination and union. Why? Because any system of religious ideas built upon elements of historical distortion must, by its very nature, calibrate the mind towards serious difficulty. Such an outlook may carry the naive believer some distance, but in the end there is no escaping the repercussions of ideas that limit rather than expand our spiritual horizons. Too great a certainty in relation to inelastic doctrines and the kind of history that backgrounds them gets between us and ultimate reality. It is for this very reason that most Christians never get anywhere near the mystical level – their idea of Jesus and God and life is simply immature; it has remained at the infantile level of hallowed fairy tales.

The historian of religion Karen Armstrong touches on this when she admits that the God she grew up with belonged to her childhood, and remained quite undeveloped. This God did not keep abreast of her growing knowledge in other disciplines. In spite of having been a nun for years, she had never as much as glimpsed the God described by the mystics. Why? Because it was Jesus who was talked about, not God. Considering herself a failure because she had no contact with a source beyond herself, she was eventually driven to ask how anyone could know for certain that Jesus was God. She puts the whole business into sharp relief when she says, "Did the New Testament really teach the elaborate – and highly contradictory – doctrine of the Trinity or was this, like so many other articles of the faith, a fabrication by theologians centuries after the death of Christ in Jerusalem?"[30] Facing reality through the tension created by this fundamental question, her eyes were opened to the possibilities inherent in mystical transcendence.

The problem here is that our conception of God can remain at the infantile level without our realizing it, and that suggests that loss of this God, hard as it may seem, is probably the best thing that could happen to us. Some people wake up automatically to the fact that their God is infantile; most do not. Some people notice out of the corner of their eye that Jesus has usurped God; most remain blissfully unaware that they have substituted a human being for God. Others are aware that they have lost all sense of God, but may not be aware that the reason for this loss is their conscious or unconscious rejection of Jesus as a divine substitute. In losing Jesus, they lose God as well, just as those who have *too much* Jesus lose God for exactly the opposite reason. Loss of God is noticeable in the first instance because of the emptiness felt, and in the second overlooked because that emptiness has taken on an emotional (affective) overlay that clouds the senses. Whatever we think God might be, he is forever fluctuating as an experience, and for a great many may well have been snuffed out altogether.

Exploding the Mystery of Christ 6.8

The nature of Truth is that it does not stop; it has no beginning and it has no end. This places religion, *all* religion, at the disposal of Truth, but does not mean that religion, whatever its makeup, is in itself Truth in final form. There is simply no religion big enough to hold Truth in its entirety (or any philosophy for that matter); it exists *beyond* our Truth stories. As Roberts intimates in *What is Self?,* a study of the spiritual journey in terms of consciousness, "the revelation and mystery of Christ has (to be) exploded to reveal and include all Truth."[31] This is not to suggest that *all* Truth can ever be revealed; it is to direct her readers to the fact that truth filtered through the human mind can always be superseded. Our truths, however big, have to be exploded; they have to be understood always as interim truths on the road to our *becoming* Truth. "Believing" is *not* "becoming"; it is merely a stage in our spiritual growth, a stage dependent on the *size of the gap* that lies between us and God *as* Ultimate Reality, or Truth.[32] Or, as James Hillman so accurately put it at 5.1, we have to see things *in* depth and *as* depth. The only thing we can say about Truth *as* depth is that it goes ever deeper. Our Truth claims may be useful, but they do not in any final sense exhaust Truth. To believe that they do is to be caught in a state of spiritual stasis. All very well, you might say, but is this woman to be trusted? Is she in her right mind to claim that she has gone beyond her mind and her emotions?

A discovery I made when preparing this chapter was that Jacob Needleman had interviewed Father Thomas Keating when preparing to write his book *Lost Christianity,* and that this same priest had written a supportive review for *The Experience of No-Self* by Bernadette Roberts. Keating's review left no one in doubt as to the book's qualities.

> One of the most significant spiritual books of our day. One of the best books on this subject since St. John of the Cross. An amazing book, it clarifies the higher regions of the spiritual path.

St. Joseph's Abbey in Massachusetts is where Needleman interviewed Father Keating, and his description of what he found there resonates closely with the spiritual overview of both

Bernadette Roberts and Father Sylvan. There is a distinct sense of connection between these characters, and it is a connection that reverberates in their carefully chosen words and statements. And as Father Keating later moved to St. Benedict's Monastery in Snowmass, Colorado, and in the acknowledgments to *What is Self?* Bernadette Roberts speaks of sharing in the monastic life of this particular community, I think we can assume ongoing contact.

According to a lecture given by Father Keating during Needleman's stay at St. Joseph's, the plight of Christians today is that they have been robbed of the art of contemplative prayer. This was due to a movement away from prayer as *an act of listening* at the end of the Middle Ages, to that of prayer as a conscious self-disciplining of the ego. A general decadence in morals and spirituality had set in, and this change in emphasis was designed to combat the deterioration in standards.[33] And so the Church's traditional teaching faded and was replaced with "serving God" rather than "experiencing God", and the *lectio divina* (the capacity to listen at ever deeper levels) disappeared to the back of the Christian mind where it became not only suspect, but was even considered *unholy*. In Keating's view, losing this art cut Christians off from their own depths; they were left stranded in upperworld thinking where outer action and analytical thought, strengthened by Renaissance attitudes, came to dominate human behavior. Individual spiritual experience was out, rote religious expression and scientific exactness was in. Applying the analytical faculty to the spiritual life, and to prayer, the "art of listening" was progressively replaced with the highly organized, speculative thinking of the theological schools.

Jacob Needleman records Father Keating's lecture matter-of-factly, then in an aside draws our attention to Evagrius Ponticus, a 4th century spiritual master officially condemned by the Church for his views about Christ's nature. Influenced by Clement of Alexandria and by Origen (also condemned),

Evagrius introduced the term *apatheia* to his pupils, and although usually translated as "apathy", this term is, for Needleman, better served when translated as "without emotions" or as *freedom from emotion.* Also termed an intermediate state of the soul, or bridge, *apatheia* as freedom from emotions becomes for Evagrius a decisive turning point for the Christian.[34] And so we are introduced to a grocery list of evils to be avoided: passionate thoughts, gluttony, impurity, avarice, sadness, anger, vainglory, pride, and even the desire to give up. Then, suddenly, like a slap on the face, we are directed to something that leaps beyond the usual Christian attitude to such weaknesses: the fact that the arising of those weaknesses in our nature can be cancelled out, not in struggling to stop them arising, but in not allowing them to *linger on and take root after they have arisen.* Ordinary as this may sound, it is in fact a lightning-strike realization that offers us the key to bringing our low-level responses under effective control. How? By waking up to the fact that the *impulse towards weakness is not yet an emotion,* and as such has not sufficient energy to overpower us. Disturbing thoughts, ambitions and desires frequently arise in the mind, but they can be avoided if we are regularly present rather than absent to ourselves. We may not have a beeper to remind us to wake up, but with a little practice in self-presencing we can intercept and cancel out many of those weaker moments *as they arise.*

Christianity's problem since *listening ever more deeply* to our own depths was exchanged for trying to *consciously discipline ourselves as an act of will* has been just that, an exchange that has cost us our capacity for sustained spiritual growth. And prayers directed at the ceiling don't really help; if anything they must convince more quickly than anything that trying to shake off emotionally-charged reactions once they've taken root entirely misses the point, the point being that human nature isn't changed through asking for it to be changed, or by morally gritting our teeth in the face of our own weakness, but by piercing down into the depths where the tangled roots of our natures lie fully exposed. We have a vital part to play in this process, but it has nothing to do with being "good" in the sense of morally correct behavior. It has to do with opening ourselves up to forces within psyche that may have an unsuspected evolutionary base. If Bernadette Roberts and Father Sylvan are at all correct in their descriptions of how inner reality works, then we may have to redraw our whole map of what it means to be a human being.

7: Retreat to the Desert

The Church cannot exist at all without a measure of mysticism, but as soon as mysticism begins to gain ground, it begins to do away with the need for the Church's ministers and their services. In the extreme case, the mystic may dispense with the Scriptures and even the Incarnate Christ himself, and seek to relate directly with the uncreated, absolute godhead. Mysticism appears to make the Church and institutional religion unnecessary, and thus is a threat to the established Church even when it operates within a totally orthodox theology.
Harold O.J. Brown
Heresies[1]

Intro: 7.0

Father Vincent's claim that "listening at ever deeper contemplative levels" (*lectio divina*) got lost by the end of the Middle Ages requires further elaboration. It is certainly true that the Middle Ages signaled the end of an era in this sense, but it raises the question as to what was going on during the previous centuries. A turning to theology and Renaissance-driven attitudes certainly took place, but the rot had set in centuries before with the consolidation of ecclesiastical authority in Rome. Not everything in the contemplative garden was as rosy as Father Vincent's historical breakdown seems to suggest.

The conditions necessary for a contemplative life formed in the 4th century, the Jewish philosopher Philo of Alexandria having set the ball rolling in the first with his *On the Contemplative Life* (50 CE), a treatise in which he merged Jewish mysticism with the Greek mysticism of Plato. Not so for many of the Christian hermits and monks of the 4th century; their contemplative scheme was centered on affective identification with Jesus' life and crucifixion, an intoxication that transformed him into a being of ever-expanding spiritual potency. Elevating Jesus to a position consubstantial with God, his all-too-human nature was shunted off into some oblique theological tributary of mind by the Council of Nicea in 325 CE.

Then came the fusion of biblical mysticism with Platonic, and later Neoplatonic, mysticism, a fusion that helped create the contemplative platform of Christianity as it developed. The Catholic scholar A.L. Maycock may deride the mystically inclined Sufis for being adulterated by "Neoplatonic metaphysics,"[2] but the Church, West and East, was equally influenced by Neoplatonic ideas, the East in particular taking to Plato's grandiose vision of transcendent realities with alacrity. In the year 200, Clement of Alexandria admitted that "The way of truth (i.e. the Christian religion) is one, but different streams from different quarters flow into it as into an ever flowing river."[3]

In the 3rd century both Clement and Origen made Platonism the metaphysical foundation of Christian philosophy, the problem of reconciling Platonic mysticism with Church doctrine leading to a watering down of Plato's grand metaphysics. Continuing in less extreme form into the next century, this metaphysic appeared in the thinking of St. Gregory of Nyssa and St. Ambrose of Milan, and returned strongly through the writings of Dionysius the Areopagite. This renowned Neoplatonist's influence on Sufi contemplative thought is everywhere evident, and it is admitted that even the thinking of Thomas Aquinas and Meister Eckhart came under his sway. Odd as it may sound, Neoplatonic thinking infiltrated the West through no less a personage than St. Augustine, the contemplative metaphors coined by Dionysius becoming the pivotal influence on medieval mystical theology. But it was the Eastern Church Fathers who imbibed the deepest, Gregory of Nyssa developing a comprehensive theory of the mystical contemplation of God.[4]

Like Philo, Dionysius combined biblical faith with mystical

experience and expressed the whole in rich metaphors. Describing the sublimity, intangibility and ineffability of God as "inaccessible light," he created a language of transcendence in which "imageless vision" and "nonseeing seeing" helped capture something of the contemplative's perceptual dilemma. And even when images interrupted, the task of the contemplative was to "penetrate the outward sheath to the core of the holy symbol, and so behold the naked and pure divine mysteries in their essence."[5]

In his exhaustive study of contemplation in Christian mysticism, Friedrich Heiler quotes Plotinus, whom he terms the greatest religious thinker since late antiquity, in an attempt to interpret the Neoplatonic contribution of Dionysius into Christian terms, and in doing so tells us that all concrete conceptions and imaginings are left far behind. The religious and cultic symbols vanish. Even the humanity of the Son of God, the child in the manger and the sufferer on the Cross evaporate. Jesus the man is forgotten; only the God-Logos remains.[6]

Heiler's attempt to leave us with a "God-Logos" in relation to the philosophy of Plotinus is an attempt to merge the "One" of Neoplatonic experience and speculation with St. John's notion of Jesus as the Logos, and St. Paul's notion of Jesus as the Mystic Christ. But it is not an actual relationship; it is a slip of the pen. Assuming that when the man Jesus evaporates in deep contemplation what is left must necessarily be God *and* Logos as one expression of ultimate reality, Heiler inadvertently mixes Neoplatonic contemplative experience with Christian theology and makes a nonsense of both. Plotinus was not a Christian; he was a philosopher of the Neoplatonic school to whom such a notion would have made no sense whatsoever. So when Jesus disappears during high contemplative activity, it is not just the stories of Jesus' physical presence on Earth that cease to have meaning, it is the whole theological corpus built around this extraordinary figure. *Everything* goes, and that includes *all* theological constructions attached to the living, breathing person that Jesus was. This is to say that when the highest contemplative levels are reached, both religion and philosophy are transcended.

The Logos 7.1

Philo the Alexandrian Jewish philosopher uses the word Logos 1,300 times throughout his voluminous works; but not always in the same sense. There is no single, consistent doctrine of the Logos, such as in Christianity. The Logos is certainly divine, but it is not God; and that in spite of the fact that Philo sometimes uses the expression "first-born son" to describe the Logos. This is not a personification; it is merely a poetic rendering of a difficult idea. In the Gospel of John, the word "Logos" is translated from the Greek as "Word", this conception having its roots in the Old Testament notion of God *speaking* through the prophets. This is rendered in the prophetic books as "The word of the Lord came to", and was conceived of as having a quasi-independent existence; but only in the sense of an activity or power that inspires. And so the prophets uttered blessings or cursings, and their behavior signaled the presence of God among the people.

Judaism avoided anthropomorphism, stressed the transcendence of God and interpreted his contact with the world as being through divine agents such as Wisdom, Word and Torah. And so the rabbis developed a doctrine of Wisdom that was feminine in gender, identified Wisdom with Torah and came to see the Word (the Law) as divine and pre-existent with God. She (Wisdom) was also *the presence of God,* had existed before the creation of light, and was involved in the creation of the world. So it is possible to exactly parallel statements about the Logos (Jesus) in St. John's Gospel with identical statements from Jewish Wisdom literature, and rabbinic writings about the nature of Torah complete the correspondences. However personified these three agencies may on occasions be, when all is said and done they cannot legitimately be conceived of as independent metaphysical entities.

Jewish thought would not tolerate such an idea, and this fact squarely places St. John's notion of the Logos as an independent entity outside of Jewish mystical tradition. And as even Philo's Greek-influenced exposition on the Logos cannot be bent to such a view, the question as to why St. John evolved such an idea is a bit of a puzzle. But not for long, for among the Nag Hammadi scrolls the *Gospel of Truth* carries elaborate speculations on just such an idea.[7]

The Gnostic scholar Elaine Pagels refers to a tradition that makes the great orator Valentinus the author of the *Gospel of Truth;* she speaks of the book as "poetic", and reminds us that Valentinus was revered as a poet and spiritual master. Paying lip-service to the Christian tradition while believing something quite different, Valentinus claimed to have been initiated into a secret doctrine of God at the hands of Theudas, a disciple of St. Paul. This initiation is interpreted by Pagels as "theological justification for refusing to obey" the Christian hierarchy.[8] As it is Paul who presents an alternative Jesus to that of the Jerusalem Church, and this Apostle's Jesus is not necessarily that of the later Roman Church, then it may well be that Valentinus is telling the truth when speaking of a "secret doctrine" being passed on from one of Paul's advanced pupils. The Jesus of the Jerusalem Church continued to teeter on the edge of theological disaster after the fall of Jerusalem, but unlike the Roman Church's later interpretation of Paul's mystic Christ, they did not allow their Jesus to be directly identified with the God of Israel.

The whole business of Jesus being made into God resulted from the early apologists' attempts to construct Trinitarian belief out of pagan philosophy. Wishing to make Paul's "Christ" intelligible to others, and superior to all that was best in pagan philosophy, the Church developed a language based on pagan philosophy itself. But there was a problem, for no matter how hard the Fathers tried, they could not avoid giving the impression that Jesus was no more than an "attribute" or "function" of God, and as such subordinate to God. And so Justin was forced to describe the Logos as flame derived from fire, and Origen driven to express the notion of the Logos as a creature eternally generated by the Father. To combat the Arian heresy, Athanasius later picked up on Origen's idea of "eternal generation", expressed it as the Son "eternally begotten", and so sidestepped the problem of explaining a pre-existent Logos independent of God. But the problem of Jesus' nature and status would not go away, and in every subsequent generation Christians challenged the Church's claim to theological uniqueness. For what could one do with a Christian explanation of Jewish-sectarian mystical ideas expressed in Greek philosophical terms? Everything seemed to make sense, but when the ideas and insights and revelations of Christianity were seriously examined, the inherent discrepancies in their construction were immediately obvious. There was certainly more to Jesus than met the eye, but to conceive of him as God incarnated in human flesh was, for many Christians, to push that "more" beyond the pale of spiritual decency.

The Contemplative Mix 7.2

Prayers directed to this constructed figure did, however, prove spiritually potent for the monks and hermits who escaped to the deserts of Palestine, Egypt and Syria – emotional identification with Jesus' sufferings could be very rewarding. But it could also be problematical, for how could one control someone to whom being out of emotional control had become a way of life? Recommending that the impulse towards contemplative fervor be checked, St. Benedict instructed his monks in unspoken contemplative prayer *(pura oratio),* and made silence the hallmark of serious contemplative activity. Having added what Heiler terms Roman balance and restraint, Benedict's influence led Pope Gregory the Great (604 CE) to further develop the more moderate approach, the ecstasies, visions, auditions and general boilings over of the Eastern Church being abandoned for Augustinian coolness.

But not completely; identification with Jesus through his sufferings was a pattern too well ingrained to be eradicated overnight, and anyway, what else was there for the common folk? This resulted in two distinct contemplative approaches, the monks developing a route to God different from that of the common people and the ecclesiastics who had to instruct them in the literalisms of biblical truth. And then a third approach developed, for St. Benedict's contemplative scheme, like that of St. Augustine's, was predominantly intellectual (the monks' attention was taken up with "godly thoughts" during contemplation), and this completed the break from Christianized Neoplatonic contemplation where the whole point of the exercise was the *penetration of all holy symbols to their core.*

It was Bernard de Clairvaux in the 12th Century who helped correct the direction taken by the Western Church's contemplative movement, for it is with this unusual man that reflection on contemplative experience begins. Developing a psychology as well as a theology of contemplation, Bernard systematically analyzed and classified contemplative experience, and in doing so resuscitated what appeared to be the old ecstatic route in preference to the intellectual. But this is incorrect. What he actually did was get rid of the Augustinian underpinnings of St. Benedict's coolly intellectual approach. Replacing "godly thoughts" with a dynamic contemplative process based on Jesus' crucifixion as a preliminary stage, he developed a contemplative technique, or bridge, that helped carry the minds of his monks towards an imageless contemplation of the Logos. Going beyond the physical Jesus, the babe in a manger, the man who was crucified, Bernard's monks moved away from the literal life of Jesus towards that dangerous sphere of contemplative realization where Jesus was capable of evaporating altogether. As Saskia Murk-Jansen states in an essay on the Beguine mystic

Hadewijch, "The demand to withdraw from sense perceptions and the activity of the intellect as a preparation for drawing close to God is referred to in numerous texts by Bernard de Clairvaux."[9]

And yet this is the man who could say: "To know Jesus, Jesus crucified, that is the kernel of my philosophy." Are we then to conclude that Bernard's imageless contemplation of the Logos was merely another step in orthodox contemplation? Or was this spiritual and political maverick simply teasing his peers? Could his statement about knowing Jesus crucified mean knowing the *real* Jesus of history, not merely the Jesus of the Church's imagination? An astute politician wielding immense power within the Church (no one since Athanasius in the 4th century had determined the policies of the Church to such an extent), Bernard is also described as having learned more about God from nature than from books, his use of natural objects for purposes of meditation being rarely found in Christian mysticism.[10] Natural objects? Such a statement forces one to conclude that this man was highly unusual, and that his move away from established religious symbolism signified a serious break with orthodoxy. Known to have been involved in many an intrigue, Bernard was a man of parts, a man with the capacity to cloak his beliefs when it suited him.

Union with God 7.3

Detachment from the things of this world was the monk's aim, union with God, his hope. Burdened by St. Augustine's conception of original sin, and by a similar inability to escape the tendency towards sin in everyday life, monks and nuns sought to purify themselves by the ascetic route. The *via purgativa* of asceticism would lead, so they believed, to the *via illuminativa* of contemplation. Closing the gates of the senses, the contemplative entered what Bernard called the *vitalis vigilque sopor*, a sleep alive and watchful.[11] Friedrich Heiler is quick to point out that

Bernard's sleep alive and watchful was not just a matter of inner concentration and heightened awareness; it was a state of mind set up for the purpose of silent contemplation on nature and the recitation of Scripture. He is adamant, "The inner void is, on the contrary, filled again with concrete content."[12] Fixating on some ritual object or sacred image, on some verse of Scripture or even on a religious fantasy, the contemplative nudged ever closer to union with God – the God of the Catholic Church, the God who had conceived of that Church's existence and behavior even before the creation of the world.

One can only be blunt in the face of such a suggestion; Heiler is quite wrong in thinking this. The words "a sleep alive and watchful" speak volumes about Bernard's contemplative competency; he knew a great deal about meditation and contemplation. A "sleep alive and watchful" is not a preliminary stage; it is a consequence with profound implications. It is not an initial approach; it is an established condition that allows the contemplator to scan the "still point" spoken of by Bernadette Roberts. Conscious ideas, Scriptural recitations, images or objects have no place in it; it is totally and utterly self-sufficient. Heightened attention and awareness become not the means to an end (a filling up again of the mind with "concrete content"), but the penultimate point in a process within which all content melts clean away. Meditations on objects, pictures, icons, saints, altars, crucifixes or Stations of the Cross can certainly help concentrate the mind, but once the mind is fully concentrated such crutches fall away like the booster rockets on a space shuttle. Heiler seems to agree; he says: "All these objects and pictures are outward aids and stimuli to the contemplation of God's presence, His mercy, His condescension and sacrificial death; while the pictures of the saints encourage contemplation of heroic caritas and love of God." There is something peculiar about this argument; it ends by subtly denying its own premise. For is not our idea of God's sacrificial death *as* Jesus no more than a cloud of impenetrable religious reasoning? And is this perhaps why Bernard was in the habit of choosing "natural objects" on which to meditate? This wily old Christian had woken up to the Neoplatonic fact that any old object of attention could afford the same result.

Aware that only the divine could reveal the divine, Plotinus said that the contemplator does nothing and should strive to do nothing. Only an "eternal seeing" could see God; subtlety of mind via the intellect was not nearly subtle enough. And yet out of this empty seeing, unimaginable visions, sounds and intimations of Ultimate Reality could flourish; there was no telling what might happen. In the Christian contemplative tradition women – ever suspect in the eyes of churchmen – seemed to be particularly susceptible to such intimations, their sensory expressions of spiritual experience having to be handled with great theological care. But whether male or female, priest, nun, monk or lay person, if unable to cut loose from mental distractions, then doomed to remain forever untouched by contemplative insight. Mental distraction, as St. John of the Cross would reveal, was the problem we all had to face, a problem that followed us right into the center of being where "self" became the final obstacle. For how could we unite the person we were with a transcendent God when preservation of the limited self was the strongest instinct we possessed? Indeed, how could we create the conditions by which such an unimaginable thing might be accomplished? And if accomplished, how might we explain to a church bound by the limitations of that self that its religious explanations of Ultimate Reality were fundamentally inadequate?

Christian monks and hermits of the early centuries are thought to have retreated to the desert to get away from the restrictions of ecclesiastical Catholicism. Prone to orthodox fanaticism on the one hand, they were, on the other, anarchic, their theology tinged with dualism, their abhorrence of the world often reminiscent of the Manichee heretics at their most intense. Without doubt influenced by the monastic practices of the

Quietist Jews who had fled into the hills during the Maccabean wars, by the Covenanters of Qumran, and by the Egyptian Therapuetae,[13] they went about their contemplative business with a seriousness that sometimes verged on the manic. Looking back to Elijah, Elisha and John the Baptist as prototypes, they also (inadvertently) imbibed elements of Pythagorean, Neoplatonist and Stoic philosophy, their aim being to pursue solitude and soar above the contents of their minds.[14]

By the year 200, Clement of Alexandria was talking of Christians advancing by progressive elevation of the soul towards the divine, and this move towards asceticism came to replace martyrdom as an accepted ambition. The contemplative could rise towards God using free will to subdue the body and its passions, so avoiding a martyr's death. In this sense, contemplation was martyrdom spiritualized; it was "death" elevated to a new level of comprehension – the death of the ego. Here then, in embryo, is the soul's mystic union with God, an attempt to so saturate the self in heavenly things that only God, and not the self, remained.

Unlike the ecclesiastics who thought orthodox belief and behavior paramount, the monks and hermits accepted adherence to orthodox teaching as a necessary discipline, but in the seclusion of their cells or caves behaved in accordance with conscience and relied not on theology, but on their own understanding of the Bible. Thinking in non-ecclesiastical terms, St. Anthony is known to have told his monks that the Scriptures were enough for instruction, a statement in defiance of ecclesiastical control. And that in spite of his close friendship with Athanasius, champion of the Nicene formula. Although critical of both the Arian and Manichaean heresies, this seeker after God nevertheless removed himself from the organized Church, and is thought not to have received the Eucharist for most of his life. This fact alone speaks volumes, for it was the firmly held belief of the establishment that without the Eucharist a soul was damned for all eternity.

At first a loose association of groups of hermits with little discipline, the monasteries later became highly organized communities where intellectual pursuits dominated, and extremes of asceticism were discouraged. But not at first; asceticism was all the rage at first. At Mount Nitria, southwest of the Delta for instance, upwards of 5,000 monks settled down to the business of collective solitude, each monk having a separate cell in this vast settlement. Seeking out and attaching themselves to a recognized spiritual "master," newcomers found themselves engaged in "fantastic competitions in spiritual perfection."[15] In northern Syria, the desert is said to have been crowded with monks, some of them behaving more like Indian fakirs than Christians.[16] On visiting one such community in 373, Jerome was taken aback by the ferocity with which they rejected the world at large, their view of physical life being little different from that of the Manichee heretics. In Palestine, an Anchorite community was established near Gaza by Hilarion, a disciple of St. Anthony's, and in Upper Egypt 490 settlements mushroomed into existence. Free as birds, the many thousands of monks inhabiting these settlements sought their own salvation by way of unregulated ascetic and contemplative practices. But not for long. The efforts of St. Pachomius and St. Basil eventually brought regulation and a new purpose to these disparate communities.

With nine monasteries and two nunneries set up, St. Pachomius introduced uniformity of behavior on many levels, and with a soldier's reasoning established an "Order" of monks recognizable by their similarity of dress. Later, full control was established through the organizing of the monasteries in alignment with the Longer and Shorter Rule of St. Basil.

Having studied monasticism in Mesopotamia, Palestine, Lower Egypt and Syria, St. Basil drew up a way of life recognizing "full episcopal control over the affairs of the cloister,"[17] so changing forever what had been a deeply personal search for spiritual freedom into a highly controlled system. Ascetic self-sufficiency was replaced with "brotherliness", monasticism attached to, rather than separated from, town and village. Monasteries were reduced to thirty or forty members, schools and hospitals created to serve the community, the old ascetic communities transformed into places of learning.[18] Over the first three centuries of the Christian era, however, communities quite beyond ecclesiastical control flourished in both the East and the West, their spirituality directed, not by theological concerns, but by a Christianity as yet unhardened by dogma.

Alternative Gospels 7.4

Some of the early monastic settlement had in their possession gospels of an unorthodox nature. In 367 Athanasius was forced to purge the monasteries of these heretical books, and that suggests there were a lot of them around. The Nag Hammadi collection, found in 1945, was probably hidden by monks belonging to the monastery of St. Pachomius in Upper Egypt around this time. With the Gospels of Matthew, Mark, Luke and John hailed as canonical – that is, as conforming to an agreed interpretation of historical and spiritual events – texts previously considered wholesome were rejected and outlawed. As some of these texts described the virgin birth and the resurrection as "misunderstandings", the Nag Hammadi texts were singled out as subversive documents that had to be destroyed. The fact that they were buried and not destroyed speaks volumes.

Among the fifty-two Nag Hammadi texts discovered was a Gospel of Thomas, a Gospel of Mary (Magdalene), a Gospel of Philip and a Gospel of the Egyptians. There was also a Gospel of Truth presenting a very different rendition of the Genesis narrative, and a strange document called *Thunder, Perfect Mind,* which spoke of a feminine divine power. This text carried the words:

I am the honored one and the scorned one.
I am the whore and the holy one.
I am the wife and the virgin...

According to the Gnostic scholar Elaine Pagels, the main point about these texts is that the writers did not consider themselves to be heretics; they used Christian terminology, related to Jewish teaching, and claimed knowledge of a separate tradition regarding Jesus and his teachings. Pagels also points out that the term "Christianity" has come to cover an astonishing range of groups since the Reformation, and that it was much the same during the first three centuries of the Christian era. Early Christianity was much more diverse than the Church cares to admit, gospels utterly at odds with those of the New Testament being in wide circulation. Although categorized as apocryphal by the end of the 2nd century, these alternative gospels containing secret teachings, myths and poems attributed to Jesus or his disciples are known to have been doing their rounds.[19] Christian scholars mostly dismiss these texts as useless flights of the imagination, but the tendency of secular scholarship is to take them a little more seriously. Some of them are, after all, thought to contain material older than that found in the canonical Gospels, and as such are viewed as of vital importance to our understanding of Christianity's early growth and development.

But what of the men and women who regarded these rejected texts as valid, those who believed that their alternative message better served the community than the stories made standard through the legislation of a council? What happened to them? Where did they go? How did they manage to survive as Athanasius's purge took effect? By subterfuge, of course. Remaining in the settlements or monasteries to which they belonged, they became a circle within a circle, a group within a group willing to pay lip-service to the dominant cult for the sake of privacy and safety.

The question is, what was the quality of the spirituality engaged in by these monks, nuns and hermits during this period of fluctuation and change? What level of contemplative experience did they attain in their desert retreats before St. Pachomius and St. Basil rearranged their personal search for God into community service and intellectual asceticism? The monks of St. Pachomius in Egypt did not pass from community life back to that of the contemplative, but in other parts of Egypt, Palestine and Syria contemplative-based groups flourished, St. Euthymius (376-473) and St. Saba (439-532) successfully founding Eastern Orthodox monasticism in these same areas.

Elaine Pagels' description of orthodox Christianity's success over other forms of Christian belief is quite straightforward; it was a matter of winners over losers. The winners wrote the history books; the losers were denied all credibility. After accepting the model of Roman organization, the Church became theologically stable, turned imperial, and dismissed other points of view as heretical. In Pagels' opinion this caused the impoverishment of the Christian tradition – alternatives were forced outside, triumph was interpreted as historically inevitable and experience overshadowed by theology.[20] Referring directly to this other type of Christianity, the historian Karen Armstrong sums up the situation thus:

> Eventually this type of Christianity would be suppressed but we shall see that centuries later Jews, Christians and Muslims would return to this type of mythology, finding that it expressed their experience of God more accurately than orthodox theology.[21]

Some of the heretics seem to have had a better grasp of spiritual reality than orthodoxy could muster, and not a few of those heretics were living quite undetected in the mainstream monasteries. Well, not quite undetected; Athanasius knew what was going on. Issuing an order for them to destroy all of their heretical texts, he reveals the extent of the monks' interest in these texts, and in doing so opens up for us a world not quite as tidy theologically as some would have us believe. And so too does Elaine Pagels in her seminal study of these Christian radicals, for on having shown that these alternative Christians did not accept Church organization or episcopal authority, that they rejected the exclusion of women from the priesthood and considered the cult of martyrdom downright silly, she goes on to show that the Church's notion of itself as the only road to salvation was not acceptable to everyone.

What has to be emphasized is that the settlements and monasteries were at first populated by monks, not priests, that these monks were unordained individuals led by unordained abbots, and that apart from a blatant rejection of ecclesiastical hobbyhorses by some, "non-conformity" was in fact a way of life for most. Adherence to monastic discipline would have been expected, but within that discipline there flourished a variety of approaches to Jesus' nature and status stimulated by writings and traditions not yet declared heretical. That St. Anthony is reported not to have received the sacraments for most of his life confirms a quite different approach from that of the ecclesiastical establishment in Rome, and the mystery of his lasting friendship with Athanasius confirms, not that the Nicene formula was already up and running, but that that formula had not yet taken hold. A mighty debate raged around the issue of Jesus' nature and status prior to the Nicene solution in 325, and that solution was swapped for an Arian one in 337 before becoming standard belief throughout the Church West and East in 381. The Nicene formula would eventually harden into dogma, and during this hardening Athanasius would be banished no fewer than six times as the theological stew bubbled and heaved.

This of course throws a completely different light on the beliefs of the so-called heretics, for during this period of upheaval these heretics weren't heretics at all, they were just ordinary Christians adhering to views of Jesus later considered to be subversive. It's worth recapping on the diversity of approaches at this point, for it will help clarify how uncertain the Christian formula was even as late as the first half of the 4th century. The widespread notion that Christianity has, since the 1st century, carried the same simple message about Jesus is a mistake. At Antioch the tendency was Adoptionist (Jesus had been possessed by the Spirit of God at his baptism), in Asia Minor Sabellian (Jesus was to be directly identified with the Father), and in Alexandria Platonic (Jesus was the divine logos or link between God and creation). In Rome, Paul's Christology had been beefed up to make Jesus into a divine being; the only question remaining to be solved being the extent of that divinity. By 325 he would be consubstantial with the Father; by 335 he would be back to being subordinate to the Father.

In Paul's scheme of things, contemplation of God became interwoven with contemplation on Jesus' incarnation, crucifixion and resurrection, the sacraments taking on a mystical charge capable of carrying the soul into ecstatic states. So intense did such states become that contemplation on Jesus edged over into unconscious worship of Jesus, the Jesus of history being transmuted, slowly and imperceptibly, from Jewish messiah into a kind of divine being in whom faith could be invested. This is to say that Christianity, from its inception, was deeply concerned with contemplative piety in the sense of emotional identification with Jesus' sufferings, and that it was this tradition of identification that eventually caused a rupture in its historical overview of Jesus the man. With their spiritual vision towards God redirected through Jesus as the Christ, Christian perception underwent a change of focus; the intermediary, like a penny held before the sun, blocking out the larger mystery. Affectively rewarded through this refocusing of the contemplative lens, the next quite natural step was a spin-off re-evaluation of Jesus' day-to-day existence, his every move or statement being seen as indicative of his newly acquired divine status.

What has to be realized is that Jewish prophetism, the Jerusalem Temple cult, the Hellenistic mysteries and the Platonic and Neoplatonic schools constitute the roots of Christian contemplative practice as it developed. For a start, Judaism was strongly mystical, Jacob's ladder with its angels descending and ascending was a metaphor for contemplative activity,[22] his wrestling match with God at the ford Jabbok indicative of great contemplative effort.[23] Given tangible form, the Eternal is interacted with by Moses in the form of a burning bush,[24] by Elijah as a still small voice,[25] by Isaiah on a throne high and lifted up within the Temple itself,[26] and by Ezekiel as a radiant cloud surmounted by a throne.[27] This is the language of contemplation, the language of transcendence, the language of mystery, and it is completed by the psalmist's beautiful songs where soul and heart are described as panting after God. Even the ordinary Jewish people are allowed to share in such experiences, for the Temple liturgy, complex and lengthy, is said to have afforded them a sense of the presence of God, and Christian liturgy would serve the same purpose.[28] In his important essay on contemplation and Christian mysticism, Friedrich Heiler completes this picture when he describes Jesus as the conclusion of this prophetic series, the most telling moment of his life being that of his transfiguration before his disciples.[29] A contemplative by nature, Jesus eventually became an object of contemplation, a move at first useful, but later problematical.

Platonic & Neoplatonic Mysticism 7.5

This presents us with a further problem, for if advanced mystics are, as Neumann attests, and Bernadette Roberts confirms, prone to break out of the conventional religious mold, then how much more anticonventional, anticollective and antidogmatic must what we call "God", or the "Absolute", or "Ultimate Reality" be in his/its own right? You can't have one without the other, as the song goes. You can't have advanced mystics breaking the belief-conventions of centuries on the one hand, and on the other have what they are uniting with advocating through traditionally minded theologians a hemmed-in, cramped religious attitude. We may not fully understand what these extraordinary individuals were attempting to say at times, but we should have little problem in following the often explosive nature of their experiences. Neumann confirms this when he says that any mysticism that consists of dogmatically defined contents is either low-level or disguised mysticism.[30]

This reinforces the idea that Jesus' teachings about God, the Sabbath and much else were the result, not of his being God, but of his having united with God (his "father" as formlessness) during deep contemplation. His policy of religious and social reform seems to have been born in his own depths, and it is to these depths that he directs the attention of his disciples throughout his ministry. So when he says, "I and the Father are one," he is not claiming to be God in person, he is claiming to have experienced God *in* his person to the point of *unity.* This was fully understood in the early days of Christianity's development, hence the concept of Jesus as God's "adopted" son, a concept eventually jettisoned as Jesus' identity underwent the twist towards inherent divinity.

Theologians argue that Jesus was God, but at the same time keep him fully human. The language utilized is at times astonishing, the arguments presented mind-bending. And still they keep coming, highly intelligent men and women laboring dutifully to explain how Jesus was actually God, yet fully human, yet not literally God while human, yet not not God because he was human. The brain reels as category cogs clash and grind and the rules of logic are tested to destruction. And all because a belief system has become circular; that is, an early mistake in information processing has become a factor integral to the integrity of the system as a whole. Discard the mistake and the whole system fails. Discard the idea that Jesus was actually God and the underlying reason for Christianity's continuance as a religion appears to evaporate. But only in appearance, for what one is left with is not a religion shorn of its heart, as many would contend, but a religion capable of functioning as originally intended. Put Jesus back into historical, cultural and spiritual focus and the result is not chaos, or blasphemy; it is an integral honesty that allows us to place this victim of our conditioned minds in a new frame of reference. Jesus was not God come to Earth in any literal sense, but the shock of his extraordinary presence was such that we're still talking about him.

8: Gnosis

The Church long ago mis-identified the locus of human freedom. Because of this error, the whole of Western civilization is crashing against a brick wall.
Father Sylvan
Lost Christianity by Jacob Needleman[1]

Intro: 8.0

If I'm interpreting my research materials correctly, then Christianity lost contact with its original vision before the end of the 1st century. This is not to say that its original vision was in itself original, just that it had in its grasp a life-transforming process that it eventually mislaid. So when I came across Jacob Needleman's book *Lost Christianity,* and read the insightful and sometimes caustic remarks of Father Sylvan, I suspected I was on the right track. And not just because Needleman's evidence reflected my own, or because Father Sylvan's take on things seemed to support my long-held contention that Christianity's life-force was moribund, but because the evidence stacking up for such an opinion could be detected throughout Christianity's long and tortuous history. What I hadn't realized, however, was that this lost process of Christianity's was tied to what many considered to be its most boring aspect: its continual harping about moral behavior. The idea of being good seemed to have overpowered Christianity to such an extent that its whole character had become one of frowning disapproval. But buried deep in that judgmental attitude lay the kernel of something breathtakingly transformative: the realization that our greatest enemy was our wayward emotions. Father Sylvan sums up this situation with precision when he says: "Do not make a religion of your better moments. That way lies the corruption of our teaching."[2]

The teaching Father Sylvan is referring to concerns the real nature of man;[3] if a teaching doesn't reflect this real nature, then it is, in Father Sylvan's spiritual scheme, fundamentally useless in spite off being helpful in a social context. The mercy and compassion of a teaching do not reflect the heart of religion, we are told; it is "the conditions under which it brings them" that are important.[4] The language of real Christianity is not for our emotions; it is for our hearts and our minds in the sense meant by St. Paul when he says, "Be ye transformed by the renewing of the mind."[5] It is the mind that has to be renewed, and that is not accomplished through moral strictures, or through doctrines dutifully believed, but through the shock of waking up to our constantly submerged mental state and to our emotional dishonesty. The crux of the matter lies not in whether we believe in Christianity's doctrinal propositions, but in our capacity to unhitch ourselves from our deeply conditioned and reactive minds. *That* was the message of early Christianity, and it is a message scrambled beyond recognition as it developed into a highly organized religion with power and authority.

What has to be understood is that this teaching was linked to previous expressions of the same thing; it was not a revelation never before encountered. In this sense there were Christians on the planet long before Christianity appeared on the scene. And in this sense "Christ" is not Jesus' surname, nor is it a description of something that Christians have to put on like a jacket; it is the title of what was believed by the Nazoraeans sect to be their God-appointed Messiah (not the Messiah *as* God), a title transformed by St. Paul into a piece of theological wizardry to stand for that very renewing of the mind Father Sylvan draws to our attention. Theologians and historians have often wondered why Paul doesn't deal with the facts of Jesus' life, and this is probably the reason. He wasn't interested in the historical Jesus; he was interested only in the consciousness of Jesus, a consciousness he recognized as generic to the spiritual life of *all* human beings. To "put on Christ" was not, in my opinion, about possession *by* Jesus; it was about finding the equivalent of his special consciousness within ourselves.

This could be why Christianity was considered to be of universal significance early on; the discovery at Christianity's core was not that it had a better grocery list of beliefs than anyone else, but that it had a teaching that applied directly to the human condition. Hence the curious disciplining aspect of Jesus' own teachings; he was heightening the awareness of his disciples through a moment-by-moment recognition that they were asleep on their feet ("could you not watch one hour?"), that they did not know what they were doing most of the time ("Father, forgive them, for they know not what they do"), and that he, in that moment of time, was their only hope of ever finding out what their problem really was. He was asking them to wake up *inside* their reactions and catch sight of themselves as they faced the onslaught of daily life – hence his curious over-the-top moral directives. It was not enough to merely do the right thing as far as the law was concerned; it was a matter of *fully occupying the space in which they moved and had their being.* That was what mattered, and it mattered because it heralded the presence of a real person capable of making real decisions.

Christianity could be said to have been left with an empty teaching, a husk of its previous intelligence concerning the self. Realizing in the 4th century that emotional identification with Jesus could lead to all kinds of aberrant behavior, the Roman Church imposed rules and regulations on the monasteries to bring their emotionally driven monks under control, and at the same time set about eradicating ideas they considered heretical. Some very strange things were surfacing in the name of Christianity, so doctrinal standardization was necessary, but the *gnosis* (knowledge) of which genuine Christianity was composed fell under the same shadow as the Gnostic beliefs then being attacked, and that led to a rejection of anything even vaguely suggestive of an alternative spiritual system. Anything that veered from this new standardized set of doctrines was termed Gnostic and dismissed as heretical, those who persisted in their *gnosis* branded as deviants and ostracized.

By the end of the 4th century the Roman church became the central organizing influence in Christendom, its consolidated authority and literalist interpretations of Scripture carrying it away from an understanding of its own *gnosis*. As a result of the clean-up operation that followed, the idea of *gnosis* became anathema to the ruling hierarchy, and this led to Christianity being scrambled on two fronts, not one. Those aware of the faith's deeper teaching were then in as much danger of reprisal from Church authorities as those who had only a distorted or limited version of the original Christian *gnosis*, and this resulted in Christianity's core teaching being outlawed and associated with the often bizarre offerings of some Gnostic groups. Father Sylvan unravels this complicated situation for us when he says, "'Gnosticism' is not a heresy of the Church, but a 'heresy' of gnosis."[6] In saying this he shows himself to have had a coherent historical sense of what was going on beneath the surface.

The Mysterious Race of Perfected Men 8.1

But the initiates of so-called Gnosticism were not all the muddle-headed idiots Church investigators made them out to be; many were skilled scientists of the mind armed with what is now recognized as an exact spiritual vocabulary. It can be argued, of course, that the Church's reaction to these groups was to be expected – much of the imagery and symbolism used by Gnostic thinkers was so obscure as to be utterly unintelligible – but there is little excuse for that kind of reaction today. Recent research by Gnostic scholars such as Elaine Pagels and Simone Petrement have shown some of these groups to have been hugely sophisticated in their approach. Even Jean Doresse's 1958 study of the Egyptian Gnostics came to the same conclusion, particularly in relation to groups such as the Naassene, the Peratae, the Sethians and the Ophites. In Doresse's view, these Jewish-oriented Christian groups were basically the same heresy under different names, the connecting point between them being the high regard in which they held Jesus' brother James.[7] There was, Doresse believed, an underlying continuity of thought allied to Jesus that, although difficult to interpret due to complexity of image and symbol, was nevertheless coherent at base in relation to particular groups.[8] Their ideas were not unintelligible. The basic code used by these groups had in fact been broken by the Church Fathers; the problem was they did not understand the significance of what they read. And for very good reason, these related groups had resorted to subterfuge in the face of a growing persecution.

Doresse gives us the basic code being used, and it is startling because it has to do with the human senses, not with theological constructions built around Jesus. The whole scheme of these interrelated Jewish-Christian groups had to do with the human brain, with the inner landscape of consciousness and sense-perceptions allied to a system of transformation. The brain was Eden, the membranes enveloping the brain were the heavens, and the head was paradise. The Church Father Epiphanius confirms these findings in connection with the Ophites. In the same allegorical manner he observes that there is a river with branches flowing out of Eden (the brain), and these branches he identifies with the human senses. The eye is the river Phison, the ear is the river Geon, and the breath is the river Tigris. Doresse's footnotes reveal that "the land of bondage" (Egypt) equaled the evil of matter; so when a spiritual master "left Egypt", it simply meant that he had died. And a vision in the heavens (meaning high up in the head) of a coiled serpent was, equally, not a reference to evil, but to energy. So when in their teachings these groups spoke of Christ "mastering the serpent", they did not mean that he had mastered evil, but that he had, as in the yogic tradition of India, brought the serpent *as energy* under control.[9] This suggests, as stated earlier, that Christianity's original *gnosis* was not in itself unique, but concerned with a consciousness-transforming process belonging to the body as Morris Berman correctly deduces. The question being debated today, however, is whether the more disparate of these Gnostic groups were in any real sense Christian, or actually independent of Christianity in spite of their Christian gloss.

Some scholars stress the independence factor; others vindicate heresy hunters like Irenaeus by appearing to prove that the Gnostics were all heretical Christians. The truth, however, may be a little more complex. There is good reason to think that no precise source for many of the Gnostic groups ever existed, but that those of suspected Jewish origin originated in the early Ebionite sect, a strict Jewish-Christian group related to the Jerusalem Church of the Apostles through Jesus' brother James – hence their high regard for James (see 17.0). This form of Gnosticism was categorized as a low Christological formation by the Church Fathers, that is, it rejected the idea of Jesus being divine in his own right; he had been an ordinary man and a prophet, end of story. This view later became the basis for the Arian heresy, which was certainly Christian in origin, and resulted in Roman Christianity being almost displaced as the ruling faction. Other Gnostic groups may just have borrowed the myths of Christianity and woven them into tapestries of thought reflecting independent experiences of internal reality. True as I think this probably was, it overlooks the Jewish-Christian input, just as it does *gnosis*-oriented Christians hiding in the monasteries for fear of being detected.

Another factor is that not all of the Gnostic texts were of the same caliber; many of the texts did descend to the level of gibberish, a point noted by the French Gnostic scholar Simone Petrement as indicative of late Gnosticism. In her opinion early Gnosticism carried the greater coherence, late Gnosticism becoming progressively incoherent. In her references to the Naassenes and the Ophites, in particular, she sums up these Jewish-Christian groups as understanding the term Gnostic to mean Christian, and that suggests they were reading the word *gnosis* in the same sense as Bishop Irenaeus did when he described heretics as "Gnostics falsely so-called,"[10] so making Christians Gnostic by definition. Petrement's summation is that the Gnostic heretics probably used the term Gnostic in all innocence, and that this usage did not mean that they saw themselves as a sect within Christianity, but as in some sense carrying the original meaning of Christianity.

The Sheep and the Goats 8.2

Christian heretics of the early centuries are not talked of much from the pulpit; they are presumed away under the guise of deviants who do not require explanation. There was, it is believed, a single community of believers called Christians in the beginning and the heretics were those who invented grotesque notions about Christ and had to be banished from that community. It's that simple. There was a single doctrine of Jesus as the Christ of God, and in unbroken succession we are recipients of that doctrine because the Church has kept its eye steadily on the central truth of Jesus' divinity and mission. You either accept or reject the fact of Jesus' divine mission, and on the basis of your decision end up in heaven or hell. End of story. End result of two thousand years of faithfulness to a set of ideas considered to be divinely revealed truth. That, basically, is the Christian argument, and it is unacceptable. There never was a simple community with one set of beliefs; there were dozens of Christian communities, and those eventually deemed heretical were those that lost out in the power struggle with Rome. Christian thinking on and around this matter makes nonsense of the historical facts, and serious scholars (many of them Christian) reject the idea that this was the regulating will of God at work. In its early days, as the Nag Hammadi scrolls demonstrate, Christianity was multiform in its approaches to Jesus and his teachings.

It was not until the 4th century that this regulating will of God got under way at the hands of Bishop Athanasius. In his 39th Festal Letter he let it be known that only certain books were to be considered inspired, and therefore canonical. From that moment the lines of demarcation were drawn, the books not on the list being marked down as apocryphal, or heretical, and proclaimed anathema. The scene was now set for conflict, those who had considered themselves good Christians on Monday reduced to being heretics on Tuesday. The dividing line was in place, the sheep and the goats were about to be separated – with a vengeance. And all because Athanasius was "influenced by the need and advantage of the Church," a statement of simple truth laden with dire implications for the future of Christianity.

The effect of Athanasius' 39th Festal Letter on the broad sweep of Christian communities was one of fear – those in possession of the banned writings (previously termed gospels) had to get rid of them. It was either that or own up to holding a view of Jesus at variance with that of this powerful faction. And Athanasius knew what this meant for these individuals; he had experienced the same thing himself – eleven years earlier he had been forced to hide in Upper Egypt as a result of a doctrinal shift in Rome. So it can be said that ideas about Jesus and his status had been quite fluid up until this point, but that from that moment the atmosphere in Christendom changed dramatically. For it was no longer a matter of sensibly debating this approach over that approach; it was now a matter of being declared already dead (cut off from salvation) by the ruling faction if you persisted in your use of writings considered subversive. In *Fragments of a Faith Forgotten,* G.R.S. Mead says that the Scriptures eventually turned into a "literary fetish deprived of reason."[11] The textual God of the Church's first fundamentalists had appeared, and he was about to stamp his disapproval on everyone and everything out of alignment with his faction's fancies.

When he published his book in 1960, Mead wrote of Christianity's origins being imbibed with our mothers' milk, and of it being an integral part of the consciousness of the Western world. Interwoven with our earliest memories, the sheer solemnity of Christian doctrine had found its way into our heart and minds; that is, it affected us deeply without our realizing it. Even if consciously unconcerned with its ideas and beliefs, we were still strongly influenced by those ideas and beliefs at the unconscious level, and at the social level. For some, this resulted in an unquestioning attitude towards Christianity, a curious inability to shrug off the idea that, somehow, Christianity was probably correct in its pronouncements in spite of much evidence to the contrary. For others, it was a nagging doubt about their rejection of Christianity. This suggested that anyone born within the confines of Christendom had a struggle on their hands if they wished to shake off the claim that today's Christianity had been in the mind of God before the world came into existence. As Mead points out, Christianity is something we have grown used to, it has become part of us at the cultural level and is backed by the "stupendous power of inertia which force of custom carries."[12] Hence deathbed conversions and the sudden leap that some people make from unbelief to belief. We've been psychologically programmed, and our first act of waking up is to become aware of that disturbing fact.

The Lowest Common Denominator 8.3

In the first three centuries of the Christian era, Christian communities tried to develop their ideas through direct experience of God and self, some believing Christianity to be a system of knowledge that could be translated into a world philosophy. The soul could be known in the same way as the body; real Christianity was an exact science of the soul that could be made satisfying to even the most exacting intellect. Given the title "first-born of Satan", these communities were forced underground, the result being an ever-deepening resentment that spread its tentacles in all directions.

Having received the name "Gnostics" because of their insistence that *gnosis* (knowledge) was integral to spiritual wisdom, these explorers of inner reality reached conclusions about God, self and world that the Church felt compelled to reject. And they were eventually in a position to make their rejection stick, for by the 4th century previously victimized Christian bishops were in control of Rome's legal arm, any groups considered heretical defined as criminals and persecuted. So the narrow orthodoxy of the Church became the ruling norm, and Christian teaching was reduced, as Professor Stephan Hoeller puts it, to the lowest common denominator. The Roman "branch", because of good fortune (Constantine's beneficence), had taken over and was now able to dictate both the content and direction of the faith. The faith was now Roman, and would soon be Catholic, that is, universally accepted because of power-politics played to the nth degree. Accused by the Roman Church of having created doctrines allied, not to Christ, but to the thinking of Plato, Pythagoras, Aristotle, Orpheus and Heraclitus, the Gnostic communities were categorized as corrupt and dismissed as a universal danger. And this in spite of the fact that their writings made no direct reference to these philosophers at any time.[13]

Successful in terms of it being the centrally positioned controlling Christian faction, the church at Rome worked to accommodate its rapidly growing flock by further simplifying its already simple message of the "Christ". This resulted in the faith reaching its lowest ebb in spite of previous subtlety. Retreating to the monasteries, gnosis-oriented Christians adapted as best they could to the mental restrictions placed upon them; others withdrew and formed secret congregations, nurturing, in Mead's words "a hidden life of great activity."[14] Private libraries of banned books were legion, and schools or workshops were formed where a veritable science of the sacred was developed. The Church was appalled. These gnosis-oriented Christians seemed to be in every thicket, their teachings ever more dangerous to, and distant from, orthodoxy. And nowhere more so than in Egypt, at Alexandria, where the greatest public library in the pagan world was housed. Thus the Alexandrian library was probably the principal source of information on past religious systems for scholars interested in gnosis, and this may well have been the reason for its destruction by fire. Then there were the mystics, those inner travelers to whom the staid doctrines of the ruling faction were merely echoes of things deeper and richer. And not an undisciplined rabble of subversives as the Church liked to think; more often than not highly disciplined and skilled groups of individuals dedicated to a purpose which the Church had already lost sight of. Yes, there were rogues and vagabonds and charlatans in these communities, and some of them may even have been quite mad, but no more so than many of the orthodox churchmen of the day. They too had their odd beliefs, and could be said without contradiction to have perfected the art of believing some very odd things about Jesus before the close of the 4th century.

The Rule of Faith 8.4

In her seminal text *The Gnostic Gospels,* Elaine Pagels pries open the Gnostic world and confronts us with a mentality quite other than the one generally thought to reside there. Revealing what she terms "the other side of the coin", she draws our attention to the fact that not only did orthodox Christianity denounce the Gnostics, the Gnostics too denounced the orthodox as "unknowingly empty, not knowing who they are, like dumb animals."[15] Accusing orthodox Christians of having built an "imitation church", these Gnostics then elaborate fully on their grievances and voice the opinion that the Church at Rome has enslaved its flock through fear and forced it to obey earthly representatives – proving, if nothing else, that they had once belonged to the Christian fold. The Roman Church is also referred to as a counterfeit church that claims exclusive legitimacy, those who lead it described as blind because they speak of things about which they know nothing. This is their principal failing, and out of their arrogance springs the notion of doctrines which cannot be questioned by anyone. Oppressing their flock, the hierarchy of this Church is described as slandering the truth and preaching a false Christ.

Elaine Pagels captures the essence of the problem when she tells us that by the end of the 2nd century orthodoxy had established objective criteria for church membership. She writes: "Whoever confessed the Creed, accepted the ritual of baptism, participated in worship, and obeyed the clergy was accepted as a fellow Christian."[16] The heart of the Christian faith had been lost, and into the vacuum created had poured manmade doctrines backed by emotional investment. And so there arose confusion in the Christian mind as to who was telling the truth about Jesus, and with the help of a central authority complete with growing police powers, the Church eventually managed to embed her doctrinal creations in the Christian mind.

This interpretation is of course hotly disputed, but modern scholarship has blown the lid off this particular pot, and attempts by some Christian scholars to put that lid back on again have failed. Many of the Gnostic communities had set up qualitative criteria and looked for evidence of spiritual maturity in those claiming to be Christian. In contrast to this approach, the bishops did away with qualitative criteria and attempted to unify the scattered churches through standardization of doctrine. It was no longer what you experienced in your own depths that mattered; all that mattered was what you believed with your mind, a point clearly agreed with by Cardinal Jean Daniélou in an earlier chapter. And do not try to have the best of both worlds: if you belonged to an orthodox church and were foolish enough to hold a cult meal or baptize someone without the bishop being present, then not only had you separated yourself from the legitimate Church, you had also separated yourself from God.[17]

So the gospels of the Gnostics were banned, and along with the suppression of these gospels went the suppression of those who understood their message. Full of symbols and veiled language concerning interior processes, these gospels were either hidden by initiates so that their insights might survive, or destroyed by those who found those insights incomprehensible and threatening. Classified as apostate, and therefore worse than pagans, the Gnostic Christians were described as evil seducers and hounded from pillar to post. And all because they claimed themselves able to discriminate between what was true and what was false. They did not need to be told what to believe, they said. They did not require the advice of waterless canals (the bishops); neither did they need doctrines that bound the mind to fixed paths of thought. Their Christianity was founded not on beliefs but on relationship, their behavior not on the dictates of authority figures but on the presence of God in their midst. The rule of faith had displaced conscience and made the arbitrary notions of men sacrosanct.

Archetypal Energies 8.5

It was the educated Christians who divorced themselves from the Roman Church and set up their own communities. Tertullian complained that it was the cream of his membership who deserted the ship of faith for the ship of understanding. And the word "understanding" should not be interpreted as referring to a desire for knowledge in the intellectual sense – that is a false accusation made against the gnosis-oriented Christians by their bishops. Gnosis was not hard knowledge, it was insight into the things of the spirit. The human mind was backgrounded by archetypal energies, they believed, and the release of those energies automatically cleared perception of its dependence on external forms.

This carries us back to the fact that Jesus was himself a nonconformist in religious terms. So it is no surprise that those who took his basic teachings seriously were also nonconformists, that they could stand neither the restrictions nor the claustrophobia of religious narrow-mindedness. And that is exactly how the Church ended up, as a narrow-minded and altogether pompous institution. Yes, it has modernized its image, but only because it has had no option – the world streaked away from it and its foolishness became self-evident. The Apostle Paul may have considered the cleverness of the world foolishness, and the foolishness of Christian belief a mark of intelligence, but if he had lived for a few hundred years he would have rapidly changed his mind. For in spite of evidence in the Epistles of Paul to the contrary, I do not think he believed what the Roman Church ended up believing; in fact I think he would have been astonished by Catholic doctrine as it eventually evolved. Paul has been blamed over and over again for writing the Roman Church a blank check, but a careful comparison of the Epistles suggests doctrinal skullduggery right from square one. There is a phantom Paul in the Epistles, and we would do well to study his profiles.

Balance 8.6

Moral law strictly adhered to was the outcome of minds struggling to get back to God by a self-conscious route. Jesus rejected this self-conscious route and, as a result deeply angered and infuriated the upholders of Jewish religious orthodoxy. Like Jesus, the Gnostic Christians believed that each person carried a different set of needs, different levels of comprehension, and different qualities of maturity. To feed everyone on the same strict moral diet was to ignore true need and further distort an already distorted self in need of help. Forcing everything into opposition and demanding *this* choice over *that* undermined our ability to act with freedom and love – particularly when we set up *one* of those choices as an unquestionable truth.

Elaine Pagels is at pains to point out that ethical questions are just as real and as important to these Gnostics Christians as they are to their consensus-loving brothers and sisters; the difference is that they have realized that fear" disables our ability to make helpful ethical choices. Connecting this fact to his rejection of cosmic opposites, Philip says, "Do not fear the flesh, nor love it. If you fear it, it will gain mastery over you; if you love it, it will devour and paralyze you."[18] This is the dilemma facing all of us, the dilemma of how to mentally balance ourselves between our fears and our loves, between our revulsions and our desires, between our projections and what actually exists. To live with the constant restriction of fear is to be mastered by life; to live without any kind of restriction is to be overcome by one's own appetites. Push the moral question too far and we end up killing people for their own good; refuse to properly recognize the moral question and we end up doing exactly the same thing. And so we come full circle and are confronted with the problem of how to control our unruly emotions. What to do, what to do?

Pagels identifies the Kingdom of God as a state of transformed consciousness, a state of "self discovery",[19] not some future event we have to wait for. The Kingdom's appearance has to do with a balancing of psychological forces; it is a "seeing" that the Gospel of Thomas describes in these carefully chosen words:

> When you make the two one, and when you make the inside like the outside and the outside like the inside, and the above like the below, and when you make the male and the female one and the same... then you will enter the kingdom.[20]

Recognizing the significance of events (their *thereness,* and our own *thereness* as they occur) is the key that saves us from the dictates of a submerged conscious mind. Or, as the Gospel of Thomas puts it: "Recognize what is before your eyes, and what is hidden will be revealed to you."[21] Such statements may seem obscure, but they are quite straightforward if you interpret them in Father Sylvan's terms. It is a matter of balancing oneself perceptually between *self as the one who sees* with *what is seen by the self*. This is not some mystic state of consciousness; it is a basic perceptual act in which the awake mind sustains its state of being awake through conscious effort – our being *present to ourselves as we perceive either internal or external reality*. The Gnostic teacher Silvanus captures the essence of this when he says: "end the sleep which weighs heavy upon you."[22] We are mostly submerged, engaged in conscious activity and have to wake up to that basic psychological fact. And not just occasionally; this waking up has to become an ongoing discipline to be effective. Pagels sums up the situation thus:

> Such Gnostics acknowledged that pursuing *gnosis* engages each person in a solitary, difficult process, as one struggles against internal resistance. They characterize this resistance to *gnosis* as the desire to sleep or to be drunk – that is, to remain unconscious.[23]

That, I think, helps consolidate the picture I'm trying to build of the submerged self and its problems. We are mostly engaged in conscious interaction with self, other or world, and as a consequence are unconscious while conscious – a flagrant contradiction in psychological terms now recognized and understood by some psychologists and philorophers, but perhaps not yet fully appreciated as to its deeper significance.

9: Gathering Substance

Redemption is first and foremost the awakening of a consciousness which had been lost for a time.
Henri-Charles Puech
Concept of Redemption in Manichaeism[1]

Intro: 9.0

Jacob Needleman was chagrined when a colleague described Father Sylvan's manuscript as "warmed over Gnosticism with a dash of pseudomystical allegorization." And equally so when another colleague returned the manuscript and said he had been able to read only half of Father Sylvan's nonsense.[2] After similar reactions from others, and the suggestion by an old friend that he had perhaps invented Father Sylvan, Needleman began to realize that the pivotal question did not concern a lost dimension to Christianity, but rather what is a lost dimension of myself. The question was his, not Christianity's. And neither was it a question of this or that aspect of Christianity being true, but am I true to what I am. Truth in its deepest sense was not about facts, ideas or doctrines; it was about our capacity to become fully ourselves.

As with the historian Morris Berman, so with Needleman. "May God preserve us from improvements," he says, referring to the attempt by reformers to correct this or that perceived distortion in Christianity's makeup. Corrections were necessary, but only if you had first grasped the larger picture: good and evil were not about being good or being bad, they were about *the arrangement of energies and sensations within the mind.* General rearrangements of facts were at best a "screen over this movement of energies within man."[3] Theories, paradigm shifts and axial moments in history were all very well, but they offered only new sets of variables for the mind to play with; they did not get to the heart of the problem: *self exiled from being*. We were, whether we admitted it or not, mostly a vacant existential site; we were "unoccupied" in the sense of being driven by habituated responses and mental associations run riot. By this means the sensation (illusion?) of being a coherent self was held in place, our imaginative constructions, arguments, repetitions and fantasies carrying us this way and that until we were forced by circumstances to surface from our submerged state of awake dream. Rehearsal, reflection, deductive inference, correction and such like were all useful and necessary mental procedures, but our tendency to generate, over and above what was necessary for our survival, endless internal dialogues robbed us of even the inclination to sense our moment-by-moment existence. We had the capacity to do this unusual thing, this uncalled-for thing, this subjectively questionable thing, but it required a deliberate siphoning off of energy to accomplish it, and that in turn required a recognition of the necessity to even bother trying.

This was of course to take Father Sylvan's "warmed over Gnosticism" seriously. So was this priest's approach as important as Needleman made it out to be? Should we take it as read that there was a distinct difference between gnosis and Gnosticism, and that later Gnosticism's bizarre theological ramblings constituted a heresy of *gnosis*, not a heresy of Christianity? What were we to make of the notion that it was the energies of consciousness that were all important, not the idea of Jesus being God, or of his being a universal savior come to Earth in human form to save us from the consequences of sin?

The answer to these questions lay in the fact that Church doctrine stated clearly that Jesus was, apart from anything else, a flesh-and-blood human being – a point labored over by Church thinkers for centuries, and for very good reason. Jesus got tired; he got hungry or thirsty, and even angry in a stage-managed kind of way. More importantly, his self-designation in the Gospels was not that he was God come to save us from ourselves, but that he was *Son of Man,* a son of humanity with something vital to tell us about the human condition. Jesus' message, therefore, was not that he was the message, but that perceiving the Kingdom of God was what it was all about. In Judaism the coming Kingdom of God was a glorious God-centered kingdom of bricks and mortar where one would pay taxes; in Christianity the Kingdom was a spiritual edifice that would descend from heaven and settle on a world purified by fire. In Jesus' scheme the Kingdom of God was starkly different; it was something simultaneously internal and external, a state of mind *and* a world transformed because of that state of mind. It was, in other words, a "seeing" that transcended ordinary perception, a balancing of psychological forces (Pagels) that revealed a new dimension of consciousness.

But what about Father Sylvan's nodding acceptance of Gnosticism, for in spite of differentiating between gnosis and Gnosticism, and rejecting the idea of a principle of evil that is as real as the principle of good, he at the same time was willing to rationalize much of Gnostic thinking into an acceptable scheme. Clearly siding with the early Fathers against the Gnostics, he at the same time seemed able to accommodate their system on other levels of explanation. By way of countering this contradiction, Father Sylvan spoke of a teaching that directed man's attention to an experience of the very forces that dispersed his capacity to accomplish his spiritual journey. Such forces were not in themselves evil; they were in fact the means by which man learned to accomplish the higher task. There were two mysticisms, not one. Without the mysticism of "perceptual reorientation" the higher mysticism was not fully attainable.

The confusion that arose within Gnosticism was that of interpreting "the illusions, self-deceptions and egoism that distract man from the work of self-perfection"[4] with the world of physical matter. Equating the overall distractive power of matter with evil, the Gnostics progressively lost sight of the role played by matter in man's comprehension of his spiritual dilemma, and ended up with a theology of creation that literalized this evil into a malevolent God. But inside this literalism resided the original gnosis, the original understanding of how these forces of distraction and self-deception could be used to liberate the mind. Yes, the world was a house of ignorance and illusion, a domain where man moved around in a drugged and mentally intoxicated state, but it was this very state that heralded his possible liberation, for in comprehending how this state arose, and in battling with it, he slowly emerged from its clutches. But more than that, for the process of his emerging was also a process of energy accumulation (gathering), and this energy, as it grew and intensified, assisted him in his escape. And not in some metaphorical manner but in the sense of a transforming energy that reciprocated his efforts step by step. So Gnosticism should not be rejected out of hand, it should be carefully interpreted in terms of the original gnosis, understood as harboring what orthodox Christianity had inadvertently mislaid.

The Manichaean Synthesis 9.1

The picture of the many interrelated Gnostic groups presented so far would be quite incomplete without the inclusion of Manichaeism, for it was Manichaeism that attempted to synthesize early Jewish-Christianity and Pauline Christianity with Zoroastrian dualism, Mithraism and Christian-Gnosticism. First preached by Mani of Ctesiphon in the 3rd century CE, its early center of activity was Babylon, then part of the Persian Empire and a meeting place for many faiths. Mani offered what he termed "true religion", declared himself a messiah and accused Christianity of having engaged in a willful distortion of spiritual reality. True religion, he said, had been taught by a succession of prophets, and he himself was the seal of the prophets.

The universal message offered by Mani led to the development of a missionary spirit that successfully spread his ideas across the breadth of the ancient world. After thirty years of preaching, his curious doctrines continued to influence Asia and North Africa, surviving even the persecutions of Diocletian and the conquest of Islam.[5] In the 10th century his ideas were considered beaten, but they sprang to life again in the eleventh, alarming the Church by attracting priests, canons, professors and even a Queen's confessor into its ranks.

Of all the groups thrown up as a result of doctrinal tensions between so-called Jewish-Christianity, Pauline Christianity, Roman Christianity and Christian-Gnosticism, Manichaeism is the doctrinal area where close investigation affords glimpses of an underlying set of ideas both explosive in content and expressive of a line of reasoning stemming from the earliest periods of religious exploration. Although brought up in an Elchasaite community (Jewish-Christian) in Babylon,[6] Mani nevertheless fell under the influence of Gnostic ideas of Eastern origin. Here then is the doctrinal mix of Manichaeism, and in the development of this mix can be seen elements suggestive of an ancient system of thought about which we as yet know very little. Embedded often in speculations inspired by naive piety, or in what appears to be such, this system surfaces again and again to tantalize and surprise. Aware of this fact, A.B. Kuhn names Manichaeism and Neoplatonism as the two great philosophical rivals of Christianity, and asserts that they "held the ancient body of sage-wisdom to its highest standards of intellectual appreciation."[7] In relation to Manichaeism, that's quite a claim; but as we shall see – not entirely without foundation – Manichaeism does seem to harbor an advanced psycho-spiritual system embedded in a rather odd theology.

Mani appears to have adopted the Iranian version of dualism, but his ideas may have had another origin. It is reported in an Arabic source (the *Fihrist*) that he preached a doctrine of darkness and light in the form of two great beings who existed from the beginning of the world. In this version of Mani's teachings he assumes this world to be a mixture of light and darkness, and that darkness is its principal essence. And so he taught a doctrine of "mixing" and "unmixing", and developed this into a system of "dispersal" where portions of light were conceived of as having separated off and mixed with a captivating darkness. In this sense, salvation was a process of *gathering in the dispersed portions of light,* a restoration of the original unity of light scattered throughout the creation. Human creation was therefore a trick of the Dark Powers to imprison the light more firmly – release could come only when individual beings woke up to this fact.

In a fragment of the Gnostic Gospel of Eve preserved by Epiphanius, the idea of gathering light takes on further significance.

> I am thou and thou art I, and where thou art I am, and in all things am I dispersed. And from wherever thou wilst thou gatherest me; but in gathering me thou gatherest thyself.[8]

And again:

> I have come to know myself and have gathered myself from everywhere...[9]

Referring to these fragments, Hans Jonas remarks that over and above a metaphysical aspect, these quotations reveal an inward aspect in relation to unity and unification. This suggests a higher form of gnosis (knowledge); or as Jonas puts it, "The increasing realization of an inner aspect purifies the metaphysical one of the cruder mythological meanings it had to begin with."[10] He goes on to say that Valentinian gnosis (Valentinus formed an underground group within the orthodox fold) is a de-mythologizing of Gnostic symbols, and in speaking thus suggests a spiritualizing of previous literalisms. In line with this, Simone Petrement notes that the idea of self-knowledge seems to arise with Valentinus, and is not to be found in the writings of other so-called Gnostic teachers such as Simon, Menander, Cerinthus, Saturnilus, Basilides or Cerdo.[11]

The doctrine of Christ's incarnation is rejected by Mani. He envisages Jesus' redemptive role in the sense of someone who awakens, and having awakened, awakens others. The mythology backing this point is complex; suffice to say that to Henri-Charles Puech, Simone Petrement and A.B. Kuhn it corresponds to a depth-psychology embedded in a highly complex mythology that has to be carefully interpreted. For example, Mani's conception of matter as an evil, half-unconscious "force" trying to invade or engulf the realm of Light is not to be taken literally. Petrement notes this and says that Mani's depiction of matter as evil is an exaggeration of Platonic dualism, a dualism originally understood as meaning that matter causes evil only when it is mixed with the spirit in a certain manner.[12] That suggests that Platonic dualism did in fact lie behind Mani's thinking, and it also suggests that he clearly saw the absurdity of a physical Jesus being God and was forced to widen the gap between those two principles.

The Engulfing of Matter 9.2

To understand what the Manichaeans meant by light being engulfed or smothered by matter, it is necessary to read between the lines and attempt to detect the psychological principles at work. Jonas is particularly good at this; his choice of words often loosens up the issues involved. For instance, in relation to the "engulfing of matter", he speaks of gnosis, or knowledge, as an inner event of the mind. But not in the sense of "thinking"; more in the sense of transcendental experience. Linked directly to the idea of "gathering", this experience is defined Neoplatonically by Porphyr as a "gathering in from the body all thy members which have been dispersed and scattered".[13] This sets the scene by way of the senses being pulled in and concentrated. Then with a brilliant twist Jonas completes the picture by interpreting the existential meaning of dispersal as "distraction". It is through distraction that we are engulfed and smothered by "the manifold concerns and lures of the world acting through the senses of the body."[14] When rescued from the obscurity of Gnostic symbols, we are confronted with a perfectly sensible series of ideas, ideas that inform us that, in Manichaean terms, *consciousness of self dissipated through identification with matter* is what the whole bag of tricks is about.

Through the senses, a usurped state of consciousness erupts. To wake up to this is to be redeemed or resurrected – it is to awaken to the fact that the self spends a great deal of time within a prison of distraction. We function mostly in an unconscious manner when conscious, and the human body is the reason for this curious state of affairs. Why? Because it functions unconsciously, and as we are that body we tend to follow the line of least resistance. In this sense, consciousness is a battle continually won through effort, and we are engaged in this battle from the moment of birth. Spending most of our time caught in the grasp of images, ideas and sensations, we forget to remember who we are, and the result is an automaton unleashed on the world who only occasionally remembers that he or she actually exists.

The Manichaeans claimed that their doctrine of redemption and resurrection was based on an authentic science, not on authority and faith. They saw redemption and resurrection as a problem of insight objectively solved by the mind. As with Gnostic ideas in general, this is where interpretations of Manichaeism as nothing more than a rational philosophy arose, but the so-called objective approach of the Manichaeans had in fact nothing whatever to do with rational systems of thought. Their idea of solving a problem did not require extended thinking; it entailed *revelation*. Switching from one method of perception to another, the initiate came to understand how self related to world. And so, borrowing from Paul, Mani evolved the idea of the Old Man, and the New Man, and in those terms we can see the basis of a depth psychology that teases us towards an appreciation of what it means to be awake. The Old Man represents the soul suffering from "dull consciousness" and "dark insight", whereas the New Man is defined as the *I here.* This reflects quite precisely the notion of being fully present.[15] And so the idea of redemption is disconnected from the notion that Jesus' crucifixion was in some sense vicarious, and as Puech so clearly states, it becomes "first and foremost the awakening of a consciousness which has been lost for a time through the forgetfulness and ignorance induced by the flesh."[16] Or, as cited in an early Manichaean work by Theodore bar Khouni, "Then Adam examined himself and knew who he was."[17]

It is at this point that the whole idea of Jesus being divine begins to make sense, for as an awake man he carries a redemptive charge; that is, he reflects the deified state and, as a redeemed redeemer (he too had to undergo the waking up process), is an example to all mankind that deification can be theirs. How? By realizing that life is itself a transformative process, and that the world is a kind of cosmic machine, or factory, for gathering and refining the divine light buried in dull consciousness. This causes Puech to refer to the cosmos as a pharmacy "where poison and medicine lie side by side."[18] To the Manichaeans life was a battleground, an area of conflict where the Old Man (the constantly distracted "I") and the New Man (the intermittently awake "self") fought for ascendancy. Which suggests a state of suffering. And so, in the writings of Theodore bar Khouni, we have demons associated with matter, and they are described as making the first man blind, deaf, confused and unconscious.

The Manichaeans then developed the idea of two traditions, one governed by light, the other by darkness. The tradition founded on darkness created false religion, the one on light true religion. Christianity after the time of Paul is seen as in decline, the new gospel of Mani as attempting to recapture the original meaning of Jesus' message. And so the historical Jesus is interpreted as different from the transcendent Jesus, the transcendent Jesus being an archetypal emanation incarnated in the historical Jesus just as Jewish-Christian theology claimed. Referred to as "he who has awakened the Living I", Jesus' passion is changed from a vicarious sacrifice into an example of the very problem faced, the problem of full conscious awareness dispersed and crucified in matter.[19] But more than that, for as our attempts to awaken are intermittent and prone to reversal, the necessity of sustained awakening becomes the central issue, a task-oriented issue belonging to the Church proper and linked to the majesty of the law – morality as a task linked to awareness as a discipline. It is the law that awakens. The law is the "unique awakener", the moral life that which inspires the instrument that makes man an instrument for the liberation of light.[20]

This carries us back to the Jewish-Christian insistence that observation of the law could not be done away with. Faith in Jesus as a redemptive sacrifice was, in their opinion, a mistake; atonement and salvation were by and through the law alone. Only the law consciously lived out in life could reveal how unconscious we really were. The Redeemer's revelation of this was important, but believing what the Redeemer said was not enough in and of itself; it was also necessary to maintain without interruption the form of consciousness that had been aroused by the Redeemer's words.[21] And so was formed the basic Manichaean attitude towards body and world, an attitude that demanded rejection of the world and of those who found its poisonous effects to their liking. Renunciation was the key, detachment from the world and the flesh the means by which the baleful influence of matter could be overcome.

Life and Light 9.3

According to Manichaean doctrine, life is light, a luminous substance resident in matter. The purpose of creation is the rescuing of this divine substance. Functioning like a machine, or factory for the gathering and refining of light, the world's elements in conjunction with moon and sun liberate the divine substance and it rises as a pillar of light towards the moon, and is then transferred to the sun and finally to its heavenly home.[22] The mythology surrounding this subject of life and light as a substance locked up in matter is complex, but the end result is pretty clear: human beings are intrinsically involved in their own redemption, and in the redemption of the planet. And not in some airy-fairy sense, but in the sense of energy accumulation. Life and light equals energy, and energy can be stored.

The twist in Manichaean mythology is that Adam's eating of the fruit in the Garden of Eden results in his liberation, not his downfall – shades of an Irenaean doctrine we have lost sight of. Sunk in the body, he has become an instrument of the unconscious,[23] a state of captivity from which the Redeemer awakens him. Able now to see that his soul's substance is diffused throughout all matter (squandered through constant submerged conscious engagement), he determines to hold matter at bay and so rescue the divine substance. As this soul substance is consubstantial with God, the idea of redemption fans out into the creation itself, the symbol for this Living Soul imprisoned in matter being *Jesus Patibilis;* that is, Jesus in the "pathetic aspect" of his suffering. Crucified throughout matter, the divine substance or "life" *in* matter is held captive and has to be restored to the realm of light. The question is, how does one hold matter at bay? What do we have to do to stop this leakage of our life-energy? Answer: arouse the "I here", of course.

In relation to the idea of light being rescued from matter, the Manichaeans also developed the idea of feeding on the divine substance, so making human beings an essential component of the world machine, or factory, where light is gathered and refined. Strict vegetarians, the Manichaean elect looked upon themselves as digestion machines capable of purifying and releasing the light from the fruit, vegetables and grain that they consumed. Allowing themselves only one meal per day, and fasting at regular intervals, they ate just enough food to sustain life, so reflecting the equally strict habits of the Nazoraeans, Ebionites and Elchasaites.

But there were also many differences between the Manichaeans and the other Gnostic groups. The Manichaeans condemned baptism and did not seem to have bothered with sacraments or rites. Certain rituals were observed, such as the laying on of hands, the kiss of peace and the viaticum for the dying, but basically there were no sacraments, the elect believing that their transformed state of consciousness made all sacraments obsolete. It was the state of consciousness that mattered, not adherence to liturgical forms. Interestingly, though, the Manichaeans recognized confession of sin as necessary, and even had their congregations publicly confess their sins to the elect, and in turn the elect to the spirit of Mani which they believed attended their church services. Basically, however, the emphasis was on quality of consciousness and on a special kind of knowledge that helped transform the inner man. It was *gnosis* that redeemed the soul, *gnosis* that transformed consciousness, *gnosis* that produced liberation from the material body's inclination to follow the line of least resistance.

Transcendent Knowledge 9.4

The Manichaean conception of knowledge is infused with important philosophical repercussions in relation to perception. In alignment with Gnostic conceptions of knowledge, Manichaeism trained its adherents in a process of perception that, if successful, resulted in immediate redemption. This process of perception was considered sufficient in and of itself to redeem the individual due to its extraordinary effect on consciousness, and resulted in complete knowledge – absolute, universal or cosmic knowledge. Transformed by this experience, the initiate began to perceive the transcendent realities and became aware of his/her true identity.[24]

Yet when back in their normal senses, caught still in consensus reality with regard to culture and the general activities of mind and required to live in the 3rd century. In some sense truly transformed as a result of their experience of transcendent reality, but necessary to sustain this condition of mind through practice. Not a permanent state. More a glimpse that had to be repeated until it became a fixed state of consciousness. In other words, Jesus' dilemma all over again as he faced unfulfilled end-time expectations in spite of a personal transfiguration. Intimations of transcendent reality were not always in alignment with mundane reality due to the mind's need to interpret higher reality experience into useful lower reality terms. Or, as Puech puts it, "It must be stressed that this body of knowledge, which purports to be scientific and even rational, actually dissolves into a system of myths."[25] The Jungian psychologist Erich Neumann, dealing with the same problem, pushes further still and describes transcendent knowledge as belonging to the creative unconscious. Placing it at the outer limits of the ego's capacity to perceive, he says: "Any attempt to approach this central and primal vortex is a hazardous undertaking." Why? Because it is "in the very nature of such an undertaking that its object cannot be captured by the direct intervention of consciousness, but that one must seek to approach the center in question by a sort of ritual circling, an approach from many sides."[26] As with the experience, so with attempting to write about it; it also requires a ritual circling.

But this is only half of the story; the rest of the story is that the Gnostic and Jewish-Christian groups were also spiritual subversives in relation to orthodox Christianity's claim that it had the truth, the whole truth, and nothing but the truth. Defined as heretical, they acted heretically; that is, over and above what they were actually experiencing, they also resorted to allegorical polemic in the sense of a tendentious rewriting of texts to confuse and bemuse their critics.[27] This is very important, for it suggests that the more impenetrable texts belonging to these groups may in fact be coded statements to which the Church Fathers simply lacked the interpretive key. Turning many a biblical event on its head, they seem to have delighted in what Hans Jonas calls the construction of countertypes. And so what they present is often not what they actually believed, but a "rebel's view of history" consciously fabricated to oppose the Church's official stance.[28]

Behind this, however, lay an equally complex visionary system, for initiates became capable of intercepting reality in such a fashion that reality ended up intercepting them at the deepest levels of psyche. Encompassing objective reality in a series of subtle subjective moves, the initiate cracked the cosmic egg and began to perceive transcendent reality through the aperture that appeared in time and space. Previously intoxicated or numbed by objective reality, the initiate slowly realized that he/she was caught in a state of conscious sleep from which it was necessary to awaken at regular intervals. Summing up this curious state of being unconsciously conscious, Hans Jonas says:

> We are dealing here, as in the whole group of the metaphors of sleeping, not with a mythological detail, a mere episode in a narrative, but with a fundamental feature of existence in the world... The 'world' on its part makes elaborate efforts to create and maintain this state in its victims and to counteract the operation of awakening.[29]

In Gnostic literature, mankind is described as asleep in the world, and this, as Jonas points out, refers to total abandonment to the world. But as we have seen, this does not refer to moral forget-

by the mixture; given back to its nature [awake again] it can only go the way of the light."[31] This suggests that real morality results from strength of consciousness, not from moral systems. Awake, the soul can resist evil; asleep, it will probably succumb.

As the above explanation seems to be the central factor in Manichaeism, we can probably constellate everything else in the system around it. But the idea of matter as "distracting" and "engulfing" is difficult for us to detect, and as interpretations of Manichaean texts tend to literalize the ideas expressed; they tend to obscure more than they reveal. Aware of this problem, Simone Petrement berates scholars for underestimating Gnostic thinking, and reminds everyone that Manichaean doctrine rests upon a very complicated myth.[32] Acknowledging and confirming Puech's evaluation of Gnostic texts pointing to the "hidden part of each human being," she nevertheless feels that his approach is reductive in relation to what the Gnostic initiate sensed, and accuses him of spinning a quite inadequate piece of sociological theory to explain a psychological breakthrough. This seems right. What these Gnostics were involved in was not some simple imaginative exercise of the mind in relation to the shape of society, but a dynamic insight resulting from an examination of the self in relation to a religious discipline.

The Concern with Self 9.6

Simone Petrement observes that 2nd century Christian heretics did not speak of the self in the same way as the 3rd century sects did; they seem to have spent most of their time arguing about Judaism, divine beings and the Law, but not about the nature of the self. Accused by the dominant Christian group of professing to know God (an insult to God if you had been classified a heretic), they were condemned for their impudence and pushed even further into disgrace. Their concern was not with self, it was with Judaism and with whether the Law of Israel should continue to be revered. Linked directly to the Jewish-Christians by way of tradition and focus, they criticized the ruling Christian orthodoxy for continuing to conceal the God Jesus had tried to reveal. Knowledge of God was the central issue, not knowledge of self. Only later would this so modern theme appear in the heretical texts.

But what of this self so beloved of the later Christian heretics? How did it develop, and from what did it develop? Petrement theorizes that the seeming preoccupation with self stemmed from the desire to know the origin and destination of the soul. In this context, knowledge of the self implied, "knowledge of a complete doctrine concerning God, the human soul, and the world."[33] So knowledge of self is actually knowledge of the origin of the self. But this view has to be tempered by the fact that knowledge of the soul's origin comes from insight, not from theoretical constructions. So I think Petrement is correct in her summation when she says, "For these Gnostics there is a knowledge of the self... but there is not, properly speaking, a search for the self. The knowledge was given without search".[34] That is the crux of the matter; there was no searching for the self in the sense that we now understand such a search, just an experiential "seeing" that revealed the complex nature of the relationship that exists between self, other and world.

The Human Structure 9.7

In Father Sylvan's scheme of things, many Gnostic sects twisted the perfectly acceptable idea of there being a God of the developed soul, and a lesser God of morality and religious sanctity into a dualistic literalism that challenged the "unicity and harmonious structure of the universe itself." This inherent unity and harmonious structure was "a key element of a world view emphasizing levels of being in man and the universe",[35] and its loss signified a loss of spiritual perspective for both Gnosticism and orthodox Christianity. The lesser God of the Gnostics was not an actual God, he was, psychologically speaking, representative of concepts that got between "the soul and experience of its supreme possibilities."[36] So also the idea of Good and Evil as fundamental forces, a cosmic dualism in which evil was believed by later Gnostics to be as *equally real* as the Good. In such interpretations lay Gnosticism as a heresy of *gnosis*, a heresy that orthodox Christianity itself was guilty of as it gave way to the idea of evil as a fundamental force that God was at war with.

For Father Sylvan, an evil co-equal with God did not exist, just impediments to our spiritual awakening that had to be recognized for what they were: psychological stumbling blocks. There were actually two mysticisms, not one. Mysticism one was direct experience of the Higher; mysticism two was direct experience of the forces that constituted being and consciousness. Although at opposite ends of the spiritual scale, these two mysticisms constituted one mysticism, for they had to be balanced one against the other for spiritual development to take place. The whole idea of perfection in Christianity was related to mysticism number one, but perfection in this higher sense was impossible if the individual ignored *the human structure and its parts*. There was a top-half mysticism, and a bottom-half mysticism, and we knew next to nothing about the bottom half.

PART TWO: BETWIXT HELL AND HEAVEN

10: To Be, or Not to Be

> *The act of bending on itself IS the act of self-awareness – the mind's own awareness of itself. Because of this bending action we have the subject-object poles of consciousness, which is the mind knowing itself as object to itself.*
> Bernadette Roberts
> *What is the Self?*[1]

Intro: 10.0

In the introduction to his study of Gnostic mythology from early Christianity to modern nihilism, Ioan Couliano cites the fable of the Flatland devised by the Shakespearian scholar the Reverend Edwin Abbott Abbott (the double "Abbott" is not a misprint), a fable taken up by Albert Einstein in his attempt to explain why we cannot understand the world from inside out. Couliano's reason for choosing this fable is that he wants to impress on us the mind-boggling consequences of Einstein's Theory of Relativity, one consequence being how extraordinarily difficult it would be for the inhabitants of a two-dimensional world to detect the existence of a three-dimensional world. Only Flatland geniuses might suspect that such a world existed. Likening Flatland to the surface of soup in a dish, Couliano supposes that circles of oil on that surface equal intelligent beings who can move in only two directions: left-right, or forward-backward; the direction up-down being meaningless to them. Beings from three-dimensional space would then have considerable advantages over two-dimensional beings, just as fourth-dimensional beings would have similar advantages relative to us.[2]

Calling these two-dimensional beings "Souplanders", Couliano then speculates on what it would be like if someone in our dimension of space-time started to eat the soup with a spoon. How would a Souplander experience the spoon? As a soupquake, he tells us. A short line corresponding to the tip of the spoon would appear in Soupland, increase in size, then decrease in size and be followed by a portion of Soupland being absorbed into nowhere. As the spoon could be experienced only as a line, and not as a vertical object (there is no up-down in Soupland), the spoon would be experienced as *a series of phenomena in time.* Given the difficulties in interpreting what was going on, it would take a Souplander of great genius to "postulate the existence of a superior dimension – the third – in which objects of an unknown sort exist."[3]

My point in drawing attention to Couliano's Flatland is that it corresponds rather neatly with our submerged and engaged conscious state, a state of mind in which we almost constantly reside, but from out of which, unlike Flatland, it is possible to emerge, or escape. And we do not have to be geniuses to do it; we can escape at will once we realize that this country of the mind, this self-sufficient dimension of mind is not the whole of the mind; there is another higher, more complex dimension of awareness available to us. But this realization requires us to grasp the fact that we really do exist mostly in such a cut-off state, and that the non-submerged state is the more sophisticated of the two. For this to strike home, however, we have to *sense our way into* this non- submerged state, sustain the experience as best we can and allow something of its potential depths to register. Being non-submerged is, ironically, all about depth, a contradiction in terms that carries its own subtle message.

Self-awareness and Inner Speech 10.1

To bring this into sharper focus, we will now direct our attention to a study of consciousness done by the research psychologist Alain Morin. In Morin's study, inner speech is postulated as playing a key role in self-awareness because it creates "a psychological distance between the self and mental events", and can help "label aspects of one's inner life that would otherwise be difficult to objectively perceive."[4] These are important observations; they allow us to glimpse the actual mechanism of mind that allows us to recognize ourselves *as* a self. Without inner speech, or "self-talk" as Morin christens it, the capacity to become the object of one's own attention is diminished; that is, parts of the self become isolated and internal consistency (Hume's illusion of a continuous self) evaporates. In Morin's terms, lack of inner speech impedes self-awareness development, whereas extensive self-talking is said to generate a rich and well-articulated self-concept.[5]

But as Morin also shows, there is a downside to this situation; some pathological conditions can, as most of us are aware, arise as a result of dysfunctional self-talk. We can lie to ourselves as surely as we can lie to another person, accuse ourselves unjustly or foster distorted notions of ourselves as in the case of an anorexic – or invent anorexic-type evaluations of reality. But on the whole, we fare reasonably well in this two-way relationship; it helps sustain sense of self at the same time as it allows self to manipulate its world. The role of language in consciousness has of course been of interest to psychologists and philosophers for decades; but as Morin points out, the role of inner language in relation to self-awareness has not received as much attention as it deserves. Inner speech facilitates self-awareness, extends existing self-knowledge and assists in the self's sense of its own continuity.

There is however a catch: self-awareness in Morin's terms is accomplished through the sustaining of a submerged, engaged conscious state, a state within which, contradictorily, the self also hides from the self. Engaged in surface-world thinking (our three-dimensional Flatland where external things masquerade as internal phenomena), we tend not to attend to our non-submerged moments, and as a result isolate ourselves in a world where self-presence is predominantly absent. Self-aware we may claim to be, but it is a claim bought at the expense of being a real presence to ourselves, and to others. And this is not merely to advocate an overlay of tactile experience in the sense of Eric Schwitzgebel's beeper experiment; it is to raise the question of our lack of self-presence in a much more intrinsic fashion. Self-presence is not ultimately physical; it is, as the philosophers say, ontological – it has to do with the nature of Being itself. In this sense it is also Shakespearean: it is a matter of *Being, or not Being.*

Erich Neumann's observation at 1.5 that the logical statement of identity – "I am I" – is a tremendous achievement because it is an act "whereby an ego is posited and the personality identified with that ego"[6] links into Morin's more explicit observation of how self arises within consciousness. For out of this process of inner dialogue comes Neumann's self-orienting consciousness, and it is our capacity for self-orientation that underpins our success as human beings *no matter how fallacious that identification may later prove to be.* In spite of our success as individualized selves, a doubt still exists as to the efficacy of this self in spite of its accomplishments, and this doubt has to do with its intrinsic reality, not its obvious worth. Yes, we have a self, but it is at base composed of mirror-reflective principles bouncing around in consciousness. Yet it is terribly important in its own right, for without it we would not have accomplished what we have accomplished, and for exactly the same reason we would not be faced with what is potentially the next step in our evolution as human beings: the jettisoning of this self in favor of an even more sophisticated level of awareness. The appearance in consciousness of a self-orienting principle was an evolutionary event of major psychological importance; but it may be that the appearance of "presencing individuals" in our societies will, as the historian Morris Berman suspects, far exceed this event in importance.

Secret Life of Belly and Bone 10.2

The above heading is a line from the final chapter of Morris

Berman's book *Coming to Our Senses,* and that line starts with the words: "Our hidden history was *always* a somatic one..." Berman then reinforces this view by saying: "When you've lost your body, you need an 'ism'. From there it is a short step to seeing other isms as life-threatening, and to seeing the other as an enemy."[7] But he isn't finished; he senses an impasse, and he articulates that impasse with a warning: we should at the same time not overvalue the body, for "To know your own flesh, to know both the pain and the joy it contains, is to come to know something much larger than this." There is a "something" that eludes our civilization, and that something involves "a reciprocal relationship between nature and psyche."[8]

As an experience, the body as subjective field plays a vital role in our humanness, and in our humaneness, but it is not the most important factor. Bernadette Roberts agrees: "... pure subjectivity could be mistaken for the self when, in fact, the finding of the true self belongs to an entirely different journey."[9] The really important factor is the play of forces that ricochet between psyche and nature as a whole (self, body *and* world) as they are brought into a state of intentionally directed balance. The partly awakened self has, along with the body, a vital role to play in this most important of all scenarios, and it is that of *self-relinquishment.* Or, as Father Sylvan puts it: "The intellect cannot be abandoned until it knows why it must be abandoned and can theoretically agree to it."[10]

In prehistory we had to emerge from the unconscious, now we have to progressively emerge from the Flatland of submerged conscious engagement. Powerful as Flatland thinking can be, it is also our weakest psychic point due to the nature of perception as it has evolved. Clever and compassionate one day, we can be dense and brutal the next because of a slight change in our inner emotional climate. That's all it takes. We are at the mercy of our reactive emotions. And we have evolved this way for very good reason: in terms of day-to-day survival we don't need this other level of consciousness; it is superfluous to our survival needs. All we need is our old primordial survival instincts and drives, and that is everywhere evident in our societies and in our personal lives. Looking after number one, we stumble from one crisis to another wondering why it has to be this way. The answer? It has to be this way because this is how we are at present.

To advocate "self-relinquishment" as a way out of this dilemma is not to advocate a mysticism where weakened egos seek to dissolve themselves in a God imagined theologically as some kind of ocean; it is to advocate the growth of a strong ego capable of handing over the reins of self-governance to a more sophisticated level of consciousness. It is, finally, the end of the submerged self's emotionally reactive dominance and the beginning of a life in which the partly aware self learns to seriously listen to inner criteria. And the words "learn to listen" are the operative words; the submerged self is not instantly freed from its dilemma through the realization that it is living a mostly submerged life; it awakens in a series of painful stages. This is a long, drawn-out process where the bad habits of a lifetime are shed one by one. There is no easy fix here; instant salvation is not on the table. It is a matter of waking up step by step to what the next step might be, and if you have the courage, acting on it.

In terms of how the human species has advanced from its prehistoric beginnings to where it is now, submerged conscious engagement with self and world has worked extremely well. But as is now realized our very success has had its drawbacks. We are now in a position to do ourselves and the planet real harm, and have only recently awakened to the fact that the latter problem is closely related to our survival-driven behavior. What had once been a glorious strength is now a baleful influence on how we relate to self, other and world, and a rearrangement of paradigms won't ultimately solve the problems we face. And neither will prayers, soothing as they can be in fractured and tormented lives, rescue us from this situation. A dramatic opening up of the mind to what is going on in our lives, in our societies and in our religious institutions is what has to take place. A paradigm shift in religious attitudes is already under way (you would hardly believe that to be case in some quarters), but that in itself won't do the trick; we'll have to delve more deeply into the self than that.

On this score let's double back to the business of self-relinquishment, for it carries further complications. If properly integrated, this kind of depth (mystical) encounter with the self is creative and world-transforming; if poorly integrated it tends towards nihilism. Eric Neumann sums up the situation thus: "The decisive factor in this orientation is the condition of the ego after its mystical experience."[11] There are two kinds of mystics: those who return and shed a positive light on everything they touch, and those who reject the world and cast a negative light on everything they touch. In rejecting (misunderstanding) the creative principle underlying human experience, negative mystics reveal themselves to be prophets of disintegration: they advocate the paradise of the unborn infant (the infant prior to ego development), and betray their infantile personalities and their desire to "achieve beatific nonexistence in the divine womb of nothingness."[12] Another name for this disabled approach would be "death mysticism", the desire to snuff the self out in an act of psychological (or even physical) abandonment. As unwitting representatives of the prenatal stage of human development, such individuals project their own repressed natures onto the world and consign it to the devil, a state described by Neumann as "uroboros incest". Succumbing to ecstatic seizure, inflation, depression and even psychosis, they attempt to kill off their ego in mystic dissolution so as to avoid the problem of integration and the ambiguities that underpin creative experience in the depths of psyche. Attacked from within by what they fear most, the feminine, they create a frightening world of shadows and infest that world with male-dominated symbols. And all because the state of consciousness sensed to underpin the conscious matrix has been misinterpreted. Alpha has been made to replace Omega; the infant's state of perfection without mind or will now lies at both ends of the ego's archetypal journey (see 14.5).

Relinquishment of the ego (the submerged conscious self) by the ego is *not* an abandonment of self to primordial forces; it is a step beyond the evolutionary process as it is presently understood by an ego that consciously decides to become part of that process. The situation is quite the opposite in terms of ego-abandonment where the ego experiences emergence from the unconscious for no other purpose than to *regain* its infantile paradise. There is, in this scheme, no point to the lived life except the moral refinement of the creature so that it can return to the arms of its creator. The path is circular, the beginning is the end, the snake of creation devours its own tail. But this need not be the case. A progressive strengthening of the ego seems to be the functional aim of life, not a weakening. The child does not remain a child, the adolescent does not remain adolescent, the mature adult seeks ever greater maturity. This causes the ego to suffer at every stage, for inherent in suffering is the energy of change and transformation. Here, too, we stumble into the positive mystic's negative counterpart, for the negative mystic's interpretation of what he or she is experiencing is at the mercy of theological constructions allied to a whole range of distorted historical ideas

This is not to say that the negative mystic is unaware of alternatives; it is to say that the personality development of the negatively oriented mystic gets in the way of properly unpacking his experience of the psyche's depths. As suggested at 4.4, an interaction with the formless center of being is an encounter that depends on the kind of person we bring to the experience – it is *our* encounter. The personality's stage of development governs the nature of the experience had, not the experience the nature of the personality. The measure of what is realized, understood or intuited is a glimpse of something that must be unpacked by the ego as it emerges more and more from its submerged state. In being able to bear the creative tension set up between conscious and unconscious levels, the intuitions had will enable the personality to endure the approaching moment of ego-relinquishment, the *replacing* of the submerged "I" with a non-submerged "I". If unable to unpack what it is experiencing without recourse to fixed theological formulas, the personality will attempt to escape the rigidity of its submerged "I" in an act of final dissolution, a suicidal return to the paradisiacal state of the unborn infant. Neumann states his case against such an act bluntly: "The mission of man is not to plunge himself into the white primal light and lose his identity."[13]

There are, Neumann contends, many types of mysticism, and the mysticism of religion may not be the most important. In spite of its long and well-documented history, religious mysticism may be only one of many approaches to the creative center of being. This suggests, as Paul Tillich suggested, that God is "the Ground of Being", so making every avenue of approach sacred. The artist, teacher, engineer, dustman, flower-arranger or pastry cook has then as much chance of forming a deep and transformative relationship with objective reality as any mystic. But only when they wake up from the sleep of a preoccupied existence, when the eyes of psyche are open rather than shut, when the senses are properly attuned to the potential "I-here" of each passing moment. Such a condition of psyche is, however, far off for most of us; we are too caught up in the affairs of our lives to pay attention to the idea of being too caught up in the affairs of our lives! And the reason for this is not just that our lives are ultra–busy; it is also the result of a spiritual education that has fallen markedly short of its declared responsibilities.

Identity 10.3

The mission of man, according to Erich Neumann, is to sustain identity: we must not relinquish the essential point or principle of self-reflective awareness in consciousness that allows the psychophysical being we are to differentiate between self, other, and world. Yes, we have pushed the business of conscious engagement and distraction too far, but it is a process through which we have grown into the realization of that very fact. Instinctively dissatisfied with our consciously usurped selves we have searched for a way out of our dilemma through innumerable changes of mind and ended up with either the same sheaf of problems in different guise or a whole new set of problems. But this "I" that we are is not all bad; it has many strengths, and these are necessary if we are to counteract the dangers of blind faith. Blind faith isn't interested in experiencing the emotional upheaval that prefaces a questioning of the "I"; it prefers the quiet life of certainty where beliefs smooth the waters of daily life.

In our prehistory we were, as individuals, indissolubly linked to such an extent that Lévy-Bruhl's law of unconscious identity (participation mystique) prevailed between us as individuals, but we are no longer in that primitive state; we have emerged from it and should attempt to emerge further still through an appreciation of what this accomplishment might mean for our collective future. We are without doubt an "I", but we are not yet what Meister Eckhart called an "I am", that which, in Father Sylvan's terms, "bridges and encompasses all the forces of creation".[14] The "I" of regular daily activity and interaction possesses useful knowledge, but over and above this knowledge is a knowledge that involves the whole man, not just the consciously aware mind. There is a knowledge that "penetrates into all realms of the universe, a knowledge that lives and moves in everything."[15] But without a higher faculty for knowing, our knowledge must remain mundane. An inner self has to be awakened before anything spiritually serious can get through to us. Enter St. Paul's New Man, the "I here" of Manichaean heresy, the man in whom soul as accumulated energy is alive and kicking.

But we are not altogether usurped by conscious engagement; we also regularly interact with deeper aspects of the self without realizing it. We are, in this sense, two-faced, but are so taken up with the demands of conscious engagement that we hardly notice what is going on in the deeper regions of psyche. And all the while deep-seated interactions between submerged and non-submerged levels of mind are taking place, interactions accompanied by subtle realizations that flash before our inner eye. We are reading the world on at least two levels, and depending on our age and development may well be wrestling with inner encounters at the same time, encounters with psyche that challenge our conscious preconceptions about life and how it should be lived. I agree with James Hillman that not everything in consciousness has to be made conscious for it to be psychologically beneficial, but some recognition of how we move between levels of awareness should be operative – some form of coding is necessary. On this score we should be being taught to recognize those levels from an early age, and to my way of thinking the responsibility for this lies as much with the educational establishment as it is does with our spiritual institutions.

Praktikos 10.4

Doubling back to James Hillman's "journey of descent" at 5.2, what comes to mind in relation to the above is Western society's preoccupation with ascent experience. In educational terms it's the "head" that matters; in spiritual terms it's "heaven" that matters. Earthiness is out; soul as the hidden depths of the human (Heraclitus) has been swapped for a battle between soul and body as separate things that results in the soul's ascent, after death, to meet Christ in the air. But only if you've been astute enough to choose the correct Christian recipe for salvation. Get that wrong and your ascent turns into a descent of a very different kind. The soul is now a detachable thing capable of being traded between God or the Devil; it is no longer, as in Plato, *the spirit of the body itself.*[16] Hence the reason Jesus as the Christ is denied sexuality; experiences of interiority" (self as "body") had to be lifted out of their visceral context. The body was about death; the soul as extractable thing was about life after death.

Jacob Needleman's take on all of this is to say: "Sensitivity to qualities of energy is the one and only touchstone for determining the level or authenticity of Christian practice."[17] If there is an esoteric tradition, this is it – authentic Christianity is about the handling of energies within the self, everything else is "a false ecumenism."[18] This energy is the result of the self's struggle with itself; it is not the result of revelation in the sense of a fixed belief system handed out while someone is entranced. Needleman is adamant about this. "All revelation is the revelation of how to search, how to struggle."[19] There are forces at work in us of which we are totally unaware, and these forces have their own inbuilt sense of direction. Feelings of anger or happiness equal the movement of specific energy transactions within the self, and these transactions, once they take hold, are beyond our ability to control: we have to wait until they fizzle out before we can move on. But we do have a chance at control, and it lies in the exact moment that the energy of emotion arises within us. There is a tiny gap between impulse and emotional expression (Evagrius), and if we are awake to what is going on we can not only annul negative emotions before they strike, we can also benefit from the energy such effort releases. And this is not just us reaching for a higher morality; it is us undergoing change in the depths of psyche, a quality of change that rearranges psyche into a new configuration.

But there's a problem. The forgotten premise of Christianity has been replaced with a myth of salvation that leaves the individual psychophysically helpless. Spiritual warfare has become a cosmic battle between God and the Devil, or between us and the Devil; it is no longer conceived of as a state of inner combat consciously entered into by the awakened self. Dressed up in the finery of a theology that reduces the individual to the level of a cosmic plaything sandwiched between absolute good and what often sounds like absolute evil, Christianity uses our submerged conscious state as an excuse for punishment in the here and now, and in the hereafter. It being obvious that we are governed by wayward appetites beyond our control, we are thought of as having no rights; we are sinners condemned even before we are born. The truth of the situation is, however, quite different. Yes, we are liable to error, sometimes gross error due to the limitations imposed by submerged thinking, but we have the capacity to emerge from this state, and when we do everything changes. Awake, we are sensitive to another's feelings. Awake, we steer away from confrontation. Awake, we avoid prejudice. Awake, we conduct our lives in a seemly and intelligent fashion. Why? How? Because the psychophysical system of an awake individual is more attuned to self, other and world. But more than that, for the psychophysical system of an intentionally awake individual is also evolving from a basic system governed by survival needs and impulses into a system where the old self's dependence on submerged thinking is replaced with a different kind of thinking altogether: the thinking of a self that only thinks and remembers what it *needs* to think and remember. In the final stages of this transition, inner dialogue ceases, associative thinking ceases, speculation and emotional reaction ceases. The awake individual steps out of the dream of conscious interaction into a more precise and morally demanding frame of mind. Moving between two distinct levels of mind, he/she at first finds thinking in the non-submerged state difficult to sustain, but as Bernadette Roberts points out in her analysis of this state:

> By the time the journey is over, the only possible way of living is in the now-moment, wherein the mind moves neither backward nor forward but remains fixed and fully concentrated in the present. Because of this, the mind is so open and clear that no preconceived notions can get a foothold; no idea can be carried over from one moment to another... There are no more head trips – no clinging to a frame of reference... In a word, what is to be done or thought is always underfoot, with no need to step aside in order to find out what is to be thought, believed, or enacted.[20]

And so the individual's dream existence comes to an end, for that is in many ways what consciously submerged thinking amounts to, a form of dream no different from the dream state we experience while physically asleep. When not engaged in the business of reaching conclusions that affect our lives practically, we engage in processes of thought and imaginative construction identical to those used by the mind when constructing dream images and complex dream scenarios. As in dream we generate images out of images and build coherent fictions out of nothing more than the germ of an idea. Carried away by our internal creations (arguments with an antagonist or rehearsal for an interview), we can drive cars or walk from A to B and arrive with no conscious memory of the intervening territory. Or we can read a good book and cease to hear external sounds or the voice of someone addressing us. But the most interesting aspect of this submerged state is our ability to generate mental scenarios out of thin air, populate them with friend or foe, and become engaged in fantasy conversations within the self. On automatic pilot for large chunks of any given hour or day, we are, although visibly conscious and active, moving around in a state uncomfortably similar to that of physical sleep. But not so when in a non-submerged state of mind. When present to ourselves as a sensed presence, as an "awake 'I'" *conscious of being conscious,* we shift mental gear and register the world of people, objects and landscapes in an entirely new way. Suddenly, without warning, they become presences in their own right.

Nature and Psyche 10.5

But there's a deal of work to be done before Bernadette Roberts' mind that moves neither backward or forward comes online. As stated so clearly by Father Sylvan, "The intellect cannot be abandoned until it knows why it must be abandoned and can theoretically agree to it." We have to fully appreciate the nature of what we are involved in before such a state of mind becomes even vaguely feasible. A slow piecing together of the puzzle that faces all of us has to take place first, and when it does, our psychophysical system will respond. There is, as Morris Berman suggests, a "something" that has eluded our civilization, and this mysteriour "something" involves *a reciprocal relationship between nature and psyche.* We are not completely on our own. In some other dimension of being a response to personal effort will come, and this something cannot be equated with the God believed by Christians to interfere in human history, for as Bernadette Roberts shows in her experience of this mysterious something, it does not answer to the dictates and restrictions of theology or dogma.

Forty years of varied contemplative Christian experience, ten of which were spent in relative seclusion, did not prepare Bernadette Roberts for what eventuated: a falling away of everything she thought constituted a self, never mind what she had thought constituted the Christian religion. There was no warning as to what lay ahead, she tells us, and owing to a deficiency of recorded accounts (see 6.0), no support during the final years of her journey into the self that finally ceased to exist. And so two questions arose for Roberts: (1) What was the self? and (2) What remained in the absence of this self? Outside of Meister Eckhart's account of his own spiritual journey, there seemed to be little by way of explanation to account for what she was experiencing. She had undergone a process that had unraveled the consciously usurped and engaged self and replaced it with a profound internal silence, a "silence of the self and its faculties of will, thought, memory and emotions."[21] Not all in one hit, of course; this was an ever-expanding and deepening experience where these attributes of the self eventually ceased to come online.

Mystical Censorship 10.6

According to Erich Neumann, the mystic's fundamental experience of his or her creative center is, by almost all accounts, anticonventional, anticollective, and antidogmatic, so making a mysticism that contradicts these reactions either theology disguised as mysticism, mysticism of a low order, authentic mysticism usurped and reshaped to sustain the religious status quo, or mysticism intentionally disguised by the experiencer for fear of reprisal. Neumann is particularly clear on these differentiations. He nominates as low-level, for instance, the mysticism of an individual affectively overpowered by some theologically defined element of the fixed canon. Authentic to the extent that it is undoubtedly an experience, it is also unauthentic in that the experience is brought about through conscious fixation with some theologically constructed idea or image. The individual's creative center (the something that responds) is not actually at work, merely the conscious mind revolving around an idea or image to the point of delirium and/or dissociation.

Of particular interest, however, is that form of mysticism defined by Neumann as "disguised", for it opens up a world of restriction and fear where profound experiences are made subservient to canons of fixed belief. Unwilling to confront the religious system to which they belong, some mystics will unconsciously re-dogmatize their authentic mystical experiences to fit in with their belief system, whereas others will consciously disguise what they have experienced in the hope of avoiding detection by the hierarchy. So there is a conundrum to be faced, for the very area of human activity most likely to produce mystical experience is the area where censorship of such experiences is at its greatest. And there is the further complication of naive acceptance of the fixed canon triggering, at the contemplative or meditative level, a breakthrough into the very levels where the surface belief system's contents are symbolically questioned. This is a catch-22 situation. It reveals both the affective efficiency of contemplative disciplines, while simultaneously suggesting that such forms can inadvertently lead to breakthroughs capable of rearranging or even annulling such forms.

Along with Neumann, William James was of the opinion that mystical states overthrow "... the pretensions of non-mystical states to be the sole dictators of what we believe."[22] That is a strong statement, and it is one that Neumann is in sympathy with. Christians of conservative persuasion, on the other hand, feel impelled to remind us that psychology is an abstract study of human consciousness held within self-imposed limits. It is the states that psychology studies, not the relation of those states to objective reality. Neumann seems to agree, he speaks of "special limitations" in the sense of psychology's interpretation of such states being firmly anchored in the human. But he does not see this as limiting psychology, for although centered on an anthropology and not a theology, the territory of the anthropos (man) is intuited to be so vast that it becomes hard for Neumann to imagine any part of it being beyond psychology's grasp. But not just any old psychology, only those psychologies that have developed a language capable of describing the mystic's relationship to objective reality. (This, as we will see later, also applies to philosophy.) If the language of transcendence is missing from a particular psychology's vocabulary, then that psychology will be incapable of going beyond state-specific studies of consciousness. Any attempt to understand mystical man "must be grounded in a psychology that takes into account the different phases of the ego and consciousness in their development from the unconscious."[23] A system of co-ordinates is required for the psychologist to understand what is going on, and these co-ordinates need to translate into a map of consciousness showing the stages of human growth in relation to mystical experience.

But problems can arise in relation to mystical experience – not all mystical experiences are beneficial. The crossing of the archetypal zones and the encounters that follow can cause immense problems for the personality. The historian and ex-Carmelite nun Karen Armstrong says, "A journey to the depths of the mind involves great personal risk because we may not be able to endure what we find there."[24] There is a mysticism of childhood, a mysticism of maturity and a mysticism of old age and death, and this again raises the question of where the personality is in its development; it may not develop quite as it ought. It can happen that the broadening effect of mystical experience on consciousness is usurped by the desire to succumb to the formless void and close down consciousness altogether. Mystical death in the sense of ecstatic abandonment can be the result, and such episodes can lead to general sickness or even severe neurosis.[25]

Father Sylvan's observation that the intellect cannot be abandoned until it knows theoretically why it must be abandoned is, as stated earlier, dramatically different from an ecstatic succumbing of the self to the formless void that backgrounds consciousness. Such a move is the equivalent of spiritual suicide and should be discouraged at all cost; it is an incomplete mysticism that betrays censorship of mystical experiences for the sake of doctrinal conformity. But as we have seen from Bernadette Roberts' account at 6.5, the self-orienting principle within consciousness is only a temporary mechanism for the development of a certain type of intelligence that we can in fact live without. In a paper for the *Journal of Consciousness*

Studies, Robert Forman homes in on a statement made by Bernadette Roberts in her autobiographical work *The Experience of No-Self,* a statement that directly compliments Father Sylvan's view that intellectual self-reflection must cease at some point. He writes: "She experienced her interior silence as her original 'consciousness', by which I understand that she experienced it as devoid of the intellectual self-reflection that generally accompanies experiences."[26] Abandonment of the self to intense ecstatic experience is the exact opposite of this; it heralds an approaching affective breakdown of the self that can lead to derangement. We hear quite a lot about those who, in the past, enjoyed the ecstasies of mystical experience, but we hear nothing at all about those who succumbed to ecstatic extravagance and suffered psychological breakdown. Even Bernadette Roberts admits to wondering if she were suffering from a pathology at times, an explanation some of her friends were not slow in taking up when they read her early writings. And no wonder, for what she describes as having happened to her is, to use Ioan Couliano's phrase in relation to Einsteinian theory, *mind-boggling.*

Imagination, dream and vision were for Einstein ingredients of mind that exceeded scientific reasoning in importance because they helped connect us with another dimension of experience, and Bernadette Roberts' detailed descriptions of a dimension of being beyond intellectual self-reflection confirms this view. Our three-dimensionally circumscribed system of engaged thought is, on many levels, highly productive, but it also holds us captive in much the same manner as a two-dimensional system would. If it weren't for the unconscious elements in our reasoning, in our relationships and in our seeing of the world, the outcomes of submerged conscious reasoning would be even more unpredictable than they already are. This rootedness of the conscious self in the unconscious matrix of being is hugely important, and will constitute the basis of the next chapter.

In his classic 1957 work, *Tertium Organum,* the Russian mathematician P.D. Ouspensky (the same Ouspensky mentioned at 3.1 in relation to lucid dreaming) tackles the idea of a two-dimensional Flatland world and its inhabitants with the following observations:

> To make out, step by step, how the (two-dimensional) plane being would attain to an understanding of our world, lying in the region of the, to him, mysterious third dimension... would be interesting in the highest degree. First of all, in order to understand the world of three dimensions, he must *cease to be* two-dimensional – he must become three-dimensional himself... he will by so doing transcend his plane, and will never be in a position thereafter to return to it. Entering more and more within the circle of ideas and concepts which were entirely incomprehensible to him before, he will already have become... three-dimensional. But all along the (two-dimensional) plane being will have been essentially three-dimensional, that is, he *will have had* the third dimension, without his being conscious of it himself. To *become* three-dimensional he must *be* three-dimensional. Then... he can address himself to... self-liberation from the illusion of the two-dimensionality of himself and the world, and to the apprehension of the three-dimensional world.[27]

In this convoluted passage, Ouspensky carries the Gurdjieffian argument that man is asleep while awake onto a new conceptual level. He suggests, theoretically, that within two-dimensional man lies three-dimensional-man *in potentia*. We each carry, in other words, another dimension of experience and comprehension of which we are unaware, but of which we can become progressively aware if we can shake ourselves awake. Being Souplanders, however, we find it impossible to recognize the spoon as it dips into our dimension of experience. Inner encounters are not appreciated for what they are; the phenomenon of emotion as it rages through our world, and through our personal lives, remains a problem for which there seems to be no corrective solution. We are, and have always been, at the mercy of inner forces about which we know very little, and there seems little hope of change, or reason for optimism. In this the 21st century we are at the end of our tether and have no place to go. At least that's how it looks from our personal Flatland perspective. But as Bernadette Roberts, Father Sylvan, Jacob Needleman, James Hillman and many another have shown, it need not be that way. We are more than we seem, much more. Our natures straddle more than one dimension, and it is now time for us to fully occupy that alternative dimension. Failure to do so could cost us dearly on both a personal and a collective level.

11: The Underneath of Things

... as imagination bodies forth
The forms of things unknown, the poet's pen
Turns them to shapes, and gives to airy nothing
A local habitation and a name.
William Shakespeare
A Midsummer Night's Dream

Intro: 11.0

The conscious mind is deeply rooted in what is loosely termed the unconscious. The larger proportion of the mind lies in our somatic depths, in the darkness and obscurity of our physicality, in the interstices of our feelings as they range inward in search of a bearing. When not engaged with conscious thought, with rumination, decision-making or fantasy creation, our habit is to scan the horizon of mind in a kind of free-wheeling reverie, a mental probing that generally carries us back into any of the above engagements. But we may also sense, for a moment or two, our own private existence, our aloneness, our existential vulnerability. Glimpsing primordial shadows, we may feel ourselves being drawn into a silence that informs, a silence that thickens – if we happen to linger in that space, that is. In that moment it is as if the self were floating on the surface of a sea that extends downwards forever, a dark sea offering intimations and promptings that we may not wish to acknowledge. In that moment, that potentially creative moment, our knowing slips towards not-knowing, a not-knowing that opens the doors of psyche to itself, an opening downward through mythic patterns. We are more than we seem; we are composed of gods and goddesses, daemons and demons, heroes and sleeping beauties, totem animals and primordial nudgings that can be avoided only at cost. We are, in a word, *legion*. We are many both in our conscious (analytical) dealings with the world, and in our dealings with ourselves at the unconscious (mythic) level of mind (see 5.1).[1]

In his monumental study of creativity, *The Act of Creation,* Arthur Koestler defines this not-knowing as a necessary "forgetting"; an art that should not be equated with "the bliss of ignorance".[2] Knowledge is necessary, vital, but the idea of the unconscious mind being no more than a mixing machine in the basement that churns out endless possibilities is, he suggests, untenable. Henri Poincare's insistence that this was the case is a mechanistic hypothesis that we're still doing battle with. For Koestler, the unconscious mind of a poet is not a rhyme-computer, just as the unconscious of a physicist or mathematician is not a calculator. If that were the case the conscious mind "would have a full-time job rejecting them (the endless possibilities) until it went out of its mind."[3] No, something much more dramatic is going on in our depths; we have at our disposal a system of unconscious mentation that is superior to the limited jugglings we engage in consciously.[4] To get to grips with this we need to use Edward de Bono's lateral thinking technique for the unusual purpose of penetrating beyond conscious thinking altogether. Intellectual reflection has its place, but when it fails we resort to scanning the horizon of mind in the hope of a gift, and we are often rewarded.

Productive Reverie 11.1

During the summer of 1797, the poet S.T. Coleridge fell asleep in his chair and dreamed into existence two or three hundred lines of his epic poem *Kubla Khan.* I say "dreamed" rather than "composed" because of Coleridge's own reservation about the nature of that creative moment – a moment that lasted for about three hours. Writing in third person singular, he recalls that "images rose up before him as *things* with a parallel production of the correspondent expressions, without any sensation of conscious effort." After an interruption, he wrote down as many of the lines he could remember, knowing full well that many were lost.

Arthur Koestler refers to this incident as "an extreme case of unconscious production,"[5] and suggests that it originated in the hypnagogic state, the semi-awake reverie state at the entrance to sleep. His reason for thinking so is that Coleridge wrote another version of this incident in which he used the word "reverie". What interested Koestler about this story was Coleridge's emphasis on the visual images that accompanied his experience for, as is well known, pictures tend to dominate unconscious thinking. The creative person enters what the Irish poet W.B. Yeats called "a waking trance", and the result is generally some level of creative act linked to the creator's momentary interest. And you don't have to be a poet or novelist for this to happen to you; it also happens to scientists, philosophers and mathematicians.

The case of Friedrich August von Kekulé's discovery of the structure of organic molecules, and that of Michael Faraday's cosmic lines of force, perfectly illustrate this point. In 1865 Kekulé was Professor of Chemistry in Ghent. As the result of a reverie in which he witnessed a serpent biting its own tail, he realized that molecules of certain organic compounds are not open structures, but closed chains or rings. This discovery turned out to be one of the cornerstones of modern science. In Faraday's case, his ability to creatively "see" the stresses surrounding magnets and electric currents as *things* that "rose up before him" gave way to the invention of the dynamo and the electric motor. Koestler is quick to compare the scientific discoveries of these individuals with the artistic creations of certain artist-visionaries. "Kekulé's visions," he says, "resemble hallucinatory flights; Faraday's, the stable delusional systems of paranoia." Kekulé's serpent reminds him of "paintings by Blake; the curves of force which crowd Faraday's universe... the vortices in Van Gogh's skies."[6] Faraday's reliance on visual intuition and instinct for the discovery of many general theorems was declared astonishing by von Helmholtz in his 1881 Faraday memorial lecture. And rightly so, for Faraday had only rudimentary arithmetic at his disposal, and as everyone at the memorial lecture realized the discovery of such theorems required mathematical acuity.

Visual intuition? Instinct?

Albert Einstein's creative process was similar to that of Kekulé's and Faraday's; he distrusted conscious conceptual thought and relied on visual imagery. Similarly, the mathematician Jacques Hadamard was so intrigued by his own creative visual imagery that in 1945 he conducted an inquiry into the creative methodology of eminent mathematicians in America. The result was as he had suspected. Almost all of them used mental pictures, not mathematics, when thinking creatively. The primary phase of creative thought was predominantly visual; only the secondary, tidying-up phase, was verbal or mathematical. Koestler quotes Woodworth's textbook of experimental psychology in this context: "Often we have to get away from speech in order to think clearly." Thinking actually requires a regression from language to be fully productive, an abdication of conceptual thought, a momentary forgetting of what we know for the purpose of intercepting, or being intercepted by, the *unthinkable.* Out of the blue such thinking comes in the form of a "seeing" that lifts mundane reasoning onto a new level of comprehension and expression. Raw logic cannot deliver such subtlety; this is the province of reason *in the service of our experience of being alive*. It is, as George Steiner is quoted as saying at 2.2, an entering into "harmonic concordance with that which is being questioned." It is Morris Berman's "bodily engagement with the world" and Steiner's "risk of nakedness in the dialectic of prayer." Linked to the vulnerable locus of being, we transcend the limitations of conscious thought and touch upon what

Koestler terms the self's superior mind. Or as Alice put it in *Through the Looking Glass,* "How can I know what I think till I see what I say?" Guy Claxton provides us with an interesting quote in this respect. When asked for proof of a particular mathematical conclusions, Newton replied enigmatically: "… it is plain to me by the fountain I draw it from."[7] You can of course downgrade the unconscious and think of it merely as an extension of the conscious mind – the conscious mind being the important bit. But what if it's the other way round? What if the conscious mind is merely the tip of a much larger mind, a mind with a mind of its own, so to speak? The psychologist Julian Jaynes surprises with this comment: "Consciousness… is not the seat of reason, and indeed some of the most difficult instances of creative reasoning go on without any attending consciousness."[8]

What is Actually Going on Down There? 11.2

Arthur Koestler accuses Poincare of hubris because he refused to accept the superiority of the unconscious mind. On no fewer than three occasions Poincare had experienced ready-made answers to difficult problems *pop* fully formed into his mind, but was loath to accept that the unconscious was capable of discernment, that it housed what might be a subliminal self superior to the conscious self. Koestler is scathing. "He (Poincare) worked by intuition, but for all his modesty and open-mindedness… was unable to shake off the rationalist *hubris* of the nineteenth century."[9] More than willing to accept the fruits of unconscious genius, Poincare was at the same time unable to accept the unconscious mind as anything other than an extension of the conscious mind. The conscious mind might be only the tip of psyche, but for Poincare the greater part of that iceberg should not be interpreted as a mind in its own right.

Carl Jung seems to agree with Poincare when he says, "I have not discovered in the unconscious anything like a personality comparable to the conscious ego. But… there are traces of personalities in the manifestations of the unconscious. A simple example is the dream, in which a variety of real and imaginary people enact the dream thoughts... The unconscious *personates*."[10] The reason for this may be that the unconscious is, as James Hillman states, concerned with depth, not with precision (see 5.1). Precision requires the ego to "take things apart"; depth causes "an invisible fullness" to erupt within us – a fullness that *nourishes*. Interiority equals depth, just as depth equals "truth" *in its own right*. In this appreciation of truth, truth is not to be confused with content, it is not a thing; it is an experience. We do not *have* truth, we descend into truth *as* being. This is the mysterious something hinted at by Morris Berman at 10.2, the "reciprocal relationship between nature and psyche" that erupts as dream. Hades, the Greek god of depths, hides from us; he remains invisible, but he is ever present in psyche as *depth*.

To appreciate what this means, a re-evaluation of the conscious mind and its relationship to mind as a whole has to take place. Yes, we live mostly submerged, engaged conscious lives, but we are at the same time searching the horizon of mind and dipping constantly towards the core of being (the "still point" at the center of our affective system) without realizing it. The psychologist Jaak Panksepp agrees about the system in operation: "every moment of our conscious lives is undergirded by feelings, and... if the biological infrastructure of those intrinsic value-signaling systems were destroyed, one's sense of self would degrade."[11] The relationship between conscious and unconscious (self and not-self) is in operation, but we are mostly oblivious to its intricacies. There is a sacred presence, or charge, attached to moments of real creativity, real relationship and real questioning, but we are at a loss to explain what that presence signifies. Is it another self hiding in the basement of being? Is it God peeking at us in the depths of our minds? Could it be the genetic code underlying our psychophysical structure inadvertently personalized? We scratch our heads and another day passes, another week, another year, another decade, and our lives run down like old-fashioned watches with no promise of an answer to this or the myriad other questions tantalizing us. There is no doubting our sporadic interaction with forces and images at a deeper level, or our moments of authentic relating, or questioning, but we are not yet sufficiently aware to consciously shrug off our entranced state.

Listening "In" 11.3

The question we should perhaps be asking ourselves at this point is this: Is mind what it appears to be? This question immediately breaks into a series of other questions: Is mind a "self" conscious *of* itself; or is it merely a container for the self? Or is it a metaphorical iceberg with a little spike of self-awareness protruding from a submerged mass of unawareness? And what exactly is subjective experience anyway? What is this "sense of feeling" that we have, this never-ending succession of subjective physical impressions we think of as *myself alive?* To tackle these questions is no easy task; it requires thoughtful reflection and a willingness to make connections in unlikely places. Clues abound for those willing to suspend hasty judgment; but these clues have to be recognized for what they are before any advancement can be made. We have to open ourselves up to the possibility of discovery, the possibility of being surprised. Or, more precisely, to the possibility of being surprised *by* being. To be, or not to be, that really is the question.

To understand the language of being we need to pay attention to our interior life. Our interior life speaks its own language, a language that connects psyche with physical, instinctive reality, and we share these realities. We are fundamentally alike at the instinctive level, and observably similar in psychological makeup due to education and culture. But also radically different when it comes to our personal responses and choices. Our temperaments are tempered in the fire of human relationships, our ability to express ourselves as individuals either hampered or enhanced by the vagaries of personality development, education and the vicissitudes of life. We are, in other words, a conglomerate of forces, some positive, some negative, some within our control, some with a tendency to run out of control. As human animals we are driven by the instinct to survive, and as a result can be aggressive and unpredictable when threatened. As selves periodically conscious of being conscious, we are capable of behaviors that extend and refine aspects of our animal natures. As witnessed in the behavior of the higher primates, and in elephants, empathy, grieving, and even compassion seem to be evident, and these traits, among others, have been developed by us into consciously directed forms of moral and ethical concern. Regard for others (altruism) seems to be hardwired in more than one species. We've been landed with two natures blended into one, natures further complicated by theoretical constructs that compartmentalize what we are, and what we know. On the one hand, we are instinctively connected to the world and to one another by our animal natures, while on the other we are forced by the nature of perception and thought into an often not-so-splendid isolation.

Touching upon the creative level requires us to differentiate between what Guy Claxton terms the "inspiration and elaboration phases" of creative activity. He describes the inspiration phase as follows:

> Instead of progressing logically and consciously down a well-worn path in the brain, different currents of activation are allowed to mingle unconsciously, and then, when something 'gels', to concentrate around a new pattern until it is strong enough to 'pop up' into consciousness. This kind of low-inhibition brain activity shows up on the EEG as what are called 'alpha waves'... When you move into the elaboration phase of creativity, however, you want your brain to behave

> differently. You want it to be more selective, critical and purposeful... This kind of thinking shows up on the EEG as 'beta waves'.[12]

As we saw at 5.1 via the psychological studies of James Hillman, Christianity inadvertently demonized our creative interior life to such an extent that it came to resemble the Greek underworld in terms of location and content. Hades, the ancient Greek god of "depth" became both Hell and the Devil. As a place of limitless depths, this underworld/underground (*ge-Chthon*) was equated with the instinctual body and the cold, dark realm of earth, its influence considered baleful and dangerous. It became the pit of the Christian imagination. Descent into this pit was to be avoided, the tendency of the mind to sink into its obscurity and ambiguity a temptation linked to our polytheistic past. The polytheistic mind had been in the grip of demons, its reliance on multiple psychic forces an indication of its spiritually corrupt state. In his foreword to Koestler's *The Act of Creativity*, Sir Cyril Burt confirms this view when he tells us that in the Middle Ages scientific pioneers were "frequently suspected of owing their miraculous knowledge and skill to the devil rather than to the deity".[13] In this subtle backdrop to psyche lies the root of our common problem with interiority, a root from which numerous other disabling filaments sprouted as Western culture developed. And on top of it all lies an incongruous Jesus story that helps sustain our suspicion of anything to do with the deeper, darker aspects of our inner world. Although mostly secular, or only nominally religious in practice, we are nevertheless cocooned in a culture gripped by a salvation myth that offers us psychological security in much the same manner as a missile shield offers national security. We don't really believe that it works, but it's nice to think it might be there.

Our entranced state is therefore multi-faceted; it is a jungle of ideas, dreams and reveries within which we imprison ourselves through acts of conscious engagement. And it doesn't matter how serious or trivial or preposterous these engagements are; our perceptual disappearing act is the same on each occasion, it is total. Our professional disciplines are aware of this fact, but are not yet fully aware of its implications for mind as a whole: long bouts of conscious engagement rob us of our ability to relate to self, other and world – we become insensitive to what is going on around us, and within us. But more than that even. Continuous conscious engagement also fools us into thinking that thinking is more important than feeling. For what can feeling tell us? If we're not thinking, then we're obviously wasting time. And so we are governed by definitions, hemmed in by definitions, defined by definitions, lacerated by definitions. Hillman takes on this problem in a footnote: "Definition excludes by cutting out what does not belong... As much of the soul is ambiguous and as knowledge about it is still incomplete, and may always be, sharp definitions are premature." What we need is amplification, he tells us. Amplification "confronts the mind with paradoxes and tensions; it reveals complexities."[14]

Psychological and philosophical theories about self and consciousness abound, but they are mostly concerned with the problem of what consciousness is in itself, and how sense of self relates to conscious experience. Is self, for instance, generated through perception as an act, or is it an effect of memory? Is memory a bridge for integrating diverse aspects of experience into a self? Perception supplies us with a continuous flow of information about the physical self – a perceived self that eventually gives rise to a remembered self – but is this all there is to a self? Are we just the result of our perceptual interactions with physical reality, or is there, as some professionals believe, a "mental self" that forms the essential heart of personhood.[15] These are just some of the theories being considered by research psychologists and philosophers, and valuable as they are for tracking down the mechanisms of mind involved in our sense of having a self, and what mind might be in itself, they tend to ignore what may be the more important avenue of exploration: the effect sustained self-awareness could have on the psychophysical system as a whole. What would the effects of holding sense of self in place be if it were intermittently sustained over weeks, months, or even years? In 2005 the philosopher Evan Thomson considered this question while being interviewed by Professor Jim Proctor for the *Journal of Consciousness Studies.* In the context of Buddhist meditation, he said, "We don't know the developmental possibilities for contemplative mental training, by which I mean practices that cultivate attentional stability and mental well-being. We don't know how such practices change or affect the way the brain works, and how they affect the physiological regulation of our whole body."[16]

Am I Conscious Now? 11.4

In her 2002 paper "Am I Conscious Now?",[17] Susan Blackmore beats a path through many of the above theories and comes out with the question of all questions: Am I conscious now as I read the question? Am I conscious now? Or did reading the question make me conscious of myself as I read the question? If that is the case, she asks, "What does this say about consciousness the rest of the time?"[18] And so we come back to Eric Schwitzgebel's question: do we have constant tactile awareness of our feet in our shoes? And from there to the fact that Blackmore's students had the same problem as Schwitzgebel's when dealing with the question of their awareness level prior to their beepers going off. As with the beeper experiment, Blackmore's students had difficulty determining whether they were made self-conscious only because of the question, or whether they had been conscious all along. At this point Blackmore makes an interesting observation. "They (her students) always seem to be conscious when they ask the question, but become less and less sure about whether they were conscious a moment before. With more practice they say that asking the question itself makes them more conscious, and that they can extend this consciousness from a few seconds to perhaps a minute or two."[19]Interesting.

Blackmore advises her students to ask themselves the question "Am I conscious now?" as many times per day as they can remember to do it, and to share their findings with one another. To what end? To avoid the pitfalls of introspection through the discipline of shared first-person practice. If we ask the question "Am I conscious now?" often enough, and share our findings, then we can turn first-person practice into third-person science. And she isn't finished. She also talks of "looking very hard, with persistence and practice" at our experiences, and refers to first-person methods of inquiry as a "discipline". She even goes so far as to recommend meditation as a means of calming the mind for the purpose of inner observation, but does not follow Schwitzgebel in insisting that first-person reports must be immediate if they are to be considered even moderately trustworthy. That, I think, is an important omission.

Then comes the claim that asking the question "Am I conscious now?" is the equivalent of putting a conscious probe into the mind that "precipitates a backward stream" of awareness. As a result of this backwards stream, "a retrospective story is concocted about what was in the stream of consciousness a moment before", plus "a self who was apparently experiencing it." For Blackmore, however, there was neither a conscious self nor a stream prior to the question being asked. Each time we look there is something there, someone there, but only because we look. If we don't look there is nothing there, and as we don't notice this, it doesn't matter. And so the grand illusion is concocted, and we sail on thinking there is a stream of consciousness with content and a self who attends, when in fact there are only multiple processes functioning without awareness that can be prodded into momentary self-awareness. True as this seems to be, there is of course the question of what a "conscious probe" is in its own right, and what it means for us to even attempt to ask such a question in the first place.

Blackmore's experiments suggest that we can never actually lay mental hands on the present; it is forever out of reach. So what exactly is going on in those moments prior to the primary question being asked? Are we in any sense "there" at all; or is it just processes processing and no more than that? Quoting William James, Blackmore suggests we will never find out: "The attempt at introspective analysis" she says, "is . . . like seizing a spinning top to catch its motion, or trying to turn up the gas quickly enough to see how the darkness looks."[20] What we intercept when we ask the question "Am I conscious now?" or "What am I conscious of now?" is, she insists, always one step removed from the present; it is always the immediate past and never the immediate present that is being experienced.

In asking her students to ask the question "Am I conscious now?", Blackmore sets up a situation in which her students appear to have the same chance to experience the present as in Schwitzgebel's tactile experiment at 3.0, but unlike Schwitzgebel she interprets the outcome as a retrospective concoction. There is no stream of consciousness and no self prior to that question being asked, she tells us, but the moment it is asked, it *seems* as if there were. This is a problematical summation; it presents us with two questions, then assumes that the answer given to one suffices for the other. I don't think it does. The question: "Am I conscious now?" is different from the question: "What am I conscious of now?" The question "Am I conscious now?" refers to the student's experience of being conscious of being conscious *as an experience in itself,* whereas the question: "What am I conscious of now?" carries the student back to what the mind had been preoccupied with prior to the mind becoming consciously conscious of its preoccupied state. Hence the claim that the experience is retrospective. The second experience is certainly retrospective, the first is not. In the instant that question is asked, the experience had is immediate. Self-awareness is not a memory of an experience, it is an experience in its own right. But it can of course be remembered later and become retrospective. (These points are explored more fully at 14.4.)

When asked to report on the question: "Am I conscious now?" as an experience, Blackmore's students reported that being conscious in this manner (1) was a difficult task to accomplish; (2) that it was hard to remember to keep asking this question throughout a day; and (3) that as they practiced this question more and more they could "extend this immediate form of consciousness from a few seconds to perhaps a minute or two."[21] The second question, "What am I conscious of now?" afforded a quite different result; it threw awareness in a different direction. It delivered "content of mind" in terms of a memory instant, not "apprehension of existence" as an ongoing experience in an ongoing present. Thoughts intercepted in the process of being processed capture and hold awareness in a state of submerged engagement, whereas the interception of our being in existence arrests thought and allows a heightened state of awareness to form. Remembering to ask the question "Am I conscious now?" throughout the course of a day is, as Blackmore's students found out, no easy task; it takes practice to set up this kind of feedback loop in the mind. The more you look inside yourself the easier it becomes to look inside yourself, but you have to remember to look, and we mostly do not do that. Awake to the business of experiencing ourselves as consciously conscious one second, we are the next oblivious to that question because sunk again in reflective thought. Or we get caught up in reflective thought *about* being consciously conscious, and mistakenly think ourselves still awake when we in fact are not. In this sense we are reflectively dreaming that we are awake and do not notice the difference. Unless of course we happen to "wake up" in the middle of our little dream – shades of lucid dreaming in a different context. But as Nietzsche observed at 1.7, we do little to acquire greater consciousness; we just assume ourselves to possess it in full. Not Blackmore's students, however, they became practiced in extending or prolonging self-awareness; a fact not developed by Blackmore in her paper.

Streams of Awareness 11.5

Samson, on recovering his strength, pushed the pillars of the temple apart and the building came crashing down on his head, and on the heads of his enemies. Not exactly the best metaphor for awareness of being aware, one might think, but oddly apt as I hope to show. For there is a sense in which awareness of being aware causes a break between thought and thought; it forms a gap in reflective thinking that *widens* with practice. However, although theoretically possible, the dynamics involved in a pure stream of awareness lasting even as little as one or two minutes demand a great deal more practice than I think Blackmore's students had time to realise as an experience. As already shown, the business of being aware of being aware can be very tricky; things are not always as they seem. And as Blackmore disallows stream of consciousness as a mental fact, and as a corollary does away with the idea of self as a "conscious continuity", we are left with neither consciousness nor a self through which such an act could actually be initiated. So what is doing the "awaring", one has to ask: a process doubled back on itself? No one ever had a simple sensation by itself, she says, quoting William James. There is no easy way to determine what is *in* the so-called stream of consciousness in any given moment of time. Fine, but is stream of consciousness identical to stream of awareness? Is there not the same difference between these two states as between the questions: "Am I conscious now?" and "What am I conscious of now?" Disallowing stream of consciousness is one thing; disallowing stream of awareness may be quite another.

Being conscious is, in terms of our previously argued definition, to be engaged (submerged or immersed) in mental activity which we experience as a stream in spite of it not being a stream; whereas being aware of being aware" is a hybrid mental state in which, I would argue, we scan Bernadette Roberts' *still point of being*. A moment of consciously wrought self-awareness would therefore be a crossing of that still point, a lingering on that point the entrance to a mental state *not governed by time*. There is no temporal factor involved at this level of awareness. Becoming aware of being in existence sets up not a time-lapse memory of some hypothetical self, but an out of time experience of our existence in/as an unbroken present. Ego-self ceases and sense of being takes over. There is an unfolding or arising of being (our intrinsic self?) that at its height extinguishes the thinking self for the duration of the experience. Time belongs to the thinking self. The mind continues to function, but it is no longer subservient to the whims of association or the niceties of sequential thought. But not in the early stages, of course; in its early stages awareness of self as being collapses constantly back into reflective, associative thought, and a forgetting of being takes place. Once experienced, however, being is never forgotten: when the building starts to shake, it never really stops: hence Blackmore's finding that it became progressively easier to wake up. But as we can remember being, so also can we forget being.

In what appears to be a parallel claim, the German philosopher Martin Heidegger refers to our contemporary situation as a "forgetfulness of being", and as an "oblivion of being", a state described by Jeff Malpas in his challenging book *Heidegger's Topology* as "contemporary destitution."[22] For Heidegger, this is "the essence of nihilism", and it is based on our failure to grasp our own being as mortals. We are not "at home" in ourselves (Heidegger's term), we have vacated our own space as an "I-here" and are consequently robbed of "any sense of the holy, or a proper connection to the gods." Malpas quotes Hölderlin on this point: "The gods have fled... their shrines and temples are empty."[23] We have been abandoned; we have become slaves to the forgetfulness of being and lost contact with the mythic level of being. Further on in the same chapter Malpas closes in on what Heidegger is articulating when he says: "Unless man first establishes himself beforehand in the space proper to his essence and there takes up his dwelling, he will not be capable of anything essential within the destining now holding sway." If we are not at home in ourselves, then we are helpless and at the mercy of every wind that blows. Paradigm change and axial moments in history will not in themselves save us from our beingless selves; we have to "cultivate a mode of being that constitutes a 'turning back' to being, that is a 'remembrance', that is a mode of dwelling."[24] The literary critic George Steiner paraphrases Heidegger's concerns thus:

> Has beingness passed totally from human reach, or are there processes and embodiments of experience in which the primal sense of essence remains vital and, therefore, recapturable? Is there anything left on which late-twentieth century man can build if he is to seek a homecoming to 'the house of being?'[25]

In terms of properly interpreting Christian tradition Jacob Needleman follows suit:

> But who is there who can occupy the tradition in order to reconstruct the teaching? ... It can only begin with individuals who can occupy their own being.[26]

James Hillman puts this same problem in the context of soul and the awakening of psyche, an awakening in the sense of mind focused upon the soul and upon the mythical, archetypal forces that are enacted through it. This is a very different story from that of the psychological and philosophical journals where language creaks under the strain of minds doing battle with mind. With Hillman, as with Heidegger, we are hauled back to face the question of our lives as the opus of our soul's creation. In this sense the opus is psyche itself, the "awakening or engendering of soul", the fundamental aim of life we ought to be consciously engaged in.

The Creative Act 11.6

One other aspect of this puzzle has to be addressed before we can move on, namely, the creative act. As we saw with Kekulé and Faraday, and with Einstein and Hadamard, the creative mind is a mind that scans the horizon of consciousness in a kind of free-wheeling reverie. There is a side-stepping of conventional thought processes for a play of images; or, more accurately, *images at play.* Coleridge's experience of a poetic outpouring did not arrive as words, but as images "which rose up as *things.*" [27] Another language was operative, a language that could also be kinetic or auditive. Einstein speaks of elements that were "of muscular type". Arthur Koestler pulls this into perspective by quoting the German philosopher Hammen: "Language is not only the foundation for the whole faculty of thinking, but the central point also from which proceed the misunderstandings of reason by herself." [28] H.G. Wells agreed. "Our minds are clumsy things and crush the truth a little in the course of taking hold of it." Visceral thinking, on the other hand, speaks in images, in symbols, in vague muscular intuitions that have to be cerebrally reconstituted as words." Too precise formulations inhibit creative thought; images or symbols allow the mind multiple choices. We are Janus-faced in our depths, and often tread dangerously close to the flame of Being without realizing it.

The moment we close our eyes we are in a state of mental deprivation that drives us towards sleep, reverie or dream. Or if we happen to be an experienced meditator, into a stillness that progressively thickens. At the entrance to sleep (the hypnagogic level), as in the exit from sleep (the hypnopompic level), images generate images by way of association (Ouspensky), and develop into complex visual storylines. But more than that, for with our eyes open and our minds engaged in reflective thought we are also subject to the undertow of an ever-present subjectivity. Emotions and evaluative feelings ebb and flow as we think, deep-set needs tug at our intellects in the shape of unarticulated and perhaps unadmitted ambitions, hopes, desires and prejudices. Yes, we can claim moments of pure reasoning where meanings are generated out of language or mathematics, but on the whole this is not the case; we are constantly scanning our mental horizon in the hope that something not yet thought of, something entirely original, will appear of its own volition. And we are not wrong in our expectations; we are capable of astonishing insights into self, other or world if we can forgo the temptation to intellectually interfere with what begins to form. Patience is the keyword, and patience in these matters equals a meditative or contemplative state of mind.

This returns us to Hölderlin's observation that, "The Gods have fled... their shrines and temples are empty." Why? Heidegger answers succinctly: "Everywhere everything is ordered to stand by, to be immediately at hand, indeed to stand there just so that it may be on call for a further ordering." Malpas breaks open this poetically rendered insight for us:

> This ordering is . . . essentially tied to the measurable and the calculable so that, in the ordering of things as resource, the technological 'brings all beings into the business of calculation, which dominates most fiercely precisely where numbers are needed.' The compass of the technological is so wide that even the human falls within it and is taken up as another resource to be transformed, stored, deployed, calculated, consumed...[29]

As products of societies governed by scientific reasoning, we stand ready to be consumed, the deepest recesses of our natures viewed with the ruthless precision that only technological consciousness can muster. We have, as Carl Jung suggests in the introduction to *Man and His Symbols,* "stripped all things of their mystery and numinosity; nothing is holy any longer."[30] This is of course quite different from Erich Neumann's claim that psychology is sufficient unto itself for an exploration into the human. The kind of psychology Neumann is referring to possesses a language capable of accommodating the deepest aspect of the human; it is not stranded in the sphere of utilitarian values where "criteria which are at home in one context, e.g., that of experimental science, [are applied] to disciplines within which they are inappropriate."[31] Human beings are not "for the use of" in Neumann's psychological scheme; they are to be understood in relation to life as *an encounter with being.* As a fellow Jungian, James Hillman is similarly sensitive. In *The Myth of Analysis,* he says:

> ... we use the word 'psychology' quite differently from the conventional practice, so pejorative to the field and to the soul. For psychologists have regarded the soul's depths and the findings from these depths as derivations of conscious, social, or pathological processes, and the things most important to the soul have become a division of learning theory or information theory, social and economic events, or simply abnormal psychology.[32]

So it can be said that two approaches are available to us: the intellectual/scientific and the creative/contemplative. In Blackmore's science-driven scheme the stuff of reality is a grand illusion; there is no stream of consciousness and no continuity of self. Yes, we have to look harder and attempt to extend our awareness through self-questioning, but only so as to realize that what we think is the case isn't. We are just biological machines with the rather odd ability to view our own mechanicalness – a view flatly rejected by Heidegger. In Bernadette Roberts, and Father Sylvan's creative/contemplative schemes, the ego-self is experientially diagnosed as a temporary phenomenon, a useful stepping stone that for Roberts gave way to a new level of cognition, and for Father Sylvan had to be consciously relinquished. And not in the sense of an abandonment to paradisiacal (infantile) consciousness, but in the sense of the ego-self reaching a point of maturity where it willingly relinquishes dominance in favor of an entirely new cognitive arrangement. Roberts is in full agreement with Father Sylvan on this point: reflexive mind is at best "a temporary mechanism for developing a certain type of intelligence, an intelligence we must eventually learn to live without."[33] The illusory self is necessary, but it is not the pinnacle of our evolutionary development.

But when all is said and done, is there really any difference between these approaches? Is there in fact any real difference at all given that the outcome on both occasions is loss of the ego-self? Yes, there is. One is hypothetical, the other experiential. One has been arrived at by means of clinical observation and deductive reasoning, a process of dogged, hard-headed research and thinking that leaves one knowledgeable, but unquestionably diminished; the other systematically expands the ego-self's appreciation of its temporary but necessary role in psyche. In one approach the ego-self has to swallow hard and accommodate a truth difficult to accommodate given that the illusion of being a self continues without change; in the other the ego-self agrees to its own dissolution in the face of experiences that systematically dismantle its need and desire to exist. When these experiences are complete, the building falls about Samson's ears and he is released from his predicament.

12: The Intermediate State

The Question appears when I am born and is gradually covered over by the world. But it continues to sound under the surface, as layer upon layer of self-definition is formed around it. In a shattering moment, the Question surfaces and its energy transforms me. In that moment out of time, to be and to be able exists, speaking now in the sacred language of Gurdjieff.[1]
Father Sylvan
Lost Christianity by Jacob Needleman

Intro: 12.0

In *Lost Christianity* Jacob Needleman speaks of his religious nature and his worldly nature, two natures between which lay a point neither religious nor worldly where the pull of each caused him to suffer. And so he asks the question, "What is this place between my two natures? Why is it such bittersweet suffering to be situated there?"[2] An accompanying realization was that he had to constantly *choose* to be in this intermediate state, or space; he had to *go there* of his own volition. But why would one want to? It was a state in which he experienced a heightened sense of loss, uncertainty, irritation and frustration. But along with this came a strong sense of existence, a quality of inquiry experienced as "voluntary suffering". The question is, why did Needleman choose to consciously suffer? (See 4.4)

Later on in his text Needleman describes this intermediate state as "that which is between God and animal;" or, as in some traditions, "the need for something to be 'formed' in man; or 'collected' (as 'light' is collected); or purified."[3] But this intermediate state should not be associated with thought, emotion or sensation; it had nothing to do with emotion, mind or reason as they were generally experienced. The only terms applicable were *openness, sensitivity, feeling, presence, attention* and *seeing*. In this sense the intermediate level of mind was not connected to personal identity or the social self in its submerged, consciously engaged state; it was an in-between state of mind where a gritty appreciation of one's lived life began to register moment by moment.

But let's double back. A "state between God and animal" makes some kind of sense, if only poetically, but what are we to make of "the need for something to be 'formed' in man", something that can be "collected" or "purified" (see 9.0). What is Needleman getting at there? How can there be an intermediate state of mind uncontaminated by emotion and/or reason? He explains himself with this statement: "Something has to be awakened in man that is highly individual yet at the same time free from mere subjectivity, something that is intensely my own yet free of ego."[4] Intermediate indeed, and contradictory in that it defies the usual categories of mental behavior by which we live. But a valuable clue is given when Needleman plays emotion, mind and reason off against openness, sensitivity, feeling, presence and seeing. In doing so he tells us plainly that the latter list of mental states is not only different from the former, but that it constitutes experiences of reality capable of short-circuiting us out of our submerged and engaged state of mind. The intermediate is *purity of attention* (Father Sylvan); it frees us from subjective engagement. Sensitivity, openness and evaluative feelings do not isolate us in our heads; they expand our awareness to include the "other" while allowing us to remain intact within ourselves. Intact? Intact in the sense of not being displaced by mental content. In fact this is the major difference between the two lists: one automatically leads to submersion, the other to a hybrid state of mind in which empathy with others is possible only *because* we are properly present to ourselves. Apply this to oneself and a further dimension is added to the situation, a self-empathy that does not allow us to tell lies to ourselves. In that moment weak subjectivity crumbles and strong subjectivity takes over.

Weak and Strong Subjectivity 12.1

These are my terms, not Needleman's. As with the difference between emotion and feeling, they allow us the opportunity to get out of the double bind the word "subjectivity" causes for anyone engaged in this kind of research. Weak subjectivity belongs to our submerged, engaged responses to self, other or world; strong subjectivity to any experience governed by the empathy that arises when we are properly present to ourselves. Empathy? I use this in the sense of our sensitivity being more than sympathy, but rather a two-way process of comprehension that includes us as much as it includes some other individual, object in the world, or the world itself. It is of course possible to muddy these waters and claim there is no real distinction between these states, but that would be to overlook the experience of being confronted by individuals who are subjectively unavailable to reasoned argument, or similarly unavailable to the pain of others. They are observably locked up inside themselves to such an extent that all they can hear is the sound of their own voice, or the emotional roar of their own needs. Interested only in their own opinions, in their own formulations, they listen without listening, hear without hearing and see without seeing. As each and every one of us regularly falls into this category, we are quick to recognize and criticize it in others, but seldom in ourselves. Why? Because there's no one "at home" in that moment; we have disappeared into Susan Blackmore's *process of mind*.

So what happens when we resist process of mind, when we attempt to stay focused and aware of being aware? Where are we then, we who do not exist in any substantive sense beyond *calling ourselves into retrospective existence*? Could we perhaps have entered a state of mind where conscience in its truest sense reminds us of our failings, where our responses are tempered by a deep sense of common humanity? Could such a state harbor our better nature, our ability to exercise free will and real rationality? As "intermediate" men and women, could we perhaps rescue the relationship that is on the point of dying, admit to failings we have stubbornly refused to recognize for years, or find the strength of character to stand up against some unconscionable bully? If so, what does this tell us about ourselves?

For Father Sylvan the intermediate state speaks not just of new possibilities in terms of response, but of a psychological revolution that rescues us from lying to ourselves. If the intermediate level of mind isn't working in us, if we aren't aware of this level's subtle demands and can consciously choose to undergo its painful illuminations, then lying to ourselves will remain a problem. In the Gospel of Thomas the disciples question Jesus on how they should conduct their lives. Should they fast? Should they pray and give alms? Should they eat only certain things? Jesus' reply could well have come from Father Sylvan. "Do not tell lies, and do not do what you hate..."[5] Which is to say, *consciously choose how you will live.* In citing this quote in *The Gnostic Gospels,* Elaine Pagels adds: "His ironic answer turns them back to themselves: who but oneself can judge when one is lying or what one hates?"[6] Fine, but which of us is capable of such honest self-questioning? By what means do we reach this point? If it rests on a moral attitude alone, then most of us don't stand a chance of ever being quite that honest – our tendency is to hide from ourselves.

This returns us to the question of what Needleman meant when he said there was a need for something to be "formed", "collected" and "purified" in man. In his terms the intermediate state has nothing to do with emotion and/or reasoning; it has to do with an awakening of the self to the self. But what does that actually mean outside of reiterating everything that's already been said about submerged and non-submerged awareness? Father Sylvan answers this question via Needleman: "The answer lies hidden within the Christian doctrine of the soul as the intermediate principle in man and in the cosmos."[7] The developing soul *is* the intermediate principle in human nature; it is something we collect or gather in moments of real awareness. It is substantial; it has the power of growth. Real awareness (attention) brings soul into existence; sustained awareness promotes the growth of soul as a transforming energy. Soul is composed of the energy real awareness supplies moment by moment; the dispersal of soul is a loss of energy through prolonged periods of inattention.

If soul is talked about at all by mainstream Christians, it is referred to in terms of an amorphous "thing" dished out at birth and reclaimed at death. There is no mention of an intermediate state, or of energies or self-questioning in relation to soul, just a harping on and on about salvation and sin and our inability to contribute anything constructive of ourselves. We have to abandon ourselves to theological constructs and force ourselves to be good through believing what we are told to believe. And if that doesn't work, then we just have to believe all the harder. And there's the rub, for Christianity's beliefs are sold to us as moral imperatives; refuse to believe them and you find yourself classified as lacking a proper moral base. Hemmed in by a creed that disallows our natural strengths and repudiates our hard-earned capacity to see through falsity, we are expected, in spite off everything known and understood about ourselves and our world, to bend the knee and believe in a Jesus story that stretches credibility to the limit. Needleman puts this lamentable state of affairs into blunt language: "Christianity as we know it does not produce Christian results, either in the individual or in the world."[8] Why not? Because the accumulation of the force of inner attention is missing. Intermediate Christianity in terms of attention is the nuts-and-bolts basis on which real Christianity is founded; failure to deliver on this level is to have in your possession a superbly crafted engine without fuel. Father Vincent summed it up for Needleman in this manner: "In order to say, *I am a Christian,* a man must also be able to say, *I am*"[9]

"Thou Shalt Not" Without Purpose 12.2

In the opening quote for this chapter Father Sylvan says: "In a shattering moment, the Question surfaces and its energy transforms me. In that moment out of time, *to be* and *to be able* exists, speaking now in the sacred language of Gurdjieff." The intermediate state is a state of suffering; it is where we consciously witnessed our own folly and learn not to turn away. And this is the crunch: to accrue the energy of soul means to suffer. To *be* is to wake up into oneself in such a manner that *all* self-games become obvious. But more than that, for *to be* is also *to be able,* and that allows us the possibility of choosing, moment by moment, in which direction our lives should go because real will is operative. But as the 4th century spiritual master Evagrius Ponticus noted (see 6.8), we have to develop the ability to catch an emotional impulse in midair, so to speak. Allow such impulses to settle and you have no choice but to ride out their consequences. Catch them in the act, however, and you rob them of the energy on which they thrive. But this midair catching is no easy task; it hurts to be awake in this manner; in fact it hurts so much we tend to veer away from it. Hence Christianity's ongoing dilemma since around the end of the 3rd century. In the most basic of historical terms the Church, as it expanded its influence, lost touch with its spiritual base and was forced to replace hands-on spiritual instruction with authoritarian pronouncements. Falling into a "thou shalt not" mindset, it progressively hardened its attitude to practical self-suffering, and laid the responsibility for such suffering on the head of another, namely, Jesus. Vicarious sacrifice was up and running; we were off the hook as far as real moral/ethical effort was concerned. Failure in the spiritual life was now official Church policy; it was to be expected because individuals were at the mercy of their ever-erupting emotions and the temptations of everyday life. All we could do was confess our sins, submit to the regime's conception of Jesus as moral paragon (he was conceived of as sinless in spite of saying that only God was "good"), and that would see us through until our next confession. You could suffer if you wanted to, but it was suffering for no more than suffering's sake.

The problem with this moral/ethical scheme is that it has no point other than the production of a self-serving goodness, a goodness that revolves on itself for no other reason than the promotion of more goodness. In this sense, goodness is handy for crowd control in our societies, and for getting into an imagined heaven after death, but it does little else. It does not function as a bridging state between submerged and non-submerged levels of mind; it is a state of spiritual stasis allied to a carousel of wearying deeds and events that leave us dizzy and depressed, a treadmill of experiences from which there is no avenue of escape other than through confession or death. We are at the mercy of our submerged and engaged minds where emotions burble and tempers flare, never mind the pronouncements of a Church convinced of its divine right to dictate terms both in this life and in the next. Confession may lessen the spiritual suffering we carry, but as that is the very thing the intermediate state of mind promotes, we are, in Father Sylvan's terms, unwittingly avoiding the very thing we ought to be facing. And this should not be confused with self-mortification; it is a suffering composed of clarity of mind, a suffering that leads to openness of heart. Goodness is better than badness, but it has a bad habit of becoming an end in itself. The Scottish poet Robert Burns identifies the real issue when he says, "Oh wid the gods the power tae gie us, to see oursels as others see us."[10] Seeing ourselves is no easy matter; it takes conscious effort and a deal of courage to face what we are inside. Needleman sums up the situation neatly with these words: "Only this self-knowledge (the intermediate state) can generate real compassion for my neighbor and a real knowledge of him and a true sense of justice toward him. Those who love justice without long experience of these inner forces will never bring about anything but more violence and hatred."[11]

Christianity no longer talks of inner forces; it is satisfied with its scheme of salvation through fixity of belief. Theological perambulations where one historically distorted idea is used to deny or confirm some other equally suspect historical idea keeps the pot of belief churning, but when all is said and done we are left none the wiser as to how to live a moral life other than through gritted teeth. The very idea of forces within the self that have to be consciously regulated is anathema to present-day Christianity; it smacks of Gnosticism to churchmen and has to be ignored. But as Father Sylvan rightly points out, gnosis (real Christian knowledge) is not a heresy of Christianity; it is what Christianity was in the first instance. The "law of my parts" (St. Paul) is no longer understood because Christianity lost contact with its source; there is no longer any attempt to gather the energies of being in an attempt to fight off the surface self's limited (lower?) nature. Not only have the original formulations of Christian doctrine been lost sight of, even the ability to recognize such ideas when they turn up has been lost.[12] As a Christian culture we are stranded in submerged thinking and doing to such an extent that we fail to recognize the movement of energies within our bodies and minds for what they are: signals from the depths of being. Our energies are constantly rearranging themselves *in accordance with where we are at in ourselves,* but we are mostly oblivious to what is being intimated. The whole idea of there being good and evil forces in the universe that have to be combated has to do with these movements of energy; we are being asked to discriminate between those energies and behave accordingly. This raises the interesting question of what is going on with regard to moral schemes in other religions. Are they, too, hamstrung by desiccated moral systems whose demands are beyond the faithful's capacity to fulfill? If so, then they require the same opening up to the intermediate state of mind as Christianity itself. In this sense the intermediate state does not belong to Christianity alone; it is a fundamental form of knowledge without which religion, whatever its source, cannot properly function.

The Problem of Mysticism 12.3

The New Age search for meaning is heavily tilted towards mystical experience and/or explorations into the body. Why? Because experiences on both those levels are regarded as properly interior to the surface self. Mystical experience, it is believed, heralds a return to the inside, Christian prayer, in the sense of a dialogue with God, viewed as no more than an excuse to avoid real interiority. There is some truth in this, but it goes much, much further than that. In Father Sylvan's scheme, the development of interiority is not the only thing to be considered. Yes, that has to be done, but it should be balanced with an acknowledgment of organic processes: a struggle with "counter-affirmative forces" (the body) should be engaged in at the same time.[13] Ignore the body and you ignore half of the equation necessary for soul-making. This, however, does not put New Agers ahead of Christians. The formation of the soul lies between these poles of experience, develop one or the other and you end up spiritually lop sided: Morris Berman's "reciprocal relationship between nature and psyche" fits at exactly this point. Mystical experiences can be had without engaging in the rigors of the intermediate state, but by themselves they do not constitute a full spiritual engagement with reality. By all means develop your capacity for inner vision through meditation; or, conversely, delve into the mysteries of the body by this or that therapy, but do not neglect or underestimate the moral challenges you face in your daily life, for they form the interstices point of the whole affair.

The Question of Questions 12.4

The word "soul" has become a cliché; it has become a throw away word with little content except in literary terms. Clergymen use the word frequently, but only in the sense of something given to us by God at birth and taken away at death. Father Sylvan's use of the word is much more exact: he directly equates soul with the intermediate state and with the energy of attention. In this sense soul is a state of being within which a special type of energy fluctuates, an energy that is either stored or dispersed through inattention. The question of questions (am I presently real or not?) generally arises in relation to grief, sadness and the proximity of death, but through inattention is quickly forgotten. In that moment of moments, soul-energy flares into existence, but is quickly extinguished due to our haste to escape any disturbing emotion. In relation to openness of heart, Needleman identifies the intermediate state (availability to what would generally be avoided) as *the* most important "channel to the development of man's deepest possibilities":[14] a channel forever open to us in our daily lives. Then comes that astonishing statement made by Needleman at 4.5 concerning the center of the Christian cyclone: "Through containing this special psychic energy that is activated in the experience of deep self-questioning, the soul comes into existence (the energy of attention begins to accrue) and gathers itself into an independent entity."[15] There is, it seems, a great deal more to soul-making than meets the eye – it is also a process whereby an entity (another kind of self?) independent of the ego-self begins to form and develop.

I bring this point up again because it can be too easily overlooked: Christianity harbors teachings on an afterlife that seldom see the light of day – particularly from the pulpit. Clergymen occasionally refer to St. Paul's teaching on the spiritual body that is raised up after death, but only in terms of an amorphous spiritual entity linked to the saved ego-self. There is no mention of soul in this context. Soul is a separate something to an ego-self that goes either to heaven or hell; that is, it enters the bliss of a life with God plus soul, or it suffers the punishment of eternal separation from God minus soul – that is, it's loss of soul that is the core of the punishment. Hell is, in other words, to exist psychically in a state of inconceivable spiritual emptiness, a state of *soullessness.* Whatever the result, this psychic self continues to exist because there has to be something to experience one or other of the afterlife states; at least that's the theory. If Father Sylvan is right, however, then today's Christianity has lost the meaning of St. Paul's words and all but scrambled an earlier, more advanced teaching about the afterlife. This is of course to hypothetically accept that an afterlife is a feasible proposition, a point I ask you to bear with as we explore the ins and outs of this fascinating subject.

What has to be kept in mind here is this idea of soullessness. In an ordinary Christian context this cancels out as our being alienated from God after death, whereas in Father Sylvan's context it means to be alienated from life. With a little tweak of its tail, lack of soul has been transformed from an activity we should attend to while alive into that of a state of being after death in which we have no say whatsoever. In a word, we have been robbed of a basic spiritual right: the right to spiritual self-determination. We are not the helpless victims of sin we have been made out to be; we are capable of initiating our own salvation through the process of soul-making. This is of course heresy to Christian ears, but only because we have come to accept our moral failings as something beyond our capacity to rectify. We're only human, we say, and in saying that allow ourselves off the moral hook because conditioned by Christianity to interpret "only human" as meaning utterly dependent on spiritual forces outside of ourselves. Even at our best we are liable to slip into soul-destroying error because of unruly emotions and linked patterns of thought.

Father Sylvan, on the other hand, speaks of a "passage from Intermediate Man to Spiritual Man",[16] a journey he describes as the beginning of the spiritual life in that a spiritual life cannot get underway without acknowledgment of the intermediate state. The intermediate state is the goal we have to aim for; any other state (mystical, theological, ideological) has no spiritual efficacy unless the process of soul-making (accruing the energy of attention) is already underway. And that requires us to wake up to ourselves and what we're up to moment by moment through a process of voluntary suffering. Christianity is not about beliefs in this approach; it is about the energy that constitutes soul and how to consciously accrue it as we live out our lives. It really is possible to gain the whole world and lose one's own soul; that is, be so distracted by, so submerged in and so identified with submerged ruminations and imaginings that soul-making never properly gets under way. No sooner has a little energy accrued from our creative scanning of the still point, or from our momentary glimpses of reality when driven into ourselves by emotionally demanding events, than it is used up again in ordinary, everyday processes of mind.

But what happens if we fail to accrue sufficient energy for soul-making, or manage to build only a bit of a soul? Well, if Father Sylvan is right about the intermediate state and its ability to nurture an independent entity, then two possibilities face us: (1) a full-blown afterlife in some other dimension of being; or (2) an afterlife that fizzles out due to there not being sufficient energy to sustain it. The intermediate state of non-submerged awareness where we "experience the psychological pain of contradiction"[17] has to be established in us as a working alternative to mere process of mind if we want to survive death, and that, as the above quote suggests, requires an ongoing honesty in relation to our own thoughts and actions. And it can't be a half-hearted scrutiny: it's *all* or nothing. Leave things to trundle on as they are and death will simply snuff us out like a candle; or if only the beginnings of a soul have been accrued, abort us in exactly the same fashion as we abort soul in ourselves moment by moment. Sheer fantasy? Who can say for sure? But perhaps not as fantastic as it sounds when the experiences described by Bernadette Roberts, Meister Eckhart and many other experienced contemplatives are viewed alongside Father Sylvan's claims. Something important seems to be going on here, and it behooves serious investigators to track that something to source.

The idea of "soul" has fallen out of favor, perhaps because it is too amorphous a term to be taken seriously, or because we've lost track of its real meaning and have come to view it in the limited sense of a gift given at birth and, if we've been very naughty, taken away at death. Believe the wrong things and the thou-shalt-not God of traditional Christianity will demand his pound of theological flesh. In this scheme it is purity of mind that matters, a purity founded not on a self-confronting awareness that challenges the ego-self to reconsider its position in psyche, but on a scheme of obedience that renders the ego-self subservient to an elaborately conceived external judgment. In the stock Christian scheme, the soul becomes blackened by sin and is judged after death. In Father Sylvan's reworking of that scheme, the intermediate state of awareness should precede the attempt to be pure in thought or deed. Why? Because this is the root of the problem sewn by the *Men of Salvation,* those who "walk the earth like explosive devices ready to be set off at random."[18] Such men offer the solace of salvation through belief in Christ's sacrifice, but they do not offer the means to fully develop the energies that constitute soul (St. Paul's "New Man") in any meaningful fashion. The hopes and aspirations of such individuals may be of the highest caliber, but if the directing force is their own ordinary nature, their emotions and their constantly submerged and engaged minds, then the results can be catastrophic.

As the soul is formed prior to birth in traditional Christian belief, and a human life is by its very nature fallen and unable to save itself, then God *as* Christ had to make up for this deficiency by doing what only he could do, by living a human life of complete purity on our behalf. This, in conjunction with his saving act on the cross, is the heart of the Christian message as it is now known, and over the course of centuries this approach has led to unimaginable levels of human suffering. For from out of this view of the soul has sprung Christianity's arrogance and belief in its own authority, a belief that has resulted in murder and mayhem on a vast scale. Jacob Needleman puts it like this:

> It was a disaster for Christianity, according to Father Sylvan, when it adopted the notion that the soul of man already exists in finished form within human nature. This assumption (led to) the futile and mistaken effort to perfect our being by perfecting our thoughts, emotions or sensations, i.e. the futile effort of thought to alter emotion or vice versa.[19]

That is the crux of the matter. The belief of Christians that the soul is already complete and in their possession as a thing, has led to the mistaken notion that what has to be perfected is our mind and our emotions. Using thought and emotion in an attempt to control aberrant thought and emotion, the puzzle of constant moral failure continues to depress, its baffling consequences offset by the stopgap theory of Christ's vicarious sacrifice. The intermediate state where souls are forged through an awareness that bares the ego-self to itself is swapped for a system dependent on the energies of another, namely Jesus the moral paragon. And how can it be otherwise, for this hoped-for perfecting of the ego-self to avoid alienation from God at death is the prime factor in the ego-self's failure to realize its lofty ambitions. It is, therefore, not the morals of the ego-self that have to be perfected in alignment with Christian teaching, or the submerged thinking of the ego-self adjusted to fit in with a particular vein of theology, but rather the ego-self's tendency to avoid the pain of self-scrutiny through remaining in its submerged and engaged state. What we have to escape from is not sin as such, but a disadvantageous condition of mind. Hence Meister Eckhart's injunction that real morality is dependent on "possession of self" (becoming non-submerged), not on a policy of *thou shalt nots*. A new self forms and occupies the old self's location, and this new self heralds the capacity to make *real decisions*.

But if soul is not something dished out at birth, does that mean it is possible to be without a soul while alive? Is that a conceivable notion? Could we be rubbing shoulders with individuals who have no soul, or even be one of those individuals without realizing it? And how could one tell in either case? What would it feel like to have no soul, or have so little of a soul that it hardly mattered? What would be the give away factors to watch out for? Well, we would perhaps sense that we had no center to our life, no proper core to which we could retire when by ourselves. There would be a sense of having been abandoned, of there being no ultimate point to our existence. There would be a need for constant distraction, a need to be entertained or kept busy at all cost. We would be bad listeners; we would be more interested in what we had to say than in what was being said to us. Life itself would be without life to the extent that we ignored its presence around us and in us, and our own presence would necessarily be a foreign field – we would have become slaves to *the forgetfulness of being*.

Or are we perhaps reading too much into this material? Is that not just how things are in this modern world, this world of glitzy celebrity-hood where money and sex have top billing? Isn't Father Sylvan's talk of soul-energy not just another way of describing positive feelings as opposed to negative feelings, his idea of an intermediate state no more than a quirky religious angle on a basic self-reflective honesty we are all capable of from time to time? Or has he homed in on something inherently revolutionary, something allied to a unique form of religious thought now lost to us? That is what we have to determine as we delve more deeply into the territory opening before us, a territory where the challenge to preconceived ideas mounts with every line.

13: Mount Purgatory

> *The general interpretation is that Christ gave up his self so the rest of us would not have to do so. He did it, so now the rest of us are free. That we should have a liberated self when Christ had no self, makes no sense. Self is not our true life or our real nature: It is but a temporary mechanism, useful for a particular way of knowing…*
> Bernadette Roberts.
> *The Experience of No-Self*[1]

Intro: 13.0

There are only a few references to Hermeticism in Jacob Needleman's far-ranging book on how Christianity lost its soul, but they are important. In this context he mentions Origen, the most brilliant theologian of the 3rd century[2] who, it is thought, was a pupil of the Hermetic philosopher Ammonius Saccas. Needleman nominates Saccas as the mysterious teacher responsible for spreading the teachings of Hermeticism in both Western and Eastern Europe,[3] and reminds us that the 4th century spiritual master Evagrius Ponticus (see 6.8) was influenced by both Clement of Alexandria and Origen. As Clement and Origen made Platonism the metaphysical foundation of Christian philosophy,[4] (see 7.0) and Evagrius held similar ideas, all three can be classified as exponents of a linked philosophy at odds with important elements of Christianity's theological overview as it evolved at the end of the 2nd century. In a lengthy paper dealing with the Christian mystery and the ancient mysteries, Hugo Rahner, after denying a generic link between the two, is obliged to admit that the Church "adapted itself to the Hellenistic world with its enthusiasm for mysteries and interpreted its own mysteries in the old, familiar images and words. Here, Clement of Alexandria was the leader."[5]

In her indefatigable book *The History of God,* the historian and ex-Carmelite nun Karen Armstrong presents Clement and Origen as "Christian Platonists", and explains their theoretical stance as based on contemplative experience.[6] But it is her description of Evagrius' contemplative life that pulls this stance into focus, for she introduces the idea of energies in relation to contemplative prayer, and observes that for Evagrius "prayer had nothing whatever to do with concepts or images but was an immediate experience of the divine which transcended these," (see 7.0). According to Evagrius, the soul had to be "stripped naked", the mind remain uninfluenced by the "impress of any form." The Immaterial should be approached in an immaterial manner. Prayer was a "shedding of thought" resulting in "freedom from distraction and multiplicity", a loss of ego based on a systematic weaning away of the mind from pride, greed, sadness or anger.[7]

As noted by Needleman, Evagrius Ponticus talked of *Apatheia* (freedom from emotion), and Armstrong observes that Clement of Alexandria applies this term to God. Clement believed Christians could partake of the "imperturbability of God" and become "divine, incorruptible and impassible" through imitating Christ; a belief also held by Irenaeus, Bishop of Lyon.[8] For Clement, Origen, Evagrius and Irenaeus, "freedom from emotion" became pivotal both in their description of God and in how they conceived the spiritual transformation of the human mind. And not just in the sense of being good, or in the sense of copying Christ, or in the mistaken belief that to be forever serious of disposition was what was expected of Christians, but in the more exacting sense of consciously wrestling with aberrant emotions *as they arose.* So taught Evagrius, and he defined this condition as a discipline of mind that "opened the door to deep knowledge."[9] This is not a description of the Christian mysteries as they are generally known (the Eucharist, etc); it is an insight into a specific discipline of mind in relation to control of the emotions. For Clement, imitating Christ may have been enough; for Evagrius this matter went much, much deeper than that.

But this teaching was not for everyone; it was secret to the extent that it was not to be given to those unable to appreciate its real meaning. Needleman quotes Evagrius on the matter of secrecy:

> We shall not, to be sure, tell everything that we have seen or heard, but as much as we have been taught by the Fathers to tell to others... So as 'not to give what is holy to the dogs or to cast our pearls before swine' some of these matters will be kept in concealment and others alluded to only obscurely, but yet so as to keep them quite clear to those who walk along in the same path.[10]

Karen Armstrong follows suit with a quote from Basil in which she identfies "a secret or esoteric tradition... handed down 'in a mystery' from the Apostles."

> ... which our holy fathers have preserved in a silence that prevents anxiety and curiosity... so as to safeguard by this silence the sacred character of the mystery. The uninitiated are not permitted to behold these things: their meaning is not to be divulged by writing it down.[11]

This of course only proves that there was a depth of spiritual comprehension inside Christianity that had to be kept from nosy outsiders, not that there was a secret teaching beyond normal doctrine held back from Christians themselves. Hugo Rahner takes on this problem with this observation: "The Christian *mysterion* is always a 'secret revelation': secret, because here on earth it appeals only to faith and once taken in faith permits only a slow ascent to understanding, to a holy gnosis."[12] To get to grips with this revelation you had to be Christian to begin with.

You may not fully understand the technical nature of the revelation you were being taught for many years, or appreciate its latent power, but if you put your mind to it you would eventually have a breakthrough. True, but this state of affairs changed as the clergy accrued power and authority to themselves; what had been a teaching graced by deep spiritual insight (revelation) turned into a citadel of belief where experience was swapped for an intoxicating certainty with regard to those beliefs. Needleman puts the problem that arose this way:

> One point here... concerns the wrong dichotomy between belief and reason that has gradually established itself in the Western approach to both the meaning of religion and, indeed, the meaning of life itself. The message of Tradition, in this respect, is that there is in man a force that draws him toward Truth. This force is neither the thinking function nor the emotional function as they are commonly understood. [See 16.2] The word "faith" may be introduced here. But this word simply cannot be equated with "belief", in the sense of a conviction that is emotionally charged but opposed to intellectual explanation.[13]

What had been a basic teaching went underground and became a secret teaching because emotionally charged beliefs of a fixed variety had come to control Christian thinking. So much so that teachers like Evagrius, Clement and Origen were declared heretical in their approach to spiritual matters.

Over and above what the Church taught to the masses there was a concealed teaching, a more developed "understanding of the faith" that could not be expressed in ordinary words. In this vein, it is interesting to note Karen Armstrong's reference to St. Anthony, the 4th century desert ascetic, as someone who shared in the divine *apatheia* to such an extent that he experienced "a foretaste of his future deification." She is in fact quoting the great churchman Athanasius, but offsets his evaluation of Anthony (they were close friends) with what she feels is a contradictory observation in *The Sayings of the Fathers.* Anthony, she tells us, "comes over as a human and vulnerable man, troubled by boredom, agonizing over human problems and giving simple, direct advice."[14] In relation to how Evagrius interpreted *apatheia,* however, there is no contradiction. Anthony may well have had a foretaste of deification, but the route to that experience seems to have been through what Father Sylvan calls "voluntary suffering", an experience of mental purgatory while still alive, not merely austerity in terms of the body. Historically, purgatory has been conceived of as an after death state, an intermediate realm, but that may be a distortion of a more fundamental doctrine concerning the rigors of the intermediate state of being. As with the question of soul being an energy that is gathered throughout life, not just an amorphous something dished out at birth, the meaning of purgatory may have been originally connected to the idea of the soul's growth prior to death, not its refinement in some torturous limbo after death. In this context, the biblical injunction "pray without ceasing" would refer, not to an incessant mouthing of words, but to a disciplining of the mind on two levels: (1) that of fully occupying the space in which we exist; and (2) through this, allowing our tendency to lie to ourselves to fully register. Bring those two things together and you have a psychological mix of some potency.

Of all the characters who turn up in the context of *apatheia,* Evagrius Ponticus is the most telling. In his quite wonderful book *Desert Fathers, A Journey in the Wilderness with Saint Anthony,* James Cowan addresses the question of Evagrius' contribution to contemplative thought, and, with an admirable empathy for what this seeker after truth meant by *apatheia,* further opens for us the thinking of a man who put his intellect "at the service of an ideal grounded in simplicity and existential truth."[15] Cowan believes Evagrius to have been one of the greatest theologians of the early Church. Abandoning court life in the Byzantine capital for the Egyptian desert, he spent the rest of his life in the wastes of Nitria, and later at Kellia, south of Alexandria. As in the case of Bernadette Roberts, Evagrius became a controversial figure, his experience of deep contemplative states inadvertently breaking down his intellect's allegiance to self. The self had to be abandoned, he realized; it had to be "removed from the I-thouness of immediate perception."[16] And so developed a body of teaching (the *Praktikos*) based on experiences that eventually got him into trouble with Church authorities. For who among believers in Christ's salvatory uniqueness could accept the idea that certain ascetic practices confirmed the need for Christians to become (1) equal to Christ, and (2) go beyond belief in Christ – indeed, go beyond belief in religion altogether. A simple allegiance to right belief was all very well, but it was not sufficient if you wished to experience real spiritual freedom. Such a freedom came through suffering and atonement in relation to intellect being stripped of its allegiance to the submerged self. Everything had to be consumed by *apatheia,* for only then could an individual be freed from the bondage of self and its unruly emotions.

The heart of this issue is articulated by Cowan when he says, "Anthony and Evagrius transcended their psychophysical predicament through... ascetic practice and realized a new understanding of what it was to be human."[17] The experience of no-self experienced by anchorites such as Evagrius demolished the Neoplatonic idea that philosophy alone could purify the soul. Abstract reasoning was out, spiritual insight was in. But not to the detriment of reason. The seeing that took place when the ego-self's systems of comprehension ceased to rule psyche was inevitably articulated in forms that challenged the mind, but for very different reasons. Intellectual thought strained the boundaries of language in its attempt to capture what the mind dimly saw, whereas spiritual understanding liberated the mind from its linguistic limitations. The outcome might be equally difficult to accept in terms of ideas at variance with accepted belief, but never in terms of meanings driven to the point of epistemological exhaustion. Unlike Clement of Alexandria whose Platonic-influenced theology espoused *apatheia* in terms of the Greek conception of God as remote and detached from mankind, Evagrius' experience of *apatheia* as "suffering in the service of truth" resulted in a movement of energies perceived as an inner radiance. This was not a mind in search of a better argument, it was mind forging its way beyond philosophy altogether. Church intellectuals such as Clement, Tertullian, Athanasius and Augustine thought and wrote like Greek philosophers, but not its anchorite explorers. They buckled down to the task of finding out experientially what Christianity's whole bag of tricks was about, and when they emerged from their caves and cells they had in their possession a Jesus all but unrecognizable to regular believers.

Dogma and Theory 13.1

Before moving on to the energies encountered by these practical men in their meditations, it is necessary to clear up some misconceptions concerning terms such as "reason", "logic", "belief" and "experience". The words "theory" and "theoretical" are now associated with reasoned, factually based forms of argument, words such as "dogma" or "dogmatic" to fixed and inflexible formulations of thought. In their original Greek context, however, such terms carried meanings not quite the same as we have them today. For instance, the Greek conception of theory" (*theoria*) had to do with our capacity for reasoning, but it was a capacity that had to be purified in relation to wisdom (*sophia*). To reason was to contemplate the world and our place in it, not by logic alone, but by "a disciplined intuition resulting in ecstatic self-transcendence."[18] If you couldn't do this, you had to rely instead on *phronesis*, anticipation of the future and general intelligence. In its highest form theoretical reasoning was philosophic, it was contemplation of God, a reasoned exploration into what drove one beyond the limitations of language and logical thinking. Hence the need for *apatheia*. Only a mind freed from the disturbing influence of bodily passions and appetites could transcend its tendency to see everything in terms of its own needs. But this was not the *apatheia* of Evagrius (freedom wrested from the jaws of emotion prior to an impulse taking root); it was the *apatheia* of Plato, a willful subduing of emotion already expressed. After many years of physical hardship and self-inflicted austerity, this was Evagrius' great discovery: you had to nip emotions in the bud.

In contrast to the Eastern Church, where theory was equated with contemplation, the Western Church's use of theory was more in the sense of rational hypotheses. And so Western theology could attempt to logically prove the existence of God, whereas in the Eastern Church contemplation of icons was considered more efficacious as a means of instruction. Karen Armstrong sums up the situation that arose with these words:

> They (the Greeks) had become distrustful of rationalism, finding it an inappropriate tool for the discussion of a God who must elude concepts and logic. Metaphysics was acceptable in secular studies but increasingly Greeks felt that it could endanger the faith. It appealed to the more talkative, busy part of the mind, whereas their *theoria* was not an intellectual opinion but a disciplined silence before God who could only be known by means of mystical experience.[19]

The busy, talkative part of the human mind indeed, and dangerous to the Christian faith in exactly the way the Greeks had imagined. Placed in difficulty by a theory in which God was simultaneously three persons in one, the Western Church further elaborated around this incomprehensible formula and ended up with a flesh-and-blood man coequal with God. Well, not quite. Western theologians knew that was incorrect, but so dependent on theoretical reasoning had they become that for most Christians it was an inescapable conclusion. It was, however, too difficult to explain why this theory of God's tripartite nature was not literally true, so it was left hanging in the air like a potential sword of Damocles. For the Greeks, the Trinity could be experienced only in contemplation; it was not a theoretical construct capable of logical explanation. For the Roman Church, the Trinity became a dogma they endeavored to explain with convoluted systems of reasoning. For the Greeks, the West had misused the language of Greek philosophy and inadvertently transformed the mystery of God into a series of logical propositions. The West's conception of the Trinity would lead, they believed, to the man Jesus being worshipped as God in his own right, and that, however one looked at it, would be an idolatrous act. In elevating Jesus to the level of God, the mystery that was God was in danger of being lost. From being a dogma in the sense of something ineffable being grasped intuitively, the Trinity became a dogma in the more rigid sense of a believed "belief" that could not be contradicted.

The Energies of Being 13.2

To share in the divine *apatheia* means both to suffer and to be beyond suffering. In its suffering aspect it refers to individuals who attempt to consciously bear the pain of their tendency to lie to themselves, and in its non-suffering aspect to those who through this exacting discipline of mind set in motion the energies of being. This is the intermediate level of being referred to at 12.0, and it is defined by Jacob Needleman as "the long and difficult development of the force (energy) of attention, which is the soul in its infinite gradations within ourselves."[20] In this context it is also the basis of true morality in that it supplies the energy of mind to withstand the tendency to "self-lie". A few pages further on Needleman clinches the matter of energy when he tells us that this energy "cannot appear without self-struggle of a specific, revealed nature." Then, by way of explaining what that means, he adds: "All revelation is the revelation of how to search, how to struggle. It is not the revelation of results."[21] Unluckily, the system of Christian morality governing Western societies is based on moral results – that is, it demands a high level of moral correctness without furnishing the necessary processes of mind to attain it. And so, as shown in the last chapter, we get caught in the spiral of failure and confession, if indeed we feel any compulsion to confess at all.

The energies of being have to be set in motion, and not just through copying or imitating what we think Jesus might do if faced with the same morally demanding situations, but through an internal process of discrimination (self-confrontation) that allows these energies to resonate alongside our fumbling attempts to do the right thing. The Church's obsession with goodness rests on an intuition of the intermediate state and its meaning, but it is a meaning shorn of its practical implications for daily life. The practical dimension of how to wake up within the self and deal with self-lying has been transmuted into a system where belief in Jesus' perfect goodness makes up for, and acts as a shield against, the thou-shalt-not God's uncertain temperament. Instead of opening up a path to God, Jesus as theologically designated intermediary blocks access to God, and in doing so reveals the Christian God's inherently schizophrenic nature. And so God remains out of bounds, not because he is inherently schizophrenic, but because the Jesus of the Western Church's imagination has been inflated beyond the point of spiritual decency. Unable to retreat from their view of Jesus as unsupersedable,[22] Father Sylvan's "Men of Salvation" offer their potentially explosive theological mix to all and sundry. For if there is one thing that thickly underlines Western Christianity's hubris, it is the authority it gleans from believing that only it has the power and the right to deliver eternal life to its adherents. Question that right even peripherally, and you invite the heavens to fall about your ears.

The Suffering God 13.3

This raises the question of the God who suffers, for that, in essence, is what the Christian God is conceived of as doing: he suffers on our behalf *through* his son's death on the cross. In Greek thought, God was remote, impassible, and unable to suffer or change. By the 4th century, however, Clement's and Origen's Greek-influenced conception of the Jewish God (Yahweh/ Jehovah) had changed into that of the Council of Nicea's Christian God who suffered *as* Jesus on the cross. And so three quite distinct conceptions of God nestled together in the Christian mind, and they were impossible to reconcile. The God of the Old Testament was, to use Karen Armstrong's words, "a blundering, ferocious deity… unworthy of worship" to the Greek mind. The Greek God was remote and unchanging, the Christian God of the developing Church all about love and suffering as witnessed in the life and death of Jesus, yet at the same time identical to the Jewish God in many of his less attractive habits.

Prior to Nicea's 4th century conclusions about Jesus, however, the early Church's view of Jesus had in fact been quite fluid. For Clement and Origen, the growing belief that Jesus was, in some literal sense, God visiting the planet was viewed with suspicion.[23] For Christian Platonists, salvation for the soul did not result from Jesus' bloody sacrifice on the cross; it arose as a result of ascending the great chain of being towards God by way of a special discipline that incorporated Jesus as a significant figure. There was an esoteric (inner) truth, and there was an exoteric (outer) truth, and it was the Christian's responsibility to differentiate between them. If you were serious about your spiritual life, then you had to make contact with the higher *and* the lower aspects of your own nature. A reconciliation between good and evil had to take place, a reconciliation that presented you with a forceful recognition of your lying evasions, your mental deceptions and your ingrained selfishness. Only when you had managed to face and sustain this level of self-inquiry would the question carried by being surface. Only through the medium of "total self-inquiry (could) the forces of good and evil... be reconciled within us."[24] A mechanical recognition of wrongdoing after the event carried no trace of the question of Being; it was no more than an engagement of mind within which one sheltered from the searing wind of shame. The question of Being carried us to the edge of ourselves, to the edge of our egos, and such a moment could surface only through the attempt to consciously climb Mount Purgatory.

The 13th century German mystic Meister Eckhart's claim that we were each essentially, and not just accidentally, capable of union with God removed the problem of a God who suffers, in comparison with a God who does not suffer, and how a flesh-and-blood man (Jesus) could at the same time be the God who transcends all that is human. How? By pointing out that in his experience God is love *because* he is above all human conceptions of love and affection. Being free of emotional reactions, God was identical to the self of a human being within whom the stage of contemplative *apatheia* had been fully established. In this strict sense, Jesus' "I and the father are one" claim reflected not that he was God paying Israel a visit in time and space, but that he had, by the time of his crucifixion, not only undergone union with God, but was also on the point of experiencing identity with God in this special sense. It is in this special sense that Bernadette Roberts breaks with Catholic tradition when she says: "these are two different experiences: union before the breakthrough, identity after the breakthrough."[25]

And so we have Jesus' struggle to find a language capable of conveying what had happened to him; he had experienced union with God and had to learn, by trial and error, how to handle the situation. On the one hand human and ordinary, Jesus was on the other deeply changed (transfigured) in his inner being. In the confusion experienced by his disciples as he moved through the contemplative levels and reached towards the ultimate state of union of identity, the scene was set for future misinterpretations of his life, his nature, and his teachings. Able only to partly grasp what had happened to their teacher, the disciples passed on impressions of him that the later Church came to view in a literal fashion. The question we have to ask, however, is this: Which of the three Gods previously delineated did Jesus identify with? Was it Yahweh, the ferocious thou-shalt-not God of the Old Testament, or was it Clement's and Origen's Greek-influenced God? Or did he ask himself the same question he asked of Peter ("Whom say ye that I am?") and conclude that he was himself the God who resided invisibly in the temple's holy of holies? Or can we deduce from his life and his teachings that he was not pathologically disturbed and that he united with something altogether different?

To answer this question we have to return to a statement made by Father Sylvan, a statement Jacob Needleman paraphrases so that we might properly differentiate between the God of "the developed soul," and the lesser God, "the god of morality and religious sanctity." [26] In Gnostic thinking, the lesser god was given the title "Demiurge", and in psychological terms this represented "true and good concepts about creation and life, but which, as concepts, can stand as a screen between the soul and the direct experience of its supreme possibilities." [27] And so Eckhart can pray: "Therefore I pray God that he may quit me of God, for his unconditioned being is above god and all distinctions." [28] Basically, the Demiurge is the God of the Old Testament, the God who, in mythological terms, created the world and the moral rules we vainly try to uphold, whereas the God beyond this God is the one which the mature mind unites with by way of contemplation and the intermediate state. In Father Sylvan's terms, "The doctrine of the Demiurge is a key element of a world view emphasizing levels of being in man and the universe."[29] It is therefore psychological at base and not to be taken literally. This was Gnosticism's later problem; it took psychological insights arrived at by earlier adventurers of the mind and literalized them into a cosmic dualism that threatened what Father Sylvan calls "the unicity and harmonious structure (goodness) of the universe itself."[30] And Christianity, the truth being told, was not far behind with its dangerously literal separation of good from evil - the Church's theology of evil nudged close to the Gnostic notion of two equally powerful forces battling it out for cosmic domination. In both cases a distortion of earlier insights into the energies governing human existence had taken place.

This is to suggest that Jesus' God was not Yahweh/Jehovah, or in some bizarre sense himself schizophrenically mirrored back to himself, but rather a God who, in the Eckhartian sense, was above all such distinctions. Such a God closely resembled the remote God of the Greeks, but with one major difference: Jesus called this God "Father". In being able to do so he intimated something about this God that brought him close to humanity, so giving back to the world Plato's (and Clement's) remote and intellectually defined God as an intimate experience. In this context Father Sylvan's remark that Christians existed long before Christians actually appeared on the planet begins to make sense: there were, in other words, individuals prior to Christianity's arrival on the scene who understood the energies of being and how to direct them. Christianity had not only lost contact with what it had once known, it had also mislaid a teaching Jesus had rediscovered in his own religious tradition and brought to fruition in his life, a life cut tragically short as a consequence of trying to articulate what he had experienced. Out of this anomaly had arisen the notion that his life and his death were significantly related, that his death on the cross was a cosmic event in its own right. And in some senses it was, for if Bernadette Roberts is anywhere near correct in her interpretation of that event, it probably marked Jesus' transition beyond the God of his religious tradition. The words attributed to Jesus on the cross, "Father, why hast thou forsaken me?", perfectly capture that instant's experiential/existential meaning: the theistic God that had helped bring him to the edge of himself had indeed died, not *as* himself in some ingrown-toenail sense but as the traditional Jewish conception of God in Jesus' mind. Bernadette Roberts sums up that moment with a contemplative's candor:

> Never in history has a holy man, saint, or sage of any religion gone out of this world with such a question on his lips, or ended his life on such a note. This was indeed the death of God.[31]

Ontological Reality 13.4

But we now have to consider statements made by Evagrius in relation to the forces (energies) he perceived as coursing through the human mind and heart, forces having, in his opinion, an *inbuilt direction.* Needleman interprets this line of thinking for us: "Modern man has absurdly underestimated the reality and the ontological direction of the energies within his own psyche." [32] Bernadette Roberts would agree, I'm sure, but she is, after all, an ex-Carmelite nun with a personal investment in believing that the religious life is not altogether devoid of meaning or direction.

Difficult-to-control thoughts and emotions were thought of in Evagrius' day as "demons", but the meaning behind that word was, Needleman tells us, anything but naive; it referred intuitively to "a field of forces and influences spanning the entire ontological range of forces in the universe."[33] Needleman drives this point home: "Moreover, our fundamentally Cartesian view of nature as a play of non-purposive motions prevents us from discriminating the direction of the forces within or outside of ourselves." He is of course interpreting Evagrius' beliefs for us, but one wonders to what extent he goes along with such thinking, for Evagrius' intuition of reality contradicts both today's utilitarian approach to energy and the ancient Stoic conception of cosmic processes as nothing more than aimless cycles. Push this idea of purposive energy a little further, however, and you end up with a theory of history in which events, *all* events, are part of an evolutionary build-up towards a cosmic conclusion in the mind of God. For in relation to Evagrius' vision, "These forces have a direction – a vertical direction toward or away from unity with God."[34]

So was Evagrius proposing some kind of long-term God-based plan for humanity? In spite of the above, I do not think so. The God Evagrius refers to is not Christianity's interfering God, the God envisioned by evangelicals and fundamentalists as straddling history like a puppet-master. It is the God who has to be approached immaterially, the God beyond God beloved of the contemplative. As "soul" has come to mean something other than an energy gathered into an independent entity, and "purgatory" viewed as an after-death state rather than a discipline in the here-and-now, and God's suffering through Jesus' ordeal on the cross made to replace the suffering entailed in *apatheia*, so has the word "God" been abused and turned into a grotesquely inflated projection of the ego-self imbued with goodness and love brought to the level of a utopian ideal. God has become the bearded man upstairs who looks down frowningly on our sometimes shameless behavior, the stern judge who will punish us with eternal damnation for not believing the Jesus story as it has evolved in the Church's imagination. This is patently not the God of Evagrius, Father Sylvan, Bernadette Roberts or Meister Eckhart, and given Needleman's depth of comprehension in these matters, it is not his God either. This is the ontological God, the Being of *all* beings, that *within which we move and have our being,* (St. Paul) as psychophysical beings. This God does not plan, scheme or manipulate, he is not a puppet-master. To nudge closer to what this might mean in relation to the energies of being, I can only reiterate something said at 11.2:

> Interiority equals depth, just as depth equals truth *in its own right.* In this appreciation of truth, truth is not to be confused with content, it is not a thing; it is an experience. We do not *have* truth, we descend into truth *as* being.

What's really being talked about here is the depth of our relationship with being *as* depth, our descent into being as an experience, our awareness of being as subject, an arising (resurrection) of being, an epiphany of being registering within us as *truth.* Such a moment signals the death of God as a being (as an imagined "thing"), and the rebirth of God as Being in its capitalized form. If God is that within which we move and have our being, then God is the essence of existence itself. We need look no further. We have, in Martin Heidegger's beautiful phrase, come *home.*

Karen Armstrong's approach to this question is a little more concrete. Through an examination of the word "energy" (*energeia*) she renders lines like "an epiphany of being registering within us as truth" into St. Basil's observation that, "It is by his energies that we know our God."[35] Armstrong remarks:

> As the word '*energeia*' implied, this was an active and dynamic conception of God. Where the West would see God making himself known by means of his eternal attributes – his goodness, justice, love and omnipotence – the Greeks saw God making himself accessible in a ceaseless activity in which he was somehow present.[36]

The energies experienced in contemplation signified communication with God, not in the sense of a telephone conversation, but in the sense of depth realized as an ongoing experience. Such moments are dependent on "the creation of a certain quality of being" in our lives,[37] and that quality is in turn dependent on our ability to shrug off the state of amnesia within which we conduct those lives. The whole puzzle of Christianity is not about salvation or damnation, or "guidance" in some literal sense; it is about the experience of, or the lack of the experience of, varying degrees of energy in the depths of being – energies that *calibrate our intentions in a new direction.* In the Old Testament this energy was referred to as the Glory of God (*kavod*), and in the New Testament as Jesus the man transfigured and transfused with light-energy on Mount Tabor. In this context it is interesting to note that Evagrius died celebrating the Feast of the Epiphany, an event recognized by all Christians as hugely important for Jesus, but not appreciated, I suspect, in relation to their own individual lives.

14: What Exactly is a Mystical Experience?

> *... definitions in language of mysticism are self-refuting. They are attempts to say what cannot be said, to eff what is logically ineffable. Talk of 'direct encounter' seems, seems, to conjure up an idea of stepping entirely clear of language, while yet remaining, as it must, firmly embedded in language.*
>
> Don Cupitt
>
> *Mysticism after Modernity*[1]

Intro: 14.0

The Christian preoccupation with devotional matters, and the secular preoccupation with logical categories, constitute two poles of a single problem – the problem of how to evaluate self in relation to God, or Ultimate Reality. Christianity holds a key to this problem, a key marked "transcendence", but the very idea of transcendence is so riddled with ambiguity and uncertainty that Christians themselves are apt to view it with suspicion. Nudge the Christian psyche and an avalanche of experiences to do with God, Jesus, the Virgin Mary and the saints will spill out to confound and amaze. There exists a veritable mountain of material on what has been seen, felt, smelt or heard in relation to whatever brand of Christianity happened to be operative. As a result, experiences had due to intense devotion are lumped in with experiences that transcend religious categories altogether, their extraordinary spiritual depths perceived in terms of the very beliefs they have left far behind. A basic reason for this confusion is that transcendent experiences continue to be thought of as mystical, and this term bedevils our ability to perceive them as anything other than adjuncts of religious beliefs brought to a point of experiential perfection.

The psychologist Roland Fischer splits mystical experiences into "tropotropic" and "ergotropic" encounters, which in simpler terms refer to "active" and "inactive" experiences of the mystical realm. Active experiences are said to involve hallucinations, visions, auditions and even smell or taste, whereas inactive mystical experiences are classified as lacking sensory content altogether. Mystics such as Eckhart, Dogen, al-Hallaj and Bernadette Roberts are placed in the inactive category. Citing Fischer's work in his research paper "What Does Mysticism Have to Teach Us?" Robert Forman adds the rider that the phenomena of such experiences do not in themselves constitute hard scientific proof that an experience is mystical, for they can just as easily be the result of "what one ate for dinner, a faulty memory, psychosomatic processes... or an encounter with Ultimate Truth."[2] We can, in other words, be easily fooled by the phenomenology of our own minds.

The odd thing about sensory-deprived mystical experience is that the experiencer is just as awake and aware as those who report back on having had extraordinary visions. Emerging from their non-sensory meditation (meditation in which the usual sensory connection is missing), they are nevertheless aware of what happened, and this gives rise to an abstract form of language described in the mystical literature as belonging to the *via negativa* tradition. So when the Anglican mystic Evelyn Underhill writes that mysticism is now "more generally accepted by theologians, philosophers and psychologists, as representing in its intensive form the essential religious experience of man,"[3] she is responding to the many serious studies of mystical experience that have become available over the last couple of decades. A whole generation of religious psychologists has helped theologians and philosophers come to grips with the substance of mystical experience, we are told; these professionals having discarded as accident the peculiar psychic disturbances that sometimes attend mystical apprehension. Serious students now pay less attention to the ecstatic or visionary elements talked of by mystics, for such experiences neither confirm nor discredit conservative Christian beliefs.

In her illuminating book *Ecstasy in Secular and Religious Experience,* Marghanita Laski tackles the problem of mystical experience, and with many an aside offers us an intelligent and highly informative overview. She records, for our amusement, an early medically based view of religious ecstasy, and in doing so reveals the attitudes of some medical practitioners to the idea of spiritual transcendence. St. Paul's vision on the road to Damascus is described, for instance, as a discharging lesion of the occipital cortex (epilepsy), St. Teresa's experiences as simple hysteria, George Fox as suffering from a disordered colon and Thomas Carlyle's claims as the result of gastro-duodenal catarrh.[4] Suggestions of this nature accord with some of Bernadette Roberts' friends insinuating that she was suffering from some unspecified mental pathology – how else could one explain the fact that her experience of God had gone beyond the expected religious boundaries? Experiences of transcendence had by those who deny, question or throw doubt on the accepted Christian paradigm are routinely assessed as pathological (even diabolical) because they do not conform to expected theological patterns. As these patterns have been constructed from historical accounts in which Christians claim to have experienced God in accordance with doctrinal formulations, the argument against those who experience God differently becomes circular. Theology's ancient templates have to suffice. Question those templates and you are apt to be downgraded to someone suffering from a not-so- nice mental or physical condition. At this point the difference between theological and medical templates fades – you are allowed to contradict neither the religious nor the secular status quo's conception of reality. In conservative Christian terms you are in danger of being demoted to the level of an Eastern meditator, a closet Neoplatonist, or written off as a screwy New Ager. But as Erich Neumann and others have shown, patterns of religious experience confirming fixed doctrinal notions are likely to be a distortion of reality's inherent nature, a reality we have to grace with a capitalized "R". In our present state of mind we are unwittingly defining and confining Reality within imposed conceptual limits that amputate us from the experience of Reality as such, and in doing so condemn ourselves to perpetuating the same basic mistakes that have haunted us for centuries.

Marghanita Laski seems to reject the suggestion that sectarian dogma modifies the nature of mystical experience,[5] but she does admit that, "Mystical religions and philosophies, together with poetry, have so comprehensively provided the vocabulary in which ecstatic experience is felt to be fittingly described that their words and phrases will perforce be used even by people who do not share the beliefs these words and phrases imply."[6] This adds yet another classification to Erich Neumann's categories of mystical exchange, and leaves us with terminology intrusions that obscure the reaches of mystical experience as surely as any ingrained religious or secular concept might do. But is there really any difference between the two approaches? Dogma, in whatever form it arises, is composed of word formulas, and word formulas constitute doctrinal attitudes and beliefs difficult to break away from. The tendency of believers is to believe in spite of evidence to the contrary. Only a shock to the system can knock out a well-established belief system, and *via negativa* experiences are known to deliver such shocks at frequent intervals. But having said that, recent studies to do with mystical experience have uncovered a plethora of experiential categories, and a quick look at some of those categories reveals how complex this subject has become in the last two decades.

The Technical Side of Mystical Experience 14.1

For some researchers, religious expectations are believed to play an obvious role in what is experienced,[7] and this argument is extended to include intellectual acculturation and the mystic's personal concepts, images, symbols and values.[8] This is the constructivist approach, and it tends to boil everything down to a "psychosomatic enhancement of religious beliefs and values."[9] The opposing school is that of the decontextualists where the argument rests on the constructivist's inability to explain exactly how language and background can influence mystical experience.[10] If the whole point of advanced contemplation or meditation is a letting go of mental constructs, then how can these constructs influence the outcome of experiences that by their very nature transcend the individual's mental landscape? The constructivist approach sees the mystical experience in terms of a horse-drawn cart where language is the horse, the decontextualist in terms of a space capsule pushed by the rocket of language into a mental orbit where freedom from earthly forces leave it weightless and afloat.[11] But what to do when a mystical vision is, say, of the Virgin Mary, or Jesus, or described in terms of Christ consciousness? Or as an encounter with Atman or Brahman in alignment with Upanishadic tradition? There is no doubting the backgrounding influence on those occasions, although, as Laski points out, this may only be because religion has, for some, comprehensively provided the vocabulary in which mystical experiences are eventually couched. To polarize this issue in terms of constructivist or decontextualist approaches is, however, quite unnecessary. There are undoubtedly experiences that result from emotional identification with religious beliefs and expectation (whether they can always be considered mystical is another question), but there are also those that seem quite disconnected from belief and its needs. And to add confusion to an already confused subject, there are, as Laski points out in her own fashion, decontextualized experiences described in constructivist terms for want of an alternative language.

The philosopher Stephen Katz, in conjunction with other researchers, is reported by fellow philosopher Robert Forman as placing all mystical experience in the basket labeled "subject to the formative and constructive processes of language and culture."[12] Forman himself takes more of a middle position. He does not see mystical experiences as universally constructed from previously held ideas, but as straddling both the constructivist and the decontextualist viewpoints. The cognitive philosopher Bruce Mangan picks up on this tendency in his commentary on Forman's 1994 research paper "Mysticism, Language and the Via Negativa". Mangan attacks Katz's constructivist approach to mystical experience as "applying the most standard, narrow and lifeless forms of analytic/linguistic philosophy to mystic utterances,"[13] and follows through by recognizing Forman's attempt to get experience back into the analysis of mysticism as a great leap forward. It is experience and not language that should be seen as primary in any discussion of mystical experience. Forman's analysis is nevertheless thought to be top-heavy with "language-encoded concepts", but redeemed by the fact that his linguistic engine is powered by *via negativa* utterances. *Negativa* utterances "*stop* us from supplying content," we are told; they are *evocative* rather than merely descriptive.[14] But as Forman points out, and fellow philosopher Wayne Proudfoot confirms, many mystical experiences are obviously dependent on the individual's religious orientation, so the constructivist approach has to be taken seriously. Enter W.M. Gadamer (Martin Heidegger's perceived champion) with the proposition that all that can be understood is language. Language has invaded all levels of enquiry, and that includes what we think of as productions of the unconscious mind. In this sense experience is not separate from language; it is essential to understanding and interpretation and is therefore an adjunct of language. In technical terms this means (if true) that linguistic formulations reside tacitly in all meanings.[15]

The now retired Dean of Emmanuel College, Cambridge, Don Cupitt, is in agreement with Gadamer's line of thought. He sees all of us as "always inside our own heads and inside our own language; we see everything only from our own human angle, and we cannot pretend to be able to lay aside our human limitations and contemplate God – or indeed any other supposed object of knowledge – in an absolute and perspectiveless way."[16] The theologian's response to this battening down of mystical experience is to say that the divine realm accommodates itself to our perceptual needs. And so the Virgin Mary turns up in a dress of the correct color and says the kind of things one would expect of her.[17] But do such interruptions of ordinary reality belong to the realm of authentic mystical experience, or do they spring from some lesser level? Can seeing the Virgin Mary, or Jesus, be lumped together in all honesty with experiences such as those had by Bernadette Roberts or Meister Eckhart, or are they intrinsically different? Or, in alignment with recent neuropsychological studies, can all these experiences be placed in the box marked "communal illusions and anxiety buffers" and cursorily dismissed?[18]

When I came to this chapter I knew I was headed for deep water, and as my research progressed, my suspicions were confirmed. As a subject, mysticism was being probed by physicists, psychologists, philosophers, biologists, neurobiologists and neuropsychologists (to mention but a few!), and this had resulted in a debate that veered dizzily between areas of expertise. Theologians were in there too, but given the problems they faced in trying to reconcile the difficulties of faith with the often unyielding facts of history and science, they had quite a job on their hands. Evelyn Underhill is therefore correct in pronouncing mysticism "more generally accepted by theologians, philosophers and psychologists as representing in its intensive form the essential religious experience of man," but it is an acceptance that has failed, on the whole, to percolate into the society at large. Some Catholic theologians consider mystical experience essential for a substantive spiritual life, but on the whole this is not the

Catholic Church's position. As reported by Jacob Needleman in *Lost Christianity,*[19] Cardinal Jean Daniélou is of quite the opposite opinion. As far as he is concerned, the saved are those who "believe, regardless of their level of interior life." It is belief in Church doctrine that saves us, not experience in the depths of being.

For the astute in these matters, however, experience has its own problems. In his research paper "The Truth of Mystical Experience", the psychologist Harry Hunt tells us that mysticism "regarded only as an internal 'state' remains within a potential and limited narcissism."[20] Mystical experience sought after in terms of experience alone are no more than narcissistic intrusions that leave us much the same as we were before the experience. Such experiences may be extraordinary in terms of images, sounds and even smells, but in the larger context they afford us little of lasting value – except, say, in terms of a general strengthening of beliefs already held. This throws Cardinal Daniélou's remarks about belief and interiority into sharp relief, for Hunt goes on to say that sought-after mystical states "devolve, especially with the inevitable secularization that follows any separation from the immediate sense of the numinous, into reassuring dogma and exclusionary group identities."[21] Such mystics fall back into the orbit of their belief system and tend to ignore anything that contradicts or threatens that belief system. They are interested only in mystical results, and as such are not open to the experience of being as limitless depth.

The Unknown Darkness 14.2

Many Christians find it difficult to accommodate experiences that run counter to clearly defined religious beliefs, and that in spite of the psychologist William James' 1907 claim that experience, by its very nature, tends to erode dogmatic forms in relation to "scientific, political, philosophical, and, through its mystical dimension (the) religious."[22] This presents us with a third category of experience: experience as a journey into self, other or world that has the capacity to transform all three. This is life lived as an experience in its own right. So immediate is this experience that we seldom think of it as being an experience in itself, an experience of being that we inhabit always in its totality and never just in its particulars. No fixed formula or belief can encapsulate life as a whole; it is beyond the finicky touch of any belief system to say what a life is in itself. So also with mystical experiences that blow a hole in religious formulas and threaten the fabric of beliefs held for belief's sake – particularly experiences that lean in the direction of God as unknown darkness, or depth, and away from intermediaries like Jesus, the Virgin Mary or any of the many saints in the Catholic pantheon.

A clear expression of this problem is made by Marghanita Laski when dealing with what she terms "induced ecstatic experience" in relation to mystical disciplines. Touching the core of the problem, she tells us that, "Christians insist that contemplation of Christ shall not become contemplation of God which is liable to lead to such statements as Ruysbroeck's 'so far as distinction of person goes, there is no more God nor creature', and 'we have lost ourselves and been melted away into the unknown darkness.'" Such an approach is anathema to the Christian mind because it heralds "the disastrous consequences which follow from the method of negation and self-deification."[23] In relation to the Quietist meditative tradition, the *Oxford Dictionary of the Christian Church* puts much the same thought like this:

> a certain form of mental prayer in which the soul consciously refuses not only all discursive mediation but any distinct act such as desire for virtue, love of Christ, or adoration of the Divine Person, but simply rests in the presence of God in pure faith ... the moral consequences of such teaching are almost indistinguishable from those of pantheism.[24]

To rest in the presence of God in pure faith (trust) is thought inadvisable because it undermines affective identification with Christ. Emotions such as desire for virtue or adoration of God are thought to be rendered obsolete. There has to be an affective connection for the meditation to be valid, discursive mediation – prayer/adoration – being the accepted route. Traditional conceptions of God, Christ and Church are the conduit through which the transcendent dimension is to be approached and entered, any other route perceived as leading to experiences out of step with the saintly traditions. Attempts to consciously induce transcendent states are considered subversive, the results deemed heretical if an emptying of the mind or a controlling of the breath is thought to equal spiritual activity. Eastern or Asiatic forms of meditation along with Quietist (Quaker, etc) approaches where Christian forms of prayer and adoration are dispensed with are interpreted by Catholic traditionalists as the slippery slope to spiritual anarchy.

If, however, the theological structures built around Christ *as* God are predominantly distortions of historical reality, then the Christian West's approach is at best untidy, and at worst divisive. Some Christian contemplatives have obviously managed to sidestep the doctrinal problems that arose for them, but many have probably been overpowered by the necessity to conform. Aldous Huxley's view of the mystical was undoubtedly untidy, but his argument against inappropriate means being used to justify ends has stood the test of time. He argued cogently that means should not be forced to justify ends, and this simple fact applies as much to the mystical realm as it does to the moral. For just as ends can be undermined, distorted and made invalid through processes of questionable worth, so also can the mystical be rendered flat and invalid if the route taken is hung with a gallery of belief tapestries. So it is interesting to note Laski's description of Christian attitudes towards contemplation of God, for within this attitude lies the observable fact that Christianity has all but lost its original premise, *trust in God,* and exchanged it for trust in a man assumed to have been God. Instituting a human being *as* God, Christians have been relieved of the pressure and responsibility of facing the challenging darkness of God. Stunned by too much light (classical theology or fundamentalist make-believe), they have replaced their transcendent God with a graspable image.

The Language of Appearance 14.3

One of the most pointed of Laski's observations is directed at Catholic theologians, for it is through their carefully honed sensibilities that the words of the Christian mystics have been filtered. She puts her point thus: "Catholic theologians may explain any seemingly pantheistic statement by an accepted Catholic mystic as not really meaning what it seems to mean." [25] Those who veer from the expected linguistic path describe only what they think they have experienced, not what has actually taken place. As many Catholic mystics knew the orthodox, permissible language inside out, yet dared to dispense with it, one has to wonder what was going on in their heads. On this score, Laski observes that there is "plenty of evidence that even the most respectable Christian mystics do describe experiences that are not doctrinally acceptable."[26] And so Meister Eckhart was attacked, St. Teresa tailored into theological conformity and Marguerite Porete forced to face the flames. God was a good Catholic. Mystical experience had to resonate alongside Catholic doctrine. For had not the Church's dogmas arisen from such experiences in the first place? Were not the Church's teachings merely an expression of what the Apostles and the desert Fathers had reported and the saints and mystics of countless generations so carefully confirmed?

If, as it appears, mystical experiences are open to interpretation, then who is to say that the theological overview is the only permissible one? Theologians may insist that their approach is the only one possible given the history of the faith and the supposed nature of mystical experience, but that overlooks the fact that faith and history make incongruous bedfellows. Accept the virgin birth and the physical assumption of Mary into heaven as historical events and you mix categories of thought to an alarming degree. It simply does not inspire confidence to be told that Jesus fed five thousand people by miraculously multiplying the contents of someone's lunch box!

The basic claim made by Christian theologians is that secular and religious forms of mysticism can be separately described. R.C. Zaehner, professor of Eastern religions, is of this opinion. Claiming that non-Christian mystical experience can be clearly differentiated from Christian mystical experience through the terminology used, Zaehner reinforces the Christian notion that there are two distinct mysticisms. Laski goes along with Zaehner to a point. The terminology used seems to reflect varieties, or levels of experience, but in her opinion it does not confirm an actual difference between Christian and non-Christian mysticism. Experiences claimed by Zaehner as non-Christian are often identical to claims made by traditional Christian mystics, so why differentiate? Zaehner attempts to explain this anomaly by arguing that although all mystical experience can be described as unitive, it is what one unites with that determines the nature of one's experience. It is one thing to encounter Reality, say, in the Quietist or Eastern meditative sense; it is quite another to prayerfully encounter God in the Christian sense. Laski's reply is that Christian mystics do not always "use such terms as must lead us necessarily to assume that their contact was with God."[27] I concur. Yes, there may well be a difference between Christian and non-Christian mystical experience in terms of what some Christians have been led to expect, but there are also numerous overlaps with non-Christian mystical experience, and these overlaps suggest a more complex experiential dimension than Christian theologians are, on the whole, willing to consider.

For Zaehner, the Christian mystic's use of terms such as "The Absolute", "Absolute Being" or "Absolute Reality" automatically refers to the Christian God; whereas the use of identical terminology by an atheist or Eastern/Asiatic meditator is assumed to mean something quite different. That is really quite odd given that Christians, as we saw earlier, are not actually allowed to approach God directly, but only through the personality and identity of a human being for whom divinity has been claimed. Yes, one can pray to God *as if* he were a separate being, but affective identification with God as opposed to Jesus is taboo. And yet Christian mystics did speak of being united with the God whom Jesus called "Father", and they were not speaking of Jesus by some other name. By some inexplicable means these good Catholics jumped the doctrinal rail and spoke of the Almighty in terms studiously avoided by theologians then and now. Evelyn Underhill may argue that mystical experience "requires to be embodied in some degree in history, dogma and institutions if it is to reach the sense-conditioned human mind," [28] but as the words "in some degree" signify, blind adherence to doctrine or institution is not being advocated. Inadequate doctrinal structures will by necessity be shed as individuals are drawn through the eye of the contemplative needle.

Intuitions and Suppositions 14.4

What then is a mystical experience if it does not confirm theological speculations or support age-old religious suppositions? Is the almost expected nonconformity of the mystic to fixed religious notions perhaps more to do with his/her state of mind prior to the experience? Are mystics closet subversives? Don Cupitt raises the specter of mystical nonconformity (see 9.4) arising from an already burgeoning discontent in the mystic's mind, and points to female mystics getting their own back on male-dominated religious hierarchies as an example.[29] This of course transforms mystical nonconformity into veiled, or not so veiled, forms of protest against the Church as an institution, so rendering the confronting elements of the experience mundane and explicable. A case for connecting mystical consciousness with matters of social reform has, however, been made by Richard Woods in his paper "Mysticism and Social Action".[30] Woods confirms Cupitt's suspicion that mysticism and protest go hand in hand, but he does so in terms of a three-part process that finally rescues mystical consciousness from the accusation that it is no more than disguised political unrest. There is undeniably a strong reform element in mystical experience, but it pertains to a "re-evaluation of the beliefs, goals, and values of the originating society" after a period of intense contemplative activity that can last for years. Such reforms result from depth experiences within (or beyond) psyche, not from closeted ruminations of the conscious mind spilling out into the world. To suggest that this is all that's going on is fundamentally shortsighted.

Don Cupitt also argues that the language of mysticism is due to mystics being in essence *writers* "highly conscious of language," and not reporters as such.[31] Again, there is no doubting that mystical language was/is produced by literate minds, but what else would one expect? The literate write, the illiterate do not. And to say that such people "play games with language, tormenting it because it torments them, keeping to the rules in such a *wicked* way as to get round the rules," and follow this with the suggestion that all this amounts to is a "slightly mocking and subversive commentary upon the officially approved forms of words for speaking about God"[32] is, to say the least, to entirely miss the point of what these individuals are attempting to say, and do. I agree that linguistic combinations such as "objective reality immediately perceived" do not convey meaning in any strict propositional sense, but there is nevertheless something conveyed by such arrangements, and that something is existentially substantial. Mystical reasoning cannot claim propositional coherence or be used to verify doctrinal beliefs, but it can affect consciousness in a manner that is existentially unique. Its purpose is not to intellectually convince us of something, its purpose is to open us up to *depth* in the sense meant by James Hillman – language can act as an entry point into experiences of psychophysical depth. We are all capable of dipping towards the still point of being in any given moment of time, but are generally too distracted by life and living (and language) to bother trying (see 11.1 & 2).

Bruce Mangan's observation that Robert Forman's attempt to get experience back into the analysis of mysticism is, in my opinion, vitally important when confronted by the reasoning of someone like Don Cupitt. And that in spite of the fact that Forman seems to agree with Cupitt that *via negativa* statements like "objective reality immediately perceived" are without propositional content. That being admitted, Forman then suggests that *via negativa* language serves the purpose of opening us up to the world "void of conceptions" about the world. Such language, he contends, is designed by the mystic to help unhitch us from language. In this sense the mystic as writer is, as Cupitt claims, conscious of language, but not in the sense of someone playing wicked games with language, but in the sense of our being teased by language to sense the presence of our own vertiginous depths. Propositional content such language may not have, but as suggested previously, it is nevertheless functioning meaningfully in terms of what it evokes within the reader. On examining this very point, the psychologist Benny Shanon has this to say:

> Lastly, there are facets of the phenomenology of conscousness that defy both verbal description and logical conceptualization. The prime examples of these have been noted by mystics throughout the ages. Indeed, in the mystical literature the limitation of logic to cope with these states has been explicitly noted and actually viewed as an intrinsic, and highly valued, determinant of the states at hand.

Shanon then completes his thinking on this issue with these telling words:

> In conclusion, the very existence of phenomenological patterns of these kinds indicates that even without considering the relationship between consciousness and the brain, even without delving into ontology and metaphysics, the phenomenology of human experience presents non-trivial phenomena. It is, in other words, interesting and intellectually challenging in its own right.[33]

The Polish theatre director Jerzy Grotowski may be capturing what is going on here when he describes awareness as a consciousness that is not linked to language. Language, he suggests, is *the functioning of the computer.*[34]

But Cupitt isn't finished. He then launches an attack on Descartes' proposition, "I think therefore I am," and denies us the possibility of introspectively knowing ourselves *as* a self. Knowledge of self is always mediated, he tells us. We are our own construction, and we're a botched job. We do not see ourselves clearly. We get ourselves absurdly wrong and cannot conceive what it would be like to see ourselves "immediately and with perfect clarity."[35] Embedded in language as we are, we cannot know anything immediately, neither ourselves nor God, and we just have to put up with this fact. Things known are by their very nature secondary and never primary. To think something, anything, is to be dragged down into language. This is of course to reiterate Susan Blackmore's notion that all attempts to know the self are by nature retrospective concoctions. But as we saw at 11.4, that is not necessarily the case. Something is missing in this argument – to equate thinking automatically with language reduces thinking human beings to the level of linguistic computers, hence Grotowski's separation of awareness from language. A conception of consciousness that disallows the intricacies of the experiential level is not to be trusted. As Jordan Zlatev comments in "Dependence of Language on Consciousness":

> Primary consciousness "involves awareness of the here-and-now, while ('higher order' consciousness)... involves various forms of detachment from the present, including conceptions of the past and future. The 'primacy' of the first is phylogenetic and ontogenetic, but also implicitly logical – without it language and 'higher order' consciousness would be impossible... If all 'higher order' consciousness (was) based on language... then the foundational role of consciousness would not run very deep."[36]

Don Cupitt's reasoning in relation to self and its quandary has been confirmed over and over again throughout this book, but many would take Cupitt to task on the notion that *all* forms of knowing, or meaning, are embedded in language. If that were the case, our every moment would surely be taken up with the task of articulating back to ourselves what we know ourselves to know! That is obviously not the case, hence the mysteries of memory or, to paraphrase Arthur Koestler, our knowing slips towards a not-knowing and that opens the doors of psyche to itself. On this very point Guy Claxton has this to say:

> There may be a bright pinnacle to the mind's activity, but there is always a shading off, around that peak, of activated assumptions, details and associations that comprise the margins, or the groundswell, of consciousness. And below that there is a wider set of connotations and concerns that are not conscious in themselves, but whose subliminal activity colors and nuances what and how we are seeing or thinking.[37]

For Claxton, the Enlightenment view of the mind is in urgent need of moderation.

> Its lopsided adherence to explicit, deliberate, conscious reason as the acme of intelligence is flawed. It leads to a contempt for symbols – for language that resonates in the intricate depths of the brain – and an overestimation of dull, literal prose. It leads to students being taught to pull poetry and dreams apart; to plunder them impatiently for their 'meaning', and to a neglect of Keats' art of 'negative capability' – the ability to dwell in 'uncertainties, Mysteries, doubts, without any irritable reaching after fact and reason." [38]

As an experience, meaning is also something 'sensed' or 'felt' – there is an affective level to meaning that should not be ignored. As Claxton observes, there is no hard and fast dividing line between conscious and unconscious. We have at our disposal a system of unconscious knowing (see 11.0) that can, if allowed to register, extend and refine the limited language-based jugglings of the conscious mind. Morris Berman is in agreement. Human beings cannot be fully understood in terms of 'objective' analysis, he tells us. Their "deepest and most significant experiences are lived on a level that is largely invisible, a shadowy region where the mind and the body move in and out of each other in an infinite number of elusive combinations, and that can only be evoked through allusion, feeling tone, rhetoric, and 'resonance'."[39] In *Man and His Symbols,* Carl Jung admits in his introductory essay that psychology is often accused of not being scientific because it allows for feeling as a factor of value, but it has to be so, he contends. Why? Because feeling is the link between physical events and life. Psychology's critics fail to understand the necessity of giving due consideration to feeling, and in doing so severely truncate their comprehension of what it means to be a living being. Jung concludes that the unconscious "seems to be able to examine and to draw conclusions from facts, much as consciousness does. It can even use certain facts, and anticipate their possible results, just because we are *not* conscious of them."[40] Conscious representations are sometimes "patterned" before we become conscious of them.

Jung and Karl Kerényi were of the opinion that in 'symbol' the world itself is *speaking*. In their mental scheme psyche stretched all the way down into the darkness of physical matter and was finally extinguished in the body's materiality. At base, psyche and matter were intrinsically related – psyche was world. The problem for psyche was that at the higher levels of conscious functioning, at the level of differentiation and abstraction, it automatically lost sight of its deep relationship to body and world and fell into inadequate rationalistic explanations for just about everything. The physicist Paul Davies seems to agree with this approach when he says:

> I have come to the point of view that mind – i.e. conscious awareness of the world – is not a meaningless and incidental quirk of nature but an absolutely fundamental facet of reality.[41]

Carl Jung believed that consciousness might perhaps be the prime ingredient in the formulation of a general theory of everything, and the physicist Wolfgang Pauli was in broad agreement with this notion. Pauli is thought to have later changed his mind on this point, but his private letters suggest otherwise. In his essay "Heidegger and Vedanta", J.L. Mehta refers to a world under the domination of a "profound illusion", an illusion scorned by Nietzsche as "'the unshakable faith that thought, using the thread of logic, can penetrate the deepest abysses of being, and that thought is capable not only of knowing being but even of correcting it.'" For Nietzsche, this illusion had started with the Greek insistence that thinking was sufficient unto itself, a belief that "spread over posterity like a shadow."[42] But as we will see in a moment, language can harbor subtle intimations of being as an experience. For Cupitt, everything mentally conceived is ultimately human and embedded in language, but this is perhaps to miss the point of what "human" stands for in the larger context of "psyche". As M.L. von Franz states in her essay 'The Process of Individuation', "No matter what we assert, we can never get away from the existence of the psyche – for we are contained within it, and it is the only means by which we can grasp reality."[43] This enlarges Cupitt's concept of our being embedded in language alone to include psyche as a whole (conscious and unconscious), and that, I think, offers us a much more accurate picture of what is going on in our lives moment by moment.

In *The Spell of the Sensuous* David Abrams homes in on the problem I'm worrying at here with Merleau-Ponty's observation that immediate experience is "necessarily an experience of reciprocal encounter." The only way we can objectify or immobilize this encounter is through absenting ourselves from the encounter, by "forgetting or repressing our sensuous involvement"[44] as living, breathing beings. Objectification of the "other" through language disengages us from our senses and blocks perceptual reciprocity – we are cut off from ourselves as experiencing individuals, and from the dynamic presence of the thing or phenomenon confronting us. But only when we ignore the shape and rhythm of words, the inherent affective depths in which words are themselves embedded. Abrams is specific on this point.

> Communicative meaning is always, in its depths, affective; it remains rooted in the sensual dimension of experience, born of the body's native capacity to resonate with other bodies and with the landscape as a whole. Linguistic meaning is not some ideal and bodiless essence that we arbitrarily

> assign to a physical sound or word and then toss out into the "external" world. Rather, meaning sprouts in the very depths of the sensory world, in the heat of meeting, encounter, participation.[45]

To think otherwise is to unwittingly accept Plato's notion of eternal, unchanging forms and place conscious reasoning on the throne of psyche, indeed, to perceive psyche as no more than literate reasoning writ large. This approach interprets "intellect" as a *disembodied* ideal power capable of propositional purity (ultimate clarity) due to having been unhitched from the sensory world. As Abrams points out, the older Homeric meaning of psyche as "breath" has been replaced with the Socratic-Platonic model of psyche where sensory input is discarded and replaced with a seemingly autonomous form of reflective awareness.

As already noted, the primary phase of creative thought seems to be predominantly visual, and sometimes kinetic, and verbal only in its secondary phase. As a depth experience, "knowing" something requires an actual regression from language to be fully productive. Immediacy of experience in terms of self, other, and even God, is possible, but only as we approach or pass through Bernadette Roberts' still point of being. In his role of cognitive scientist and expert on Jewish mysticism, Brian Lancaster's research is of particular interest. In a summary of his research into unconscious processes, he has this to say: "The picture of the mind which emerges... is of a preconscious realm characterized by multiplicity of meaning and intent, preceding the entry into consciousness of unitary concepts."[46] George Steiner helps unravel the intricacies of the situation further in relation to Martin Heidegger's unusual use of language, and helps cancel out the negative Platonic effect detected by Abrams.

> If we reach deeply enough into the origins of crucial Greek terms we may gain some sense of what grammar and perception were when "being" was still immediate to man, and we shall certainly gain some understanding of how it was that this immediacy came to be dissipated. The Greeks called "being" *ousia* or, more fully *parousia.* Our dictionaries translate this word as "substance". Wrongly, says Heidegger. The veritable translation would be a set cluster of significations comprising "homestead, at-homeness, a standing in and by itself, a self-enclosedness, an integral presentness or thereness."[47]

This suggests that words can carry something of our original "immediacy of being" in their grammatical form, and that the dissipation of this immediacy can be traced to a breakdown in how we relate to ourselves in terms of self-presence. Steiner is specific. Immediacy of being is *an integral presentness or thereness* experienced beyond mere existence. To merely exist is to stand outside of being, or be in a state of non-being. In terms of how we live our submerged and engaged conscious lives, this exactly captures our plight, for it describes with surprising accuracy our estrangement from being – the deep relationship of psyche to body and matter that we have lost sight of. Through words termed crucial by Steiner – words Cupitt would probably find propositionally suspect – we are brought to an appreciation of being that would otherwise remain undetected. For Steiner, Heidegger is attempting, through the medium of language, to "separate the authenticity of 'being' from the factitiousness of 'existence'",[48] and that, in a nutshell, is our existential problem. We exist mostly without knowledge of being in the present – we lack a present *tenseness* (tonos/energy) in our individual and collective lives.

A further refinement in relation to Heidegger's use of language is to be found in Jeff Malpas' book *Heidegger's Topology,* a study of being, place and world in which Heidegger's highly original use of language gives Malpas reason to address what some see as a prime example of language devoid of real propositional content. In this vein Malpas quotes Thomas Sheehan as saying that contemporary scholarship has no clear understanding of Heidegger's philosophy due to its supposed lack of linguistic clarity, whereas Malpas is of the opinion that clarity in this sense "may constitute a mistaken philosophical ideal in general."[49] Why? Because Heidegger perceived language not as an arrangement of fixed linguistic pointers, but as a system of multiple meanings that overlapped one another. In this sense his curious etymologies (at-homeness, self-enclosedness, etc) were meant to "stimulate a way of thinking with language that is not restricted to the literal and yet is not simply metaphorical either." [50] My own reading of Heidegger suggests that he was aiming at something beyond propositional clarity, his use of simple, everyday words his attempt to reintroduce us to immediacy of being through language itself, a reaching into language that could carry us beyond the inbuilt limitations of language.

J.L. Mehta, on the other hand, tells us that Heidegger probably interpreted mystical pronouncements "as gestures of thought, as happenings on the path of thinking, never in the sense of finding access to a realm and an experience which lie beyond the reach of thinking, never as the necessary or even possible abrogation of thought."[51] This is to say that thought in some delicate sense never ceases, that it is always integral to awareness, but it is not to say that everything thought is ultimately embedded in language as form. For as already shown, thought necessarily straddles conscious and unconscious processes, and can on occasion taper out into a profound inner silence without halting acts of awareness. As the depth experiences of Bernadette Roberts show, such experiences can be described afterwards, and that suggests some form of ongoing comprehension. Heidegger's aim was to help us heal ourselves through a form of thinking that freed us from the Greek insistence that thinking was sufficient unto itself – that is, a 'thinking' grounded in the limitations of linguistic manipulation alone. As pointed out by Otto Poggeler in his essay "West-East Dialogue", "Heidegger demands a language in which it is not primarily a question of univocal concepts and their coherent connections, but rather of images whose meanings are multidimensional and inexhaustible."[52] Poggeler adds two pages later that Heidegger saw thinking as a *laying of furrows in language.*

In *Wittgenstein, Grammar and God,* Alan Keightley captures something of what is going on here when he says, "Wittgenstein may well have thought that something 'ineffably' shows itself through the language of religion." And through poetry. "... something may ineffably 'show itself' through the language of poetry," he tells us.[53] In reference to a poem sent to him by a friend, Wittgenstein's own words break open the puzzle of the role played by language.

> The poem... is really magnificent. And this is how it is: if only you do not try to utter what is unutterable then *nothing* gets lost. But the unutterable will be... unutterably *contained* in what has been uttered.[54]

Benny Shanon helps clarify the situation further.

> Meaning is not a quality that is added to cognitive structures and dynamics. Rather, it is the stuff that makes such structures and dynamics be in the first place. With this, the ground is established for semantic and actional operations.[55]

Jordan Zlatev, a specialist in linguistics, follows with:

> ... the linguistic turn implies an exaggeration of the power of language over consciousness, since it is far from obvious that 'the limits of my language mean the limits of my world'.[56]

The Japanese philosopher Tetsuaki Kotoh also squares up to this problem in his paper "Language and Silence" by touching on what he terms *the linguisticality of human experience of the world.* With reference to the notion that Heidegger's philosophical approach was based on language as the primary force in human comprehension (as found particularly in the thinking of W.M. Gadamer), he suggests that this is to misinterpret Heidegger's thoughts on language. Kotoh's argument is complex, but it comes down to this: "Can the entire reality of our being be grasped from the level of language?" In reply to his own question he says, "Self-transformation can... be described as a process in which the normal relationship between language and reality breaks down into silence, and language then revives through such silence." It is only at the shallow end of everyday experience that language restricts our comprehension of reality; at the deep end of experience language breaks down into silence and gives rise to our creative capacities. Sound familiar? The ground of self is silence (Roberts), not language, and it is our capacity for creative silence that constitutes the basis of Heidegger's thinking. In Heidegger's own words, this creative state can be described as the "echo of silence (*Gelaut der Stille*), and is by definition the echo of our own reality. But note the progression – language gives way to silence and then silence gives way to language – language by its very nature must remain secondary to the primacy of Being as an experience in its own right, and constitutes a response to the soundless voice of Being. Silence is the source of language.[57] For all its power, language must by its very nature conceal the world it attempts to reveal through a process that standardizes reality and habituates us to that reality.

From the Undifferentiated to the Undifferentiated | 4.5

In an attempt to sort out this kind of problem, Benny Shanon allows for three basic levels of consciousness. Level one (termed Cons1) is sensed being of the most rudimentary type. This level of being lacks definite structure, does not exhibit differentiation, and thus has no specific contents associated with it. Cons1 is all pervasive and non-local. Hardly anything substantial can be said about this state, *but it is there throughout our lives in every situation.* (Author's italics) Level two (Cons2) is mental awareness, and consists of subjective experiences that are distinct and differentiated. This level constitutes the totality of our articulated life and comprises all internal events of which we are aware. Level three (Cons3) consists of meta-mentations, productions of mind inspected further through reflection. Meta-mentations are distinct from 'consciousness of the self' because consciousness of the self is an act of cognitive-mentation, not meta-mentation. *Cognitive-mentation requires us to relate to our own cognitive activities, it does not involve mentations that take other mentations as objects of observation* (see 11.4).[58] This is an important observation that should be kept in mind, and it is echoed in Bernadette Roberts' study of self in relation to consciousness when she says "self does not mediate self-knowledge, but is ITSELF the essence of self-knowledge or self-awareness."[59]

These levels or states are of course interrelated; we are constantly shifting between them, and, as it turns out, beyond them if we happen to be an artist, a meditator or a contemplative of any skill. And this simple tripartite system can be transcended; it is not the end of the line – there are two further levels (Cons4 and Cons5) which Shanon designates as *non-ordinary* in that the latter of those extra levels is experienced both firsthand and theoretically as the ground, or foundation of being, the *fons et origo* of all existence. Cons1 and Cons5 are the opposite ends of this integrated system, the difference between them being that those who experience Cons5 have *moved entirely beyond the distinctions and differentiations that govern* Cons2 and Cons3.[60]

These levels or states of consciousness are, according to Shanon's scheme, an integrated system exhibiting a whole spectrum of experiences "between the undifferentiated primitive quality of sentience (Cons1) and the full-fledged domain of articulated internal experience (that) may be encountered" (Cons2 and Cons3). The basic types or levels mark key points, or prototypes, in this spectrum, but they do not exhaust it. Similarly, at the end of the spectrum between Cons4 and Cons5 there are also intermediate variations. These mark a progressive, graded diminishing of differentiation in the non-ordinary manifestations of experience."[61] And so we enter the territory described by Bernadette Roberts, Meister Eckhart and Kotoh Tetsuaki, a territory where, in Shanon's words, "The distinction between self and non-self [is] no longer pertinent." He adds: "Conceptually, these states imply that with high levels of consciousness the mental turns into the ontological."[62]

But let's double back to that extraordinary observation of Steiner's when he tells us that Heidegger was trying to "separate the authenticity of 'being' from the factitiousness of 'existence'," for this, surely, is what concerns many of us throughout our lives. We sometimes sense that we've become unauthentic in relation to self, or other. Or, as is generally the case, we do not perceive our merely existing in the world as problematical. We simply fail to notice that our state of merely existing is closely related to the "mere existing" of others. We remain content with our submerged and engaged state of mind and discount our periodic *moments of emerging* as of little importance. Heidegger refers to this state of being as *Verfallen* (Fallen), and in doing so allows us to glimpse an alternative meaning to that generally given in Genesis to our First Parents' *fall into sin*. There is, he is saying, an alternative way of seeing self, other or world, but it is up to us as individuals to find out what that alternative seeing entails. What we're waiting for, in essence, is not Christ's expected *parousia* (his grand Return as a being of substance) at the end of time, or history, but our own *parousia* in the original Greek sense of *presentness,* or *thereness* of being in any given moment. This is the challenge of our time, the challenge Christianity must respond to if it is to retain any level of credibility in the 21st century.

But all is not lost in this respect, for there are churchmen to whom such a challenge has become self-evident – Archbishop Rowan Williams for one. Quoting from Walter Davis's *Inwardness and Existence* in his deeply realized book *Lost Icons,* the archbishop writes: "… a self is only really definable in the act of self-questioning; reflecting on the self cannot be a way of thinking about an 'item' that will stay in focus while we look at it. The act of questioning is the act in which the self is itself."[63] That, as we saw earlier, is a vitally important observation, and we will unpack it further in the final chapters. But one more thing of interest. Three pages further on in the Archbishop's text we find him quoting from none other than Jacob Needleman's book *Lost Christianity.*

15: Back to Bernadette

> *... we use the term 'consciousness' (or awareness) to include the entire system of consciousness with its various levels of experience from the unconscious to God-consciousness. By 'consciousness' or 'self' we mean the whole of the psyche, which, in Jungian terms, includes the conscious ego and unconscious self.*
> Bernadette Roberts
> *What is Self?*[1]

Intro: 15.0

In Bernadette Roberts' mystical scheme, conscious and unconscious processes are not separate systems; they are one and the same system functioning at different levels of psyche. So also with reason and the senses. They too are intimately connected and function as a unit or singular whole. And if for some reason the senses don't develop, then neither does consciousness – we are fundamentally dependent on our senses for the sense of personal existence that we have. Our unconscious subjective sense of self arises from the integrated body-mind being that we are, consciousness of self *as* a self from the same physiological base.[2]

Such statements encapsulate something I've been trying to get across throughout this book: terms like "conscious" and "unconscious" have to be reassessed in relation to self and its functional elements. The very ideas that the conscious self is, when physically awake, perpetually conscious, or that the unconscious is actually unconscious in the sense that consciousness is thought to be during sleep, are almost certainly mistaken representations of how psyche functions in relation to self and its experiences.

In his 1998 paper "What Does Mysticism Have to Teach Us About Consciousness?" Robert Forman mentions Bernadette Roberts twice, and touches on a series of points relevant to this book's basic argument. His opening point is that mystical experience may constitute "the least complex encounter with awareness *per se*," and for that reason be invaluable to consciousness researchers. Why? Because meditative or contemplative procedures systematically reduce mental activity in the sense of quieting down or eliminating the complex stew of thoughts, feelings and sensations that accompany human experience. As pointed out by Forman, the humble bacterium *E. coli's* contribution to our understanding of gene functioning in complex species is now acknowledged, and mystical experiences may prove equally seminal in our understanding of human consciousness.[3] Forman's basic argument is this:

> ... by reducing the intensity or compelling quality of outward perception and inward thoughts, one may come to a time of greater stillness. Ultimately one may become utterly silent inside, as though in a gap between thoughts, where one becomes completely perception and thought-free.[4]

Meditative and contemplative experience is termed the "pure consciousness event" by Forman, and dubbed a "PCE". This in itself is informative, but what comes next helps cancel out the problem cited at 14.3 with regard to Christian and non-Christian mystical experiences being viewed as radically different from one another. The pure consciousness event experience, we are told, has been identified in almost *all* religious traditions, and although only occasionally experienced by non-meditators, is regularly experienced by some practitioners. Similarly, long-term meditators seem to experience pure consciousness events in advanced form, their relationship to perceptual objects undergoing profound change.[5] The question is, can these reports be trusted? Where is the proof or evidence that these experiences are what they are being made out to be? How do we determine the truth-value of mystical experiences?

Forman's reply is simple and straightforward: we determine their truth-value in the same way we determine the truth-value of experiences described by anyone we happen to communicate with. Do they seem delusional, unconnected, paranoid or psychotic? Does the person behave in an unusual fashion? Does he/she sound right, or do we sense something untoward in their attitude? If none of these, then the chances are these individuals are attempting to describe real events and not just concocted fantasies. And if their description of mystical events can be closely correlated with the experiences of practitioners from other religious traditions, then there is no good reason for out-of-hand rejection. Even then, however, what we glean from the experiences of others cannot be passed on as "conclusive evidence for or against a particular thesis." Forman is clear on this point: phenomenology is not science. But in conjunction with the competent research of other professionals we can hope to verify or deny many of the elements of mystical experience that confront us. And as some professionals are themselves skilled meditators/contemplators, then a double-check factor can be added to this mix.

In Forman's terms a pure consciousness event describes a wakeful but contentless (non-intentional) state of consciousness experienced in two sequential stages: (1) an experience of ongoing inner stillness; and (2) a perceived unity of one's awareness with the objects one encounters. These experiences are in turn defined as a "dualistic mystical state" (DMS), and described over all as a "unitive mystical state" (UMS). So far so good, but pure consciousness events (PCEs) are also described as an *awareness of one's own awareness* while simultaneously remaining conscious of thoughts, sensations and actions,[6] and that is a highly unusual description of mystical experience and meditative procedure – at least it is in my experience. The mystical state is generally described in what I would term mono-directional language – that is, as an experience of unity with some exterior object of attention such as a tree, a person, or the world as a whole. Or even with oneself in sensory terms. But Forman's dualistic mystical state is much more than that; it is in effect an advanced description of what takes place during *via negativa* experience. Unity in run-of-the-mill descriptions of mystical experience refers to a blending of self and other to such an extent that the line of demarcation (the dualistic sense of self and other) vanishes, and this refers in particular to meditative states in which visions and auditions occur to the exclusion of any sense of self. In these deep and often intense meditative situations, the experiencer is *caught up* (disappears) inside the experience he or she is having. So taken up are they with the experience that all sense of self evaporates. In contrast to this, *via negativa* experiences lack any form of perceptual hook; they are truly *pure consciousness events* in that the experiencer's awareness of being aware remains intact *alongside* the perceived experience.

Guy Claxton captures the flavor of *via negativa* experience without hooks in *The Wayward Mind* by quoting D.T. Suzuki's appraisal of Hui-neng the 7th century Patriarch of Chinese Ch'an Buddhism's experience of a state of mind in which "action, feeling, perception, thought, all continue to arise, but 'I' am neither 'doing' them nor 'having' them."[7] And in an earlier passage dealing with Christian mysticism, Claxton describes the experience of God not in terms of "a transcendent 'being' Out There somewhere," but as "a radical transformation in the quality of experience, in which all sense of a knowing, questing, controlling, separate 'ego' or 'I', busily perceiving, planning and doing, drops away, and yet the up-rush of experienced life continues, miraculously, by itself."[8] Claxton also describes a telling experiment done with experienced meditators where two different forms of meditation produced quite different responses in the control groups. Both meditational forms were Buddhist in origin, but quite different in terms of process. One form used "the [meditator's] ability to inhibit the spontaneous ramblings of the mind," whereas the other maintained a "stance of disinterested observation while allowing the mind to run around as much as it likes." When presented with the Rorschach ink-blot test and asked to describe what they saw, the first group "could not be induced to make any projected elaborations, whereas the second group "spewed out dozens of highly fanciful and often obscene 'interpretations'." The second group's disposition to create meaning had been disinhibited, whereas the "meaning-seeking tendencies" of the first were under control.[9]

In close alignment with this, Robert Forman draws our attention to the non-sensory, non-imagistic language of mystics like Eckhart, St. Teresa, Dogen, al-Hallaj, Shankara and Bernadette Roberts. These individuals are all identified as *via negativa* mystics, St. Teresa's, Eckhart's and Roberts' descriptions of the contemplative process receiving particular attention in that they each speak of states in which feelings vanish, thinking ceases, breathing all but stops, memory comes to a halt and all faculties of attention are suspended. There is no sensory content, we are told, yet these individuals are awake and aware and able to describe their experiences afterwards. And such experiences are cross-cultural. Those who penned the Upanishads and the Buddhist texts talk of "sheer contentless presence" or an "abiding in the fullness of emptiness" (descriptions that would surely frustrate constructivist theorists like Don Cupitt and Stephen Katz) and in doing so reveal themselves to be on a par with Christian mystical writings past and present. Professor Zaehner would of course reject this correlation on the basis of the Christian God not being mentioned, but as Forman makes plain in a footnote, theistic thinkers like Zaehner define mystical experiences far too narrowly.

The claims made by Bernadette Roberts in her books are not questioned by Forman; they are taken at face value because they resonate with what is already known about mystical silence states, loss of sense of self and much else besides. As a meditator of some experience, Forman gets down to the business of carefully delineating mystical states for his readers, and with dexterity concludes that self-awareness (whether ordinary or mystical) "may have a non-localized, quasi-spatial character, much like a field."[10] This suggests that self-awareness is not a *thing* in consciousness that is aware of itself (Cons3 in Shanon's theoretical construct), and this fits reasonably well with the Roberts quote at the head of this chapter, for she equates self with the whole of psyche, and not just with some element in psyche. Self-consciousness, she tells us, is not something a self HAS; it is what a self IS in relation to experience.[11] Consciousness, self and experience are for Roberts one and the same thing, they are not separate entities. One's life or self is not a collection of experiences had by an individual self; it is one big seamless experience and it constitutes what we ARE as a person. Personal existence is, in this sense, all of a piece; it is at every point in time *everything* we have ever experienced, known or felt moving as one towards a point beyond time. Our memories and senses may give the impression of an individual bearing our name having experiences, thoughts and feelings in isolation, but we are in fact an experience unity traveling through time and space that can, under certain circumstances, be intercepted experientially. For Roberts, self or consciousness is "an experience and only secondarily a word or an idea that expresses this experience,"[12] (see 11.4). Even with our eyes wide open, we are constantly teetering on the brink of knowing self in a *via negativa* fashion. To know this as an experience, however, we have to shut up, watch and listen.

Rooted in the Unconscious 15.1

In relation to what I've just said about awareness of awareness in terms of Forman's suggested dualist mystical state (DMS), I was fascinated to find Bernadette Roberts similarly differentiating between ordinary conscious states and those in which we become aware of being aware. But being the kind of mystic she is, she pushes further and tells us that our ordinary, engaged form of awareness is as it is because it is firmly rooted in the unconscious. Conscious we may think we are, but we in fact function predominantly at an unconscious level. What is important is the realization that our so-called conscious thoughts are in fact conceived in the darkness and obscurity of unconscious processes. When we think we do not add words together as one would add numerals, we conceive of something (become pregnant with it) and give it form (birth it) through the act of speaking or writing. Enter Don Cupitt saying, "I told you so!" But that is to miss the point of the point being made. It is not that we only know something, or know that we do not know something when it is articulated or put into writing, but that *all* our articulations exist in some unconscious form prior to their being articulated. In other words, we know that we know something before we know it in any strict propositional sense. We may not know in exact terms what that thing is prior to saying or writing it, but the very fact that it can be said or written proves beyond doubt that it was in some sense known. You simply can't say or write what you do not know – experience comes before words. Meanings reside in language only because of our ability to "conceive meaning" at the unconscious level. Roberts puts the core of this problem succinctly when she says:

> There could be no self-awareness if this awareness were not, first of all, unconscious. As someone once noted, nothing rises to the conscious level that is not first on the unconscious level of consciousness. This fact tells us that self-awareness on the conscious level is not sufficient to account for self or consciousness, and that we must look to a deeper level if we are to find the true source and origin of self-awareness.[13]

Roberts is in good company when she makes this kind of statement. The philosopher Michael Polanyi expresses much the same idea when he says, "We know much more than we know we know,"[14] and the Cambridge philosopher Ralph Cudworth is not far behind with "[the] Cartesian implication [is that] if you cease to think then you cease to be is plain silly."[15] Something other than language-directed thought is at work here, and ignoring that something won't make it go away. Guy Claxton pulls the whole business of conscious versus unconscious into strict focus when he says, "Conscious experience is just one kind of manifestation of unconscious brain activity, and it may well be suited to the moment, or it may not… the primacy of the unconscious brain, as we get to know more about it, is becoming increasingly evident."[16] Just how evident becomes evident later when he adds: "Through inhibition the brain can arrest and attenuate its own natural outflow, and thus allow its *internal* pools of activation to deepen and widen… Speech, dampened, becomes *sotto voce,* and this enables us to engage in that kind of talking to ourselves that we call thinking. Action, dampened, becomes the internalized, mental rehearsal of action, while perception, dampened, becomes the internal visualizing, hearing and feeling that are the embodiments of imagination."[17] Without this dampening, or inhibiting effect, creative thought would be impossible, the route to contemplative and meditative experience equally unattainable.

The plot thickens. As creatures grounded in unconscious mentation, we are all capable of intuiting even the most obscure of Bernadette Roberts' meanings. To do so, however, we need to sink a little more deeply into ourselves. There is a surface self, and there is a deep self. The surface self is surface only because it deals predominantly with surface issues, the deeper self is naturally deeper because of its attempts to plumb difficult questions. But there is a still deeper self, and out of it come formations that defy the surface self's attempts to fully explain everything in surface self terms. And deeper still there is yet another self, and this self senses things beyond the grasp of all the other selves put together. I'm not absolutely sure who said it, but a quote springs to mind that perfectly sums up what I'm attempting to say here: "Flotillas of meaning coming across the horizon of consciousness that should not be intercepted too soon." (Anton Ehrenzweig?) Not only are we the recipients of useful intelligence from deeper levels of psyche, we should learn to wait upon these intimations and not interfere with them before they've fully formed. Why? Because they are knowings we do not know ourselves to know until we tease them into language from out of our own depths, and they are not to be confused with *new combinations of already known things.* This of course raises the question of just how deep one can go in relation to psyche. How many focal levels of the self are there?

And so looms a definitional problem: What is the difference between a submerged, engaged self, a deep questioning self, an artistic self and a meditative or contemplative self? Well, as suggested above, it's a matter of focus. Imagine the self as a lens that can change focus in relation to unconscious processes. The surface self (Cons2), the self of everyday activity, is, as are all the others, grounded in the unconscious, but its preference is for the shallow end of conscious experience. Its prime reason for being submerged is to realize propositional clarity (what something might mean until a better explanation is offered) as quickly as possible. All the while engaged with surface issues, it busily probes its understanding, or lack of understanding, and arrives at what it hopes are answers to problems. The deep questioning self (the self that reflects on its own reflections: Cons3) is similarly engaged, but it has the habit of stumbling into questions that drive it deeper still (Cons4), and in this sense it is confronted by realizations that push propositional reasoning to its limits. So also with the artistic self, for in its encounter with unconscious processes the realizations it comes to are to do with the deep end of life and living. Probing the question of what it means to be a human being through poetry, the novel, painting or the play is a sure fast way of experiencing unfamiliar depths. But when we touch on meditative or contemplative experience, this picture changes dramatically; for as the surface self is recalibrated into the self that can bear the thickening silence of the psyche, it is progressively stripped of its propositional-seeking identity (Cons2). Frozen in terms of its normal sensory reactions, its seeing becomes fixed and immovable, its tendency to scan the horizon of mind reduced ('dampened' in Claxton's terms), step by step, until it ceases to be perceptually hooked by what it sees and senses. And that, simple as it may sound, is what the whole meditative/contemplative process is about: it is about contentless seeing, seeing and experiencing in a non-attached, non-identifying manner. Freed from the need to get consciously involved with what we perceive and experience, we look unblinkingly into the heart of what it means to be alive. Tetsuaki Kotoh sums up this complicated situation with these telling words:

> There is no more urgent or basic concern for a human being than the conversion by which the everyday self becomes aware of its self-concealment, returns to the dark bottom of life and seeks a solid place on which to reside peacefully. However, self-transformation does not mean that the self changes into another self, but that the self whose true existence is concealed returns to the non-vacillating self, and in this sense means the birth of the true self.[18]

In alignment with the observations of Eric Schwitzgebel and Susan Blackmore, Bernadette Roberts speaks of our not always being conscious of our own consciousness, and this, she says, proves how rooted self-awareness is in the unconscious. This rootedness of the conscious in the unconscious is responsible for the continuity of self-consciousness across all levels of consciousness, "including the level we call 'unitive" or 'God-consciousness'." In Roberts' very exact scheme, self-awareness on the conscious level is insufficient to account for self or consciousness, so we have to "look to a deeper level if we are to find the true source and origin of self-awareness."[19] But this is not something *in* consciousness descending; it is, as suggested, a lens-like calibrating or focusing of consciousness in terms of awareness intensity. As happens to all of us at some time or other, we change consciousness levels depending on experiences at the conscious level. Working, as we mostly do, at the unconscious level in terms of dealing with conscious needs and demands, we are constantly experiencing different levels of awareness intensity without realizing it. We often "feel" our awareness levels change, but are so used to these different focusings taking place that we sort of ride them out unconsciously. Convinced that we are a separate "thing" *in* consciousness, a "something" residing in the head, we live *as if* the conscious self and the body are two different things.

This is not so, says Roberts. The unconscious is "the root level of physiological functioning" for the whole system. We do not *have* a body, we *are* a body. The mind's ability to "bend on itself" in terms of self-awareness is possible only because consciousness is rooted in physiological unconsciousness. In this sense self-awareness does not depend on our actually being conscious of self, for it is a characteristic of the mind-body relationship that when self-awareness is required it appears when summoned just as Susan Blackmore suggests. But not because it has no existence prior to that summons as she contends. If self-awareness did not in some sense exist unconsciously prior to its summons, *we would be incapable of self-directing behavior when it wasn't around.* Hence the stability of perception we so thoughtlessly enjoy whatever the circumstances.

Bernadette Roberts has written extensively on the problem of the self in relation to contemplative experience, and it would greatly benefit those involved in consciousness studies to take a closer look at her theoretically sophisticated arguments. What she has to offer is not, as some may think, introspective guesswork laced with religious preconceptions; it is a first-hand assessment of consciousness offered with an unusual level of academic clarity. What she has to say allows us insights into the mechanisms of self that the intellectual approach finds difficult to match. The intellectual assumption is, as we saw with Don Cupitt, that we cannot know anything about self or consciousness (or anything for that matter) beyond the confines of language, but if what produces language (the conscious mind) is itself rooted in unconsciousness, then something a little more complicated than that is going on. And as correct as Susan Blackmore is in her assertion that it is only because we look for self that we find self to exist, this too could be said to overlook the vital role played by the unconscious in the puzzle of self-awareness and self-continuity. Blackmore's recognition of the multiple physiological processes underpinning self-awareness do not emerge in the same light as Bernadette Roberts' view of the same processes. In Roberts' scheme these blind processes of the body constitute, in aggregate, the unconscious mind within which the conscious mind is rooted, and without which it could not function as an awareness system. Self, in this sense, is essentially a physiological system capable of multiple focusings, or intensities, topped by an evolutionary ability to perceptually double back on itself. We did not always have this ability, and if Bernadette Roberts can be trusted, as I think she can, then there is the distinct possibility of developing a whole new system of awareness to take its place.

Revisiting the God Beyond God 15.2

There is a "knowing" self, and there is a "feeling" self, and in spite of their being so different they constitute one system of awareness. If robbed of the knowing self, the feeling self would cease to exist, and conversely, if robbed of the feeling self, the knowing self would cease to exist. Why? Because the feeling self, rooted as it is in the unconscious, is what the knowing self is embedded in – you simply can't get rid of one without disabling the other.[20] As previously pointed out, we are an experiential unity that cannot be broken apart without disastrous consequences. But we can function *as if* broken apart, and can believe that this is how it ought to be. Feelings are all very well, we may say, but they have a tendency to backfire on us. Get too emotionally involved with something and the chances are you'll make a mess of it. And so we work toward developing the clinical approach, the emotionally drained response, the carefully constructed sentence, research paper or book that heralds objectivity over subjectivity. In this sense, loss of the subjective self is a holding of that self at bay so that we can function without subjective interference. At least that's the theory as conceived by those wishing to avoid the accusation of being subjectively unreliable. Seriousness of intent is to be measured by our calm, unruffled demeanor, the quality of our work by its equally staid and starchy appearance on the page. This is the knowing self in full flight, and its disdain for the feeling self sometimes reaches the level of a fetish.

As we saw at 3.3, however, emotion and feeling constitute two poles of our affective life, one evaluative, the other reactive. Emotion in the service of evaluative feeling is a positive, not a negative, experience, whereas emotion in the purely reactive sense is always potentially disruptive. In the first instance, an overly emotional life is obviously not the best way to go. You may struggle through, but the chances are you'll be beset with problems that waste precious time and effort. The manner in which we hold and execute our ideas signifies the manner in which we evaluate ideas and experience, and this, too, breaks down into roughly three categories: (1) Those whose ideas are deeply influenced by, perhaps even formed by, their emotionally intense natures; (2) those who lack or scorn emotion and rely on logic and rational thought to the exclusion even of feelings that suggest an alternative course; and (3) those whose natures are in greater balance with regard to emotion and rationality. No one is of course stuck in one or other of these categories; we are all of us liable to slip and slide between them from time to time. But when sailing along we do tend to exhibit more of one category than the other, and become known among friends and enemies for our particular personality mix. But there is a fourth category of individual, and they are highly unusual in that they can tap directly into the treasure chest of their psychophysical natures via the meditative or contemplative process. Bernadette Roberts is such an individual.

Roberts has however suffered the penalty of being gravely misunderstood by her religious peers. Classified as mentally unfit by some, she has by others been pronounced mentally deluded, intellectually incompetent, illiterate, ignorant of the available classics and lacking in formal knowledge of the path. Having read her books with some care, I personally have come to exactly the opposite conclusion. What this extraordinary woman has to offer is both relevant and pertinent to the human condition as presently understood, and may in time prove to be seminal in our understanding of what a religious life can mean beyond the confines of belief and dogma. Not only is she highly literate, she has had experiences that help authenticate the challenging approach to religious matters taken by both Jacob Needleman and his mentor Father Sylvan.

This is particularly evident in what Roberts has to say about God. "Nothing," she tells us, "rises to the conscious level that is not first on the unconscious level of consciousness" – not even God. Even the experience of being united with God is rooted in the unconscious. Then comes a Needlemanesque statement with a twist:

> Because its deepest nature and experience is unknown some people identify self or consciousness as the mystery of the divine, or identify it AS the divine... Thus, for example, we believe our experience OF the divine to BE the divine when, in fact, what we experience is the unconscious responding to the divine.[21]

Which is to say that what we experience in such a moment is ourselves having an experience that eclipses any previous experience. Hence Needleman's take on this in terms of Christians seeking not God through prayer and meditation, but *their own presence as such.* This presence is the unconscious self in Roberts' contemplative scheme; it is US experiencing our own reality at the *affective deep end* of consciousness. This is not God, but in Roberts' overview it is the route to God.

Imagine the problems that can arise for the religiously minded if this situation is misread? Interpreting their experience of the unconscious self's highly charged presence in contemplative prayer as a visitation from God, such individuals could only too easily be seduced into thinking that this experience of their own deep reality authenticated their particular religious viewpoint. In this sense verification of a belief system would arise, but it would rest on a subtle misinterpretation of psychophysical events, not on some form of divine communication. Similarly, in interpreting this event in such a manner, the experiencer would miss out on the realization that their own psychophysical presence was, if intercepted, a life-transforming experience in its own right, and one through which an even greater experience of reality could be had. Blown away by this experience they might be, but they would nevertheless be in a state of ignorance concerning processes that could lead to all kinds of religious nonsense at the conscious level. The whispering God of Protestant evangelicals and fundamentalists can be downright problematical in terms of society's hard-fought-for freedoms, but the intuited approval of the Catholic God can also lead to bizarre theological claims and pronouncements. Add to this the heavily censored contemplative literature that has been handed down to us, and the courage required by experienced contemplatives to shrug off the Church's restrictive influence becomes self-evident.

Self *as* presence is, for Roberts, the experience of life and being, which together with the reflexive mechanism or knowing self (the "I-think") composes the whole of consciousness and the entire self-experience.[22] At the surface level of consciousness where we dip or dive in engagement with thought, fantasy or imagination, the feeling self is termed "ego" due to its preoccupation with its own needs and wants, whereas at the deep end of awareness the self is referred to as the "true self" (Kotoh) because of its maturity in such matters. From out of this mature self comes our definition of God as being beyond description and definition (the God beyond God), for in its maturity this unconscious, affectively concentrated self knows that it itself has to fall away in preparation for something that is beyond the propositional self's ability to grasp or describe. And so we face the conundrum of an experience that is not an experience, for the God beyond God cannot by definition be grasped in terms of an experiencing self. As indicated by Father Sylvan, self has to be abandoned at some point. Why? Because it is composed of experience (reflexive consciousness), and as such cannot continue to exist in a non-experiential space. Hence the non-propositional nature of advanced mystical statements – if not composed of experience as it is generally understood, what else can they be but non-propositional!

We exist mostly at the conscious level without any sense of ourselves as a self, but the backgrounding haze of feeling that we carry with us is in fact the unconscious self's aura of existence, a sense of something that becomes known when we pay attention to it. Bending the mind back on itself and sustaining the condition that arises is what the whole religious quest is about –

it is about us being regularly resurrected in and to our own minds. We are not biological machines devoid of intrinsic meaning; we are psychophysical beings with a capacity to wrest ourselves out of mechanicalness and conformity and experience ourselves as limitless depth. There is, however, a limit to how much limitlessness we can take on board. There is a point where subject and object converge, a focal point of the mind where, with practice, we can slip into other dimensions of experience, but in the final analysis we have to leave such dimensions far behind. Through the still point at the center of the affective system we have to go, and when this happens the self as known and understood is faced with its greatest challenge, the challenge of a final letting go of everything it is. In this sense the self dies to itself and is reborn as a contentless seeing that infiltrates every level of perception.[23]

The Evolutionary Puzzle 15.3

Thomas Merton was encouraged by a Hindu friend to study the Catholic mystics. As a result of exhaustive studies in Christian mysticism, he then turned to the Eastern contemplative tradition, and after a while made Zen the focal point of his research. As with Father Keating, Merton was aware of how Christianity's contemplative tradition had suffered historically at the hands of those engaged in the practicalities of the faith, and he came to the opinion that Zen practice might offer a way out of this dilemma. This becomes evident in his book *Zen and the Birds of Appetite* where he says: "The real drive of Buddhism is toward an enlightenment which is precisely a breakthrough into what is beyond system, beyond culture and social structure, and beyond religious rite and belief."[24] This is an important observation; it helps define what it was Merton saw in Zen. This was not a Christian selling out to Buddhism; it was a Christian recognizing the vital elements missing in his own faith. Buddhist meditational practice, he realized, could be used as a tool to reintroduce the Christian mind to contemplative prayer beyond the restrictions of belief and dogma, but the old scholastic distinction between "grace" and "nature" was nevertheless still operative for Merton. Grace in terms of God's responsiveness to his creatures remained uppermost in Merton's mind. The Oriental approach was, for him, fundamentally utilitarian by contrast; it was a system designed to help free the mind from distraction, and as such was the highest contribution human nature could make to the spiritual life – the rest was up to God. For precisely this reason there was no God in Zen Buddhism. Christianity, on the other hand, was a revelation that by its very nature united the human and the divine in and through Christ's life and teachings. Hence the mystery of Christ's double nature in the New Testament – he was, in a sense, *us in potentia*. There was little danger in grafting Zen practice onto Christian practice, for Zen was not a religion; it was a psychological system designed to get the best possible result out of human consciousness. And so Merton was able to say:

> Buddhist meditation, but above all that of Zen, seeks not to *explain* but to *pay attention,* to *become aware,* to be *mindful,* in other words to develop a certain *kind of consciousness that is above and beyond deception* by verbal formulas – or by emotional excitement.[25]

Thomas Merton's thinking seems to support Professor Zaehner's concern with what it is the contemplative ends up uniting with. God and Ultimate Reality are not the same thing for Zaehner; there is an intrinsic difference between those experiences that only Christianity can explain. So the question has to be: What does a Buddhist or Hindu unite with if it isn't, in the end, the Christian God? The answer to this question is *something beyond the doctrinally constructed idea of God.* Zaehner is correct in his assumption that Buddhists and Hindus do not unite with the

Christian God; what he fails to understand is that neither do Christian contemplatives following the *via negativa* path. The Absolute, or Ultimate Reality is no different from the God beyond God experienced by Bernadette Roberts or Meister Eckhart. It is merely a quirk of the Christian imagination that it thinks its definition of Ultimate Reality superior to any other definition of Ultimate Reality. Christianity's claim that Jesus the Jewish teacher was actually the Second Person in a Divine Trinity of which Israel's God was both part and whole is a gross misreading of contemplative experience. Given his Jewish identity, Jesus' statement "I and the Father are one" was hardly likely to have been his way of saying that he was, in some incomprehensible sense, Israel's God shoehorned into a human body; it was an Eckhartian-type statement that drives us to reconsider what was going on in this extraordinary man's life.

One of the throwaway lines in Bernadette Roberts' introduction to *What is Self?* stopped me in my tracks. On having said that we cannot know what is missing from the mystical literature in terms of the no-self event, she goes on to say: "This does not mean that millions of people have not come upon the no-self event; indeed, sooner or later everyone will do so."[26] What exactly did she mean by that, I wondered. Did that statement not unravel the *salvation by vicarious sacrifice* premise underlying Christian belief? And who were these millions who had probably experienced the no-self event already? Why hadn't we heard of them? And if everyone was going to have such an experience *sooner or later,* what did that mean in terms of what the Church was presently teaching?

I realized immediately that what Roberts was saying, in a veiled kind of way, was that experiences of no-self were in fact taking place across the world's societies, but that that hadn't been realized yet, indeed, that she was one of the first (in our time) to speak up and fully describe such a condition, and that others would follow. And in relation to mystics of the past not mentioning the no-self event (apart from Eckhart), the reason for that had been fear of censure from the Church's spiritual directors. The theology governing mystical experience had, in relation to inflexible doctrines and the later rise of the Inquisition, stifled any chance of a more advanced teaching reaching the public ear, and that, in a modern context, was still the case. It was not then a matter of Roberts having been singled out for censure by her religious peers; it was a matter of that having been the way things had been handled for centuries. As noted by Erich Neumann in his essay "Mystical Man", any mysticism consisting of dogmatically defined contents is either low-level mysticism, disguised mysticism or mysticism intellectualized by others after the event (see 7.5). Mystics of advanced experience are prone to break out of the conventional religious mold, not because they are closet social revolutionaries, or heretics in the making, but because they have entered a new, dynamic relationship with truth *as* being.

16: Dying Like a Dirty Dog

...the best word would be awareness, that is, a consciousness which is not linked to language, to the functioning of the computer, but to presence. Certainly, one could also say that awareness is linked to the mind, but in such a case, surely, this refers to another mind. In it, there is a meeting with the heart, with the domain of the soul, of the emotions, but in this case distinct from the soup of projections, repulsions, and attachments. It is of the same domain, but much higher and, at this point, there no longer exists a perceptible difference between the higher "psyche" and this higher "mind". The two aspects are very linked and perhaps identical.
Jerzy Grotowski
A Kind of Volcano[1]

Intro: 16.0

Jerzy Grotowski's radical explorations of the meaning of theatre are widely known in theatrical circles, his Stanislavski-influenced conclusions often identical to those advanced by the Armenian philosopher G.I. Gurdjieff. Before exploring some of these conclusions, Grotowski's view of what conscious awareness is in itself should be considered, for in suggesting (as he does in the above quote) that awareness is not linked to language, but to the body's mind (heart, soul, presence, etc) Grotowski breaks with the tradition in which language is our only means of knowing that we know something. In his interpretation of consciousness and its workings, language itself is identified as the mind's computer, not the unconscious mind as presumed by Poincare and many a neuroscientist. Poincare's conception of the unconscious as a "mixing machine in the basement" is replaced by language functioning like a computer program, a program that sifts the essence of thought within the confining rules of grammar and syntax, so automatically limiting it. Attended by awareness, language can then be described as manufacturing language out of itself by way of an associative juggling. That is its functional limit, however; it is not in itself the root cause of our ability to think. Reduce or extinguish the influence of language in consciousness through meditation or contemplation (self-talking in particular), and another dimension of the self begins to form, an experience of self quite different from the one we are accustomed to.

What we generally do is conceive of something *then* clarify its meaning through the words we choose. We in other words test bits of language against other bits until some level of clarity is achieved – particularly in writing. It is this stumbling and sometimes incoherent process that leaves the impression that everything belongs to language, when in fact what we started with belongs to a much deeper level of coherence, a deeply subtle level where psyche works alongside language and informs language of its next optimum move. But we can of course get caught up in the act of manufacturing language out of language and ignore the promptings of psyche. We can get distracted (seduced?) by the logic of language, and end up with meanings estranged from their psychophysical base. This need not lead to an immediate debacle of thought, but if it becomes a habit then that will almost certainly be the case. Why? Because language-dependent concepts endlessly pursued lead us into a linguistic desert, a dry, lifeless place of the mind where inspiration and insight give way to feats of linguistic gymnastics. This is the tormenting of language Don Cupitt unfairly attributes to mystical expression, and the same reasoning can be applied to mathematics and philosophy when the somatic element is all but missing.

The aware conscious mind does not think in language, or math, it expresses its realizations *through* language or math. In this sense the unconscious mind takes on a significance not generally attributed to it, namely, that within which there is a meeting with the heart, with the domain of the soul, of the emotions. This is in contrast to the conscious mind's tendency to indulge in raw logic, in addition-like knowings that breed situations of conflict linked to the "soup of projections, repulsions, and attachments" belonging to the personality. The unconscious mind is our "other" mind, the one within which we *move and have our being* but tend to denigrate as "un" because it functions contrary to how everything known is conceived to have become known. For Don Cupitt, this is a non-argument; there is only one way to know anything, and that is through language representations, the rest is by definition psychic mush. To my way of thinking that is to overlook the role of evaluative feeling (see 3.4) in thought and ignore its pretty obvious role as that which backgrounds comprehension. There is no doubting how powerful language is, but the belief that only language can carry meaning is a false conclusion. We "think" *in a marrow bone,* to borrow W.B. Yeats' lovely phrase. To think otherwise is to ignore the psychophysical nature of thought; the fact that thought in its primary stage grows into language, not out of language. In its primary, undifferentiated state, thoughts haunt and tantalize us with the weight of their presence, a psychic weightiness that drives us to express in language what we sense and feel forming in psyche. In speech we blurt our thoughts out into the world *through* grammar and syntax without awareness as to how they arose, and when writing spend most of our time struggling to express what we sense ourselves to already know. And if by chance we get stuck and attempt to wrestle meanings out of psyche by sheer force of will, then we invariably end up with a big fat nothing for our efforts. Forced by the nature of psyche to wait on the good auspices of psyche as it realigns awareness with psychophysical reality, we have little option but to submit to the sheer magic of interior processes.

I will be accused of subjectivism by some for daring to say what I've just said about language and meaning, never mind many of the other things said about psyche and body throughout this book. So be it. The barriers put up to thinking like this are beginning to come down, and philosophers like Jacob Needleman, R.K. Forman, Bruce Mangan, Jordan Zlatev and the psychologist's Benny Shanon and James Hillman (to name but a few) are leading the charge towards a more experientially based appreciation of psyche. Self-reflectivity is now part of the push towards an informed scientific investigation of consciousness (Schwitzgebel/Blackmore), and you can't get anything more basic than a re-evaluation of how meaning arises in the mind. Get that right and just about everything to do with consciousness falls into place. Get it wrong and we end up with a skewed comprehension of what it means to be a human being. Meaning stranded in language leaves us with a meaningless subjectivity and a truncated understanding of self. If all we can know is what's known in language, then we are governed by the very obvious limitations of language and incapable of ever venturing beyond linguistic constructions.[2]

But this is not the case. Language itself gives way to intimations that stretch beyond the horizon of language; we are forever straining at the linguistic leash, and do sometimes break free. Great poetry is a breaking free. Great literature carries us into the depths of the human psyche as it battles with life and death. Great mathematics opens before us vertiginous vistas of space and time. In sleep we cast aside the restraints of logic and experience psyche in the raw, and in meditation or contemplation we probe to the very heart of what it means to be human and emerge transformed in attitude if nothing else. But it is in our relationships that the most insightful moments occur, for it is there in the daily tussle between minds that we see ourselves reflected in our entirety. Mystical experience may afford us glimpses of another dimension, but it is our experience of each other that affords us, moment by moment, the chance to see ourselves as others see us. The question is, what do we see when we look at ourselves in this way?

Sleepwalkers Awake! 16.1

If George Ivanovitch Gurdjieff gave the world anything of value, it was a system of ideas whereby human beings could intentionally witness their own state of mind in the behavior of others, and in how they themselves behaved in relation to others. Throughout this book I have explored the tendency we have to disappear into consciously engaged thought, and through the writings of Jacob Needleman, Father Sylvan and others have moved towards the realization that this is a serious matter. So serious, in fact, that to not be aware of it is to be without proper bearing in terms of how to behave, think, or feel. Usurped by thought and deed, we surface only occasionally during any given hour, and may remain submerged for hours, indeed days at a time. Moving impulsively from one thought to another, from one deed to another, we resemble sleepwalkers in our actions and reactions. We are awake and aware to the extent that we are not asleep and in bed, but we are not intrinsically awake and aware (real to ourselves) as we sometimes find ourselves to be. In moments of real awareness we exchange our usurped conscious state for a sense of self that is immediate, a *thereness* of the self that can leave us feeling vulnerable and uncertain. Or elated. It depends greatly on what triggers the experience, on how we are *way down deep* in ourselves. Conversely, we can experience ourselves as being so near to the surface of what we are that nothing seems to be of the slightest importance. In such moments we are empty of self in a manner that is existentially dangerous, possibly suicidal. So it can be said that loss of self as an experience lies at both ends of the awareness spectrum, and that depending on the end experienced this loss can lead either to insight or despair.

Gurdjieff plays an important role in Jerzy Grotowski's scheme of things because this man of the theatre discovered for himself important aspects of Gurdjieff's thinking through theatre and what it takes to be an actor of substance. This is not surprising, for Gurdjieff, too, was a man of the theatre; he saw all human beings as involved in role-playing, and used actual stage performances (sacred dances and movement configurations) to get his ideas across *as* experiences. He was also recognized as an actor in his own right because of intentionally wrought behavior designed to impart aspects of his system beyond the confines of language. Aware of how predictable human beings are in their reactions, he set out to destroy the automatic thinking responses of those around him through situations that embarrassed and sometimes alarmed those attempting to work with him. This earned for Gurdjieff the reputation of being a bit of a madman, and caused not a few to regard him as mentally unstable. As it is the chief desire of most of us to appear sane and sensible, Gurdjieff's willingness to suffer the bad opinion of others for a greater purpose speaks of someone within whom the usual requirements of ego had perhaps been brought under conscious control. But more than that even, for he was also pushing Evagrius' *apatheia* (the intermediate state) to new heights in the sense of creating that subtle form of suffering in the psyches of those around him. So powerful was this form of instruction that even those who knew what he was up to could not escape the pain of such situations. In relation to the originality of Gurdjieff's approach, Grotowski's own words are revealing:

> There, all at once, appeared a person who brought a rigorous practice and a rigorous research. I mean it when I say research. For me, there is a very strong element of research. It is not like implanting a branch of the ancient tradition; it is also, on the same level, contemporary. After all, the traditions are only founded in this way.[3]

What Gurdjieff was up to went far beyond the instilling of some ancient system into those who worked with him; it was also an attempt to extend and refine what was already known about that system through ongoing experience and an examination of first principles. The temptation to engineer that knowledge into a system that could be learned, like a foreign language, was anathema to Gurdjieff; it had to be conveyed through hands-on work on oneself, a confronting of what we were at the deepest levels of being. In *The Heart of Buddhism,* Guy Claxton sums up this situation rather well:

> The function of much teaching and instruction is to try to speed things up by giving you hints and clues as to where to look and what it is you are looking for. But the danger with this, of course, is that, if you are prompted too much, you may get too fixed an idea of what it is you are supposed to be seeing, and see your idea, rather that what is really there.[4]

For this reason Grotowski says that P.D. Ouspensky's great work on the Gurdjieff system, *In Search of the Miraculous,* is both useful and potentially destructive because it is too clear by half. Clarity is all very well (see 14.4), but too much clarity leads to a false security, the security of thinking that believing something is the same as experiencing something. Caught up in the dream of believing that we are awake because involved with ideas about being awake, we fail to notice the difference between belief and experience and die, to put it in Gurdjieff's confronting language, *like a dirty dog.* Or, in Meister Eckhart's equally brutal words, *rot with the body* because we do not have the power *to do.* There has to be a substantial accumulation of the energy (tonos) of attention for real change to be possible, and because of our natures and the mechanics of perception we are deficient in our ability to accrue this energy. This, too, was the core of Father Sylvan's thinking: without an accruing of the energies that accompanied sustained acts of awareness no new entity can form within us. To accept that this entity continues after death is neither here nor there; what matters is our awareness of the huge difference sustained acts of attention make to the quality of our responses. Gurdjieff avoided questions at the theoretical level; he asked them at the practical level of everyday experience and interaction. It is in the rough and tumble of everyday life that work on oneself begins, not just in the organizing of one's ideas into a coherent and satisfying form, or system.

My reason for leaving Gurdjieff's system of ideas to the very end of this book is because there is a plethora of books on Gurdjieff already available, and another book solely about his ideas would offer only a rehash of the questions and answers he posed. Hence our journey into so many highways and byways of thought and research. I wanted to illustrate as fully as possible the nature of the problem facing us as human beings, the problem of what consciousness is in itself. That is the question bothering everyone at present. We are, it seems, a problem waiting to be solved, a problem Christianity thought it had solved a long time ago, only to discover that its answers were not as clear-cut as it had assumed. We are, on one level, more than we seem, and on another less that we hoped we were. Gifted in that we can know what the animal kingdom seems incapable of knowing, we are at the same time blind to the fact that our engagement with knowing robs us of the next level of knowing, that of mind freed from its engagement with knowing through signs and ciphers alone. There's nothing wrong with knowing, or with attempting to know, but there is something deeply problematical when that engagement usurps the whole mental landscape.

When that happens our humanity progressively leaks away and the result is a blind automaton who gets around by radar. We do awaken to ourselves every so often, but it is the equivalent of someone awakening from a sedative-induced coma – no sooner are we awake than we are comatose again. We may do the right thing, say the right thing, even think the right thing, but it's all hit and miss and done inside a dream-like state of awareness that only a shock can awaken us from. And that's the rub. As we're all in the same boat there's little chance of anything other than grief, pain, psychological suffering or the threat of death acting as the shock we require. Anything less leaves us blissfully unaware of our predicament. Hence the power of Christianity's crucified Christ; he is a rude, crude awakener for many within whom the Question of existence has arisen. Such individuals sense that this man was properly awake and aware, and that makes them question the quality of their own awareness in terms of moral behavior. But as we saw earlier, moral issues in terms of our being good are not what this puzzle is about, and neither is it about using Christ as a shield against a God angry with us over moral issues; it is about our inability to embrace real change in our lives because our awareness level is calibrated to only one focal level. There are numerous awareness levels available to us, but we are far too involved in thought and action to try them out. Religion, as we know it, is undoubtedly helpful to those for whom questions of being or not being are meaningless, but that does not excuse our religious institutions from not facing up to their own meager grasp of spiritual reality.

Jacob Needleman cuts to the heart of this matter when he asked if we can hear the voice of conscience speaking within us. This was Gurdjieff's question, and it had nothing to do with moral injunctions. And neither had it anything to do with the voice of our social conditioning. Conscience was not the voice of parent, teacher, clergyman or policeman whispering in our ear, nor was it the voice of Christianity's tripartite God instructing us personally from some unknown dimension. It was, rather, "the feeling of the whole truth in any situation" surfacing within us as a friction between our deep-seated sense of truth and our automated natures – we were awake, and the gift of being awake was the gaining of real conscience. It was conscience alone that had to be awakened. Discover real conscience and morality and ethics took care of themselves. So also with the attempt to teach "love", "hope" and "faith". Such attributes were impossible possibilities until the intermediate state was established. We had to open up to the intermediate state of being, and that meant opening up to the force of conscience as it arose in our awakening minds.[5] To consciously awaken was to undergo intrinsic change at the center of being, it was to wake up into a new mind and perceive things in an entirely new way. And in waking up what did we see? We saw that Christ had been turned into a monster because of our emotions and conditioning and had to be chased out of our minds.[6] Only with the arising of real conscience could he be allowed re-entry, and real conscience was the psychological friction experienced by mind as it glimpsed itself slipping constantly into unaware responses. With reference to Jacob Needleman's book *Lost Christianity,* Archbishop Rowan Williams picks up on this theme when he says, "Authentic religious... practice begins in the attempt to attend to the moment of self-questioning – to refuse to cover over, evade or explain the pain and shock of whatever brings the self into question, to hold on to the difficulty before the almost inevitable descent into pathos and the personal drama begins."[7]

Three Centers of Perception 16.2

To help us with the problem of conscience, Gurdjieff postulated three centers of perception: (1) the thinking center; (2) the emotional center; and (3) the moving-instinctive center. It is through these centers that we perceive, think or move in any given moment of time. In our consciously engaged state of mind we are unaware of the functioning of these centers, and equally unaware of our perceptions being organized and filtered through what Gurdjieff called the "formatory apparatus", the mechanical functioning of the mind that organizes all physical and mental experiences as they occur. Place this alongside Grotowski's idea of language functioning as a computer program in its own right, and "formatory apparatus" begins to make sense – it aptly describes our perceptions of self, other and world as being under the control of automatic processes difficult to detect, and equally difficult to bring under conscious control. As each center is said to perceive only one aspect of reality, and we perceive reality through only one center at a time (thinking, feeling or organic sensation), we end up with a truncated comprehension of reality that can be righted only through an *intentional spreading of attention into those other centers.* Needleman puts it like this:

> … the body needs to be penetrated by a quality of attention that is quite distinct from the mainly intellectual function which we usually designate by 'mind'.[8]

If, however, this penetration of the body by attention does not take place, then we are at the mercy of the center that happens to be in control. We are, therefore, not just half the person we ought to be, we are only one-third the person we ought to be in terms of the center we happen to be functioning through. We're either *all* mind ("intellect") or all feeling ("emotion") or all sensation ("body"), but hardly ever a conscious mixture of all three. That is perhaps the deadly fascination drug addiction has for us; it allows us a glimpse of reality not generally experienced, and it is such a revelation some of us are willing to slowly die to repeat it. At the most basic of levels a single cigarette can change the consciousness of an addict, and alcohol and sex can become addictive for the same reason. Even intellectual matters can become addictive in the sense of an over-dependence on verbal schemes.

So what to do? How can we escape the dictates of our own natures as they have evolved? And what does this say about Christianity's spiritual premise? If the penetration of attention into the body can bring about a radical transformation of what we are and what we perceive, and this was well understood and practiced by Christians in the early days of the faith (witness the core realizations of Evagrius and the desert Fathers), then how are we to evaluate that faith's evolution when dependence on vicarious sacrifice has turned its original contemplative genius into a theological excuse for us to stay exactly as we are? For that, in essence, is what Christianity offers the world: the ability to legitimately ignore the deep-seated knowing that moments of real awareness afford. Don't you dare question the Christian plan of salvation, or cast doubt on whether Jesus walked on water or fed five thousand with the contents of someone's lunch box. Salvation comes to those who believe, then believe some more. It is the experience of *believing without question in what you've been taught to believe* that saves you from the wrath of God, not some philosophically obscure notion about truth being allied to the experience of being. But hang on a minute. The wrath of what? God? Does this mean that God too is emotionally unstable, that he is liable to react in unpredictable ways? Is that why we need Jesus? Would God destroy us all if left to his own devices?

In terms of conscience, what we're talking about here is not some kind of mental struggle in the sense of trying to be good and avoiding bad behavior. That's not it at all. That's bootstrap conscience, and it belongs to anyone within whom attention has not, to some degree, been developed. Yes, there is a struggle involved, but it has nothing to do with sin, guilt or fear; it has to do with *impulses recognized for what they are as they arise.* It is a state of attention within which we sense (because we are momentarily awake) an impulse toward behavior that could be problematical and manage to deal with it before it takes hold. If we don't, then like everyone else we have to ride it through until the energy of the impulse dissipates. *That* is conscience at work, and it is altogether different from what an engaged mind does when confronted with the same impulse. When we are engaged in (mesmerized by?) mental or physical activity, habit tends to rule the roost – we are at the mercy of ingrained patterns of behavior. When not so engaged the slide into habitualized responses is less likely. So what we're doing battle with is the impulse to go along with behaviors triggered into existence by a host of subtle, and sometimes not so subtle, urges of a well-established nature. Such urges can, on occasions, be conquered through mental stubbornness reinforced by prayer or New Age affirmations, but few individuals are capable of sustaining that kind of control, and when their steely resolve fails the result is generally catastrophic. Father Sylvan puts it like this:

> The most dangerous people... are those who have achieved inner being without the corresponding development of soul.[9]

And again:

> Man must reverse the... dispersal of the soul by drawing unto himself the attention which he unnecessarily gives to his thoughts, emotional reactions and sensations, and which results in the deformation and distortion of the entire human organism, to the extent that he has fallen to the level of a sick animal. This work is the basis of religious asceticism and is the authentic meaning of religious morality.[10]

The dispersal of the soul refers to the losing of soul through an inability to accumulate the energy of attention. We in other words fail to withdraw attention from mental and emotional experience and suffer the consequences of being continually overpowered by such experiences – we have the habit of feeding them and don't know how to stop. For those who achieve a sense of inner being through moral uprightness alone, their morality is by definition bigger than their soul in the sense that they have invested all their energies in the idea of moral uprightness at the expense of the energies they ought to have accumulated. They will achieve much in pursuing this path (moral uprightness seems to confirm the claims of faith), but as these powerful energies are still attached to submerged and engaged conscious minds, and to emotionally governed natures, the result is religious leaders or charismatic personalities who at the flick of an eye can exhibit unexpected tendencies. Hence Father Sylvan's observation that these "men of salvation walk the earth like explosive devices ready to be set off at random." This is "mysticism without a soul," he tells us,[11] and according to Needleman it can lead to religious fervor (the "caricature of love") and to fear, hatred and violence. Orthodoxy has a role to play in society, but on its own it offers a system of moral idealism and belief that in itself is not enough in terms of personal transformation. Christ may be held up as the example we ought to follow, but the meaning of Christ's life and death have been trumped by a theology of dependence that leaves the individual existentially bankrupt.

For Jerzy Grotowski, P.D. Ouspensky suffered from the problem of being too clear in his breakdown of Gurdjieff's ideas, but as we shall see, a certain degree of clarity is necessary when dealing with the challenges that system of thought represents. Misunderstand attention and everything falls in a heap. Whatever one thinks of our having three centers of perception, it is the idea of attention being ultra-important that makes Gurdjieff's ideas unique – unique to the extent that Father Sylvan relies on them to explain the relevance of contemplative practice for the modern world. So also the philosopher Jacob Needleman who, as co-editor of *Gurdjieff, Essays and Reflections on the Man and His Teachings,* tells us in the introduction that Gurdjieff's diagnosis of the human condition "integrates psychological, social, cultural, and ontological approaches to life."[12] The surgeon Kenneth Walker (see 1.4) was no less certain as to Gurdjieff's importance, for on meeting with P.D. Ouspensky in 1923 he spoke of stumbling into Gurdjieff's ideas and described them as capable of "taking possession of us and of propelling us in a direction in which, at the beginning, we had no desire to go."[13] Likewise Jerzy Grotowski whose radical explorations of the meaning of theatre splice almost seamlessly into the Gurdjieffian perspective of what makes a human being human. And as I discovered when reading the book of essays on Gurdjieff edited by Needleman and George Baker, many others were of the same opinion. Peter Brook, director of the International Centre of Theatre Research in Paris, had, like Grotowski, come under the sway of Gurdjieffian thought, as had Henry Leroy Finch, philosopher and Wittgenstein authority. Also Roger Lipsey, historian of art and classical literature; Basarab Nicolescu, theoretical physicist and specialist in the theory of elementary particles; Ravi Ravindra, professor of physics and comparative religion; Robin Skynner, psychiatrist and pioneer in the development of family and group therapy in England; and last but not least Charles Tart, professor of transpersonal psychology. This varied collection of individuals had given the Gurdjieffian scheme a firm nod of approval, and their reason for doing so rested mainly on one thing: the discipline of *self-remembering* as taught by Gurdjieff to Ouspensky, and through Ouspensky's seminal book *In Search of the Miraculous* to a host of others across the planet since 1949. So maybe Bernadette Roberts wasn't far off the mark when she suggested that there were millions of people out there who had, like herself, experienced the depths of being, and that eventually all human beings would experience what she had experienced. In an evolutionary sense we were perhaps on the cusp of another huge change in perception of self, other and world, a change already well established, although not yet self-evident.[14]

The Skill of Self-Remembering 16.3

Those familiar with Gurdjieff's ideas may think the word "skill" in this context inappropriate, but I think it has its place, particularly as Ouspensky himself refers to self-remembering as a "deliberate" act.[15] If something is deliberate, it is intentional, and if it is intentional it is brought about by an act of will. We may not have a developed will, but we are not exactly will-less. As self-remembering is, in its early stages, an extremely difficult thing for many people to grasp, it takes an active will to set it in motion *as an experience*, that is, it takes conscious effort to start the wheel of awareness turning. Once that wheel is set in motion, however, everything changes, for self-awareness then becomes part of a loop in the conscious mind that can spring into action when least expected. But there's a problem here, and it has to do with how we interpret "self-awareness", for becoming self-aware is something we all experience from time to time, and that, strictly speaking, is not self-remembering in the sense that Gurdjieff taught. Self-awareness and self-remembering are different experiences; there is without doubt self-awareness *in* self-remembering, but there need not be, and seldom is, any level of self-remembering in a moment of self-awareness. Why? Because self-awareness as an experience is by definition mono-directional, that is, it is reflective of the self alone, whereas self-remembering incorporates the context within which self-awareness takes place *alongside the experience of self-awareness*. In this sense self-remembering is duo-directional, not mono-directional, and it is this fundamental factor that makes it into the problem many people experience when experimenting with it. To get around this problem, Ouspensky produced this simple diagram:

I —————————————> the observed phenomenon.

and

I <————————————— the observed phenomenon.

This intimated that self-remembering requires *a division of attention between self and object.* Self-remembering is therefore not just you becoming aware of yourself, it is you becoming aware of yourself *and* what you are looking at or interacting with in the same moment of time. It is a form of double-attention in which two objects of attention are paradoxically attended to simultaneously. Ouspensky's own words confirm this point:

> Having defined this I saw that the problem consisted in directing attention on oneself without weakening or obliterating the attention directed on something else. Moreover, this "something" could as well be within me as outside me.

Hence my interest when I came across Robert Forman's definition of a "pure consciousness event" (see 15.0) as a "dualistic mystical state" (DMS) that gives way to a "unitive mystical state" (UMS). And then more directly still as *an awareness of one's own awareness while simultaneously remaining conscious of thoughts, sensations and actions.*[16] I did a double-take when I read those words, for Forman was articulating something not generally understood in meditational circles. I was also intrigued by his two-tier approach: that a dualistic mystical experience subsequently *gives way to* a unitive mystical experience. The reason for my interest was that a form of awareness capable of going in two directions simultaneously defied the philosophical notion that two objects of attention could exist in the same conscious space in any given moment of time. That seemed to put the mockers on the whole business, except that Forman had come to the same realization I had come to: it was a two-tier process that *resulted* in an experience of mystical unity. First came the intentionally aroused state of two-way attention (the attempt to scan self and object simultaneously), followed by the unity experience in which self and object *appeared* to fuse into one experience. But how did one explain what had happened given that the first tier of this experience had been declared philosophically impossible to attain? Accept that that was the case and one had to admit that it was simply not possible to scan two objects of attention at the same time. And what's more, it could be proved to be so by anyone in two seconds flat. So what was going on?

For myself, the answer to this problem came from experimentation followed by the realization that there was an "as if" in the experience of dualistic scanning *as it is initially experienced.* Choose two external objects of attention, say a book and a flower, or two objects of thought, and the process of double scanning could not be initiated – it was truly impossible except in the most defused sense of looking at a room in which both objects happened to exist. In relation to "self" and "other", however, things were quite different; there were two distinct levels to the experience, and it was only when the first level had been perfected that the second level began to emerge. There was, in relation to self and other as objects of attention, a slow ricochet between the two that became progressively faster with practice, and this resulted in a motion that was so incredibly fast that it seemed *as if* a simultaneous scanning of each had taken place. The first level was that of experiencing the physical self and the other as alternative objects of awareness at growing speed, the second level what appeared to be a momentary fusion of those levels.

The question that arose at this point was this: Why does this fusion result from a mind that loops presence of the physical self into its internal or external perceptions? Is the experience had a mystical experience, is it a reward of some kind gifted by a beneficent universe? Or is there a more mundane explanation? Could it be that the experience of unity had has more to do with the tension set up in psyche than with anything overtly spiritual? The experience would then be the result of a mind that had blown a psychic fuse, not a mind in contact with some transcendental source. Such an explanation tends to take the gloss off such experiences, but it need not be viewed as such, for we have no way of telling how or when the phenomenon of self-consciousness arose, and how those who first experienced consciousness of self reacted to that development. The self-conscious loop would have given a huge advantage to those within whom it first developed.

But what kind of unity experience are we talking about here? Robert Forman's description of a "dualistic mystical experience" suggests a moment in the meditative process when self and other come together as a result of successfully holding in place awareness of one's own awareness alongside whatever one happens to be looking at or dealing with. But that should be understood as a moment prefaced by many such moments that can hypothetically result in a full-blown fusion experience – this is not something that happens once and that's it; it is an ongoing series of experiences that progressively strengthen. There are degrees (qualities or intensities) of the self-other fusion experience to be had, and the *via negativa* experience (contentless seeing) is the beginning of a whole new way of knowing oneself. This is quite different from identification with (being hooked by) internally projected events leading to ecstatic experiences aligned with religious beliefs or experiences of at-oneness with nature; it is an altogether different experience in that it has no emotional content and no doctrinal hook. If the eyes are closed, there may be visual content, but it is content witnessed rather than identified with. The meditator/contemplator is not at the mercy of religious bias or imagination; they are instead open to the mythic level of being where symbols dominate. Having said that, it is possible for someone of a definite religious persuasion to find themselves experiencing something that carries them beyond their religious orientation – in fact if they persist it is almost inevitable. It is at this point that after-the-event interpretations can be placed on the experience to bring it into line with theological expectations. Conformity to religious norms can even bedevil someone who has experienced the depths of psyche.

To suggest that the fusion experience may be the result of the psyche blowing a fuse should not be seen as in any way diminishing the importance of such an experience. Why? Because we don't actually know what blowing a psychic fuse means in this context. The tendency to romanticize such experiences and make them part of some grand spiritual scheme governed by something outside of ourselves is not uncommon, but we may have to lower our sights and accept that most fusion experiences belong to fairly rudimentary, but nevertheless important, levels of meditative experience. There are, in other words, numerous levels of fusion, the final levels being described by people like Meister Eckhart and Bernadette Roberts as unitive on two levels. At the more mundane levels fusion experiences can be described as instances where the mind manages to cast off its constant busyness, and through the conscious attempt to hold self and other in the same perceptual frame of reference, experiences the tiny jolt of becoming momentarily real to itself in the sense that consciousness of the self is an act of cognitive-mentation, not meta-mentation. As we saw at 14.4, cognitive-mentation (awareness) requires us to relate to our own cognitive activities; *it does not involve mentations that take other mentations as objects of observation.* In this sense we are fundamentally free of the philosophical objection cited above: awareness of self is *not awareness of an object in consciousness,* it is, as defined at 11.4 and at the end of 14.4, an experience, not a thing. Or, as J.L. Mehta puts it in Heidegger and Vedanta, "... Being and thinking belong together in a deeper unity (inaccessible to any form of dialectic), from which they both derive their nature and which exhibits itself, while yet concealing itself, as the proper manner of thinking that is no more a grasping, no longer a striving to form a system of concepts for what is beyond conceptualizing."[17]

The discipline of being aware of being aware in conjunction with either internal or external reality is the key to a wholly other kind of mental life, and it can be initiated with a blink of the eye. But it is the sustaining of the condition that arises that is important. Without effort nothing is reciprocated. Reciprocated? I use this loaded term in the sense of a higher system of awareness being switched on. No, sorry, not "switched on", that is a mechanistic way of talking that has no place here. This is not the experience of a switch being thrown; it is the experience of Being registering at ever deeper levels.

There is, however, little reason to call these initial experiences "mystical"; they are the result of little more than a subtle mental game, albeit a game with serious consequences. Ouspensky uses the term "novelty" to describe the deliberate production of such moments,[18] and that just about sums them up. But not quite. For to scan self and other simultaneously is to inadvertently scan the still point of being, and when one consciously accomplishes that there is always the chance one might thread the ontological needle of existence and pop through. When that happens the as-if factor in fusion experiences gives way to a new experience of self and other, an experience that changes sense of self into something altogether different (see 10.2).

17: "In the Blink of an Eye"

It is, at heart, a question of the approach to the feeling of presence – the strange and yet so intimate sensation of closeness, always lost, always near – 'eternal generation', if one dare adopt the expression of Meister Eckhart. According to a holy hadith transmitted by the Prophet... this work of 'becoming aware with all one's presence' needs always to be renewed.[1]

Jacques Choisnel

An Unfinished Creation

17.0

In Christianity's scheme of self-awareness, the individual has a moral role to play, but no actual say in the salvation process as promised by the Church – salvation is a gift, it is not something we achieve. Yes, there is a decision to be made in this regard, but it is one of abdication to a greater power, namely, Jesus in his role as propitious sacrifice. It is Jesus who saves us from ourselves, Jesus who helps us fend off evil, Jesus who stands between us and the God who would otherwise do us harm because of our daily sins *and* our "inherited" sinful nature. The Church is adamant about this sinful nature and has been so for many centuries: we are powerless in ourselves to bring about intrinsic moral change, and that is what the puzzle of salvation through faith in Jesus is all about. Above all, it is about being good. Without Jesus we are doomed to fail because we are morally deficient by way of disposition. If you're not "good", God doesn't want you.

But there are now two distinctly different versions of the Christian faith in operation, and I'm not referring to the difference between Catholic and Protestant theologies. I'm referring to the conservative and liberal camps on both sides of the theological divide, camps in deep disagreement with one another. The conservatives believe in the Jesus story as it has come down to us, the liberals in a greatly modified version of that story. The conservatives continue to view Jesus as the transcendent God's son physically present in the 1st century, the liberals as an extraordinary human being who tried to radically modify the religious perceptions of his time. To the conservative mind Jesus is unsupersedable (there has never been anyone like him on the planet); to the liberal mind he is an individual of great spiritual potency who made an indelible impression on those who encountered him (see 5.3).

This is of course a simplified version of what is actually the case; there are in fact numerous conservative and liberal camps, each with a view of Jesus that is subtly different from the others, but the above differentiation holds reasonably well when discussing the more extreme approaches to Jesus' life and intentions.Why bring this up now? Because it is important to recognize why one might think being aware of one's own awareness is an act of little consequence. Accept the conservative Christian viewpoint and there is little reason to think we have anything to do outside of being good and believing what we're told to believe. Accept the liberal Christian viewpoint and things are not quite so straightforward.

And again we have two camps: the liberal Christian and the non-Christian. The difference this time is that unlike conservative Christians, liberal Christians and non-Christians of sensibility shoulder their moral responsibilities not for fear of God's wrath, but because they want to better relate to their societies, and to one another – the idea of a God capable of punishing an individual for all eternity is simply too absurd a notion for either party to take seriously. The idea of God being in some sense there probably persists for many liberal Christians, but he has undergone a transformation. He is no longer the ogre in the sky from whom Jesus has to protect us; he is that within which everything manifest moves and *has its being*. The old theistic conception of God as a someone who interferes in human history has evaporated for most liberals; he has been jettisoned along with the mythologies that have grown up around this problematical idea.

Some liberal Christians go so far as to question the idea of God altogether; they turn into Christian humanists for whom Christ's extraordinary humanity is the greater revelation. But if the historian Morris Berman is correct in his contention, that paradigm shift is not enough (see 1.0), and Jacob Needleman and Father Sylvan are correct when they call into question our quality of self-awareness, then even the advances of liberal thought over conservative thought may not be sufficient to save us from ourselves. Christianity has had its chance and failed, not because of evil forces overpowering the human mind, or because no one took its message seriously, but because it came to depend on inadequate historical conclusions about Jesus' life and intentions. This set of conclusions has inadvertently helped keep us consciously unconscious, and in doing so they have all but shorn us of the capacity to wake up to that uncomfortable fact.

What has to be admitted, however, is that secularism in the West (that which informs Christian liberalism) has also failed spectacularly on many fronts, and that in spite of the obvious gains had from a robust science and an equally robust democratic system. What we've done is taken the idea of personal freedom and all but tested it to destruction, our desire for equality and fairness creating a situation where just about anything is permissible. And all in the name of rights for the individual, a worthy notion that has backfired to the extent that unscrupulous individuals have used it for dubious ends. The individual has rights and ought to have them, but when those rights inadvertently tear at the heart of a society and systematically disable its capacity for self-reflection, then something is surely amiss. And so we try to rectify the imbalance with an injection of conservative Christianity, or with theories of ethics, or with mild censorship, and when things get totally out of hand we bring in the police, the doctor or the psychiatrist. It's all a bit of a muddle, and it's becoming more and more muddled by the minute. As an integral part of this mix, Christian liberalism too finds itself headed for trouble, its critical stance with regards to long-accepted Christian doctrine often leading its exponents to express a form of Christian atheism, a late apology for theological excesses that also tend towards the extreme. In a homily, Origen (see 7.0) addresses our deep-seated collective problem when he says: "One is not able to offer vows to the Most High without having in oneself, in one's substance, something to offer."[2]

This brings us full circle in terms of conservative Christianity's claim that we fail *because* our natures are oriented towards evil, not because of honestly made mistakes. And so we shuffle backwards and forwards between rejecting conservative Christianity's sillier notions and enlisting its services when threatened by social upheaval. It's a game we play, and it leaves people deeply confused and bemused. Add to this the possibility of terrorist attack, a backgrounding war that is draining the West's resources, and the erosion of our financial institutions through unbridled greed, and you have a recipe for potential psychic disaster on a massive scale.

But as we've seen when viewing early Christianity through Father Sylvan's eyes, there is at the heart of Christianity a clear recognition of our dilemma. There was once a central doctrine dealing with the manner in which we relate to ourselves on the moral level. And not just in the sense of our being good because that's what God wants, but in the sense of a carefully constructed discipline of mind leading to a gradual transformation of the mind. Christianity's preoccupation with moral issues has therefore a different theoretical base from the one generally supposed; it is not about goodness, it is about *a raising of conscious awareness by way of acts that help sustain our level of awareness at a high level.*

An intriguing verse in the Epistle of James seems to touch on this issue: "For he (man) beholdeth himself, and goeth his way, and straightway forgeteth what manner of man he was."[3] Has any modern-day Christian preacher ever paused to ask him or herself what these words actually mean? A verse such as this would, I imagine, be made into a homily and interpreted as having something to do with our falling again and again into sin, but it could equally have to do with our habit of becoming lost to self as we go about our daily business. We are all in the same boat. Being Christian makes not one whit of difference to the situation we find ourselves in. Whether Christian or atheist, we are caught in an identical conceptual/perceptual trap.

The fact that James was Jesus' flesh-and-blood brother is conveniently overlooked by most Christian scholars (See 8.1). His epistle is placed in the too-hard basket because of the theological problems it contains; it does not fit neatly into the New Testament canon. In fact it was rejected by many of the early Christian Fathers because of its strong Jewish overtones. James is seen as placing too great an emphasis on works; he sounds more like a law-bedraggled Pharisee than a follower of the Pauline Christ. Why is this so? It is so because James was not a follower of the Pauline Christ as he is now understood; he was a devout Jew and leader of the 1st century Nazoraean sect in Jerusalem called The Way, a desert-based offshoot of Judaism at loggerheads with St. Paul over the question of faith taking precedence over works. This historical fact is interpreted by Christian scholars as the Jerusalem Church of the Apostles falling back into Judaism's law-driven conception of the religious life, but the situation was much more complex than that. The Apostolic Church in Jerusalem led by James did not fall back into orthodox Judaism; it never at any time ceased in its close affiliation with Jewish orthodoxy. As a Jewish sect traveling parallel to Judaism, the Nazoraeans just happened to nominate someone as the Messiah of Israel that orthodox Judaism did not accept, and after the Roman invasion of Judea in 66 they found themselves hated by Jews, Romans and Paul's Christians alike. James would have had immense difficulty in perceiving his older brother as an aspect of Israel's transcendent God packed into a human body. The anointed, priestly Messiah of Israel, yes, that would have made perfect sense to this ascetic Jew, but not a being consubstantial with Israel's God as would be proposed by the 4th century Council of Nicea. That, as James' rejection of Paul's more adventurous theology of the "Christ" shows, would have been too much for this highly respected Nazoraean leader to swallow. It was James, after all, who tricked Paul into taking Nazarite vows in the temple, an act that saw Paul attacked by devout Jews for the dangerous literalisms he had allowed to accrue around the figure of Jesus.

What James believed about his brother Jesus was not at all the same as what Paul believed about the same man – they held what appear to have been divergent theologies. Or maybe it was just that Paul the maverick theologian developed a strain of theology in which there were two levels, one for the pagan mind familiar with the idea of men being gods, and one for the more discerning pagan mind capable of seeing his enigmatic Christ-consciousness as an advanced mental condition in the Platonic mold. He did after all speak of "milk" and "meat" in terms of his teachings, and that suggests exoteric and esoteric levels of instruction. This perhaps explains how James and Paul were able to put up with each other's company in the early days; they were experimenting with a teaching with astonishing ramifications, a discipline of mind that in their separate hands took on different forms of expression. There was no secret teaching as such, but there were levels of sophistication within what James and Paul taught about Jesus that only later ceased to gel. The faith grounded in Jesus' teachings was, in essence, a progressive revelation in the sense that each individual traveled the route of *apatheia* ("works" as a discipline of mind); it was not, as it later became, a rote formula of beliefs *about* Jesus intoned prior to baptism. As Paul himself intimated, being a Christian could be equated with "the pains of childbirth" whereby a different order of self was born, *a new self with a new mind.* In these terms it is I think fair to accept Father Sylvan's suggestion that the more demanding levels of *apatheia* were later mistakenly identified by the evolving Church as Gnostic-influenced extensions of Christian teaching and outlawed – the faith's original insights, dynamic and life-transforming, were transformed into a grocery list of beliefs that one either accepted or rejected. Christianity had turned into a language-driven religion, a religion of the word where a simple mistake in interpretation could rob you of your life, the idea of a progressive revelation changed into an excuse for the development of an elaborate theology around Jesus as vicarious sacrifice.

Excavating Our Foundations 17.1

Where does this leave us? It leaves us with Father Sylvan's "unconscious Christianity", a Christianity that often hinders even as it attempts to help. It is, as the French writer Alain Forget says in his incisive little book *How To Get Out of This World Alive,*[4] a game of cosmic hide and seek that has to be seen through for what it is – an illusion, a lantern show of the mind. Highly complex in structure and ever changing in what it generates, this mental show, or flow, is run not by some grand central self, but by elements of psyche congregated around an idea of self that sustains the illusion of there being a continuous self, a self that is always the same. Alas, that is not the case. This helpful illusion is created out of conditioned psychic tendencies reinforced by emotional energy released in the psyche in response to life events. These tendencies (complexes) are recognized by us as facets of the self, personality traits that we exhibit under certain circumstances, but they could also be psychic elements that take on a life of their own and become autonomous. Strutting their stuff before an audience of similarly autonomous self-bits named "friend" or "foe", they strive for dominance, and, depending on what underpins them, may succeed in collaring most of the psyche's available energy. At the mercy of such elements, we veer this way and that in our responses, our dominant mode of response governing how we are perceived by others.

This returns us to James Hillman's scheme (see 5.1) in which the ancient Greek gods replace complexes. Hillman's reasoning is that it is easier for us to relate to a "being" than to an abstract idea.[5] An aggression complex does not carry the same force as Mars, god of war; it robs our psychology of useful anthropomorphisms. If, when uncontrollably angry, we think of ourselves as having turned into Mars, the god of war (or Mrs. Mars), awareness of our mental condition will be much more direct. Multiply this effect by way of the Greek pantheon's colorful inhabitants and our relationship to self (psyche) will take on a quality of awareness our complexes fail to provide. Alain Forget picks up on this train of thought in the writings of Meister Eckhart:

> Man has within him numerous skins which cover the Depths of his heart. Man knows so many things but does not know himself! Ah! Thirty or forty skins just like those of an ox or a bear cover the soul. You should therefore excavate your foundations and learn to know yourself.[6]

The idea of "excavating our foundations" is a challenge we cannot afford to ignore; it confronts us with how little we know about ourselves. Socrates' injunction "Know thy self" becomes a psychic imperative in this context, but not in the sense generally understood. Socrates (or Solon) may have had more than a psychological understanding of the conscious self in mind when he coined his famous phrase. Psychology has its place, as have all the disciplines that assist us to think clearly, relate sensitively and know our world objectively. But we also need to develop a capacity for empathic judgment (evaluative feeling), and that comes not through cerebral juggling but through an immediate and ongoing apprehension of our *being in existence*.[7] But "being in existence" is no easy thing to detect, it makes unusual demands on us. One such demand is to observe the constant parade of psychic bits that take to the stage and demand attention. We are not one grand, majestic self-ruling psyche, we are, as the ancient Greeks saw only too clearly and Meister Eckhart confirms, a conglomerate of psychic bits (skins) each with its own distinct attributes (ox or bear), each with its own emotional and intellectual agenda. Hence Eckhart's notion of "eternal generation"; staying awake is an "intimate sensation of closeness" that constantly slips away from us and has to be renewed. What we need is the will to will ourselves awake, but that seems to be beyond our reach due to the nature of perception and our reliance on conceptual frameworks. We simply don't realize that there is a problem. Our time is taken up with defending our personality bits as they flare in and out of existence in response to circumstances, the deeper needs of our nature being neglected due to the frenzy of activity we're engaged in.

Three Progressive Levels of Interaction with Self 17.2

Waking up into the presence of one's self as a psychophysical being is an achievement of profound significance. That is level one. Waking up into the presence of one's self as a psychophysical being and attempting to sustain the experience is an achievement the consequences of which only slowly begin to dawn on us. That is level two. Waking up into the presence of self as a psychophysical being and sustaining that experience for longish periods over a course of weeks, months or years, is an achievement of such profound significance it changes forever how we perceive self, other and world. That is level three.

Curiosity sets level one in motion. Deepening curiosity sets level two in motion. Curiosity blended with a growing sense of wonder sets level three in motion. Why wonder? Because by the time we get to level three we know that self, other and world as experienced when awake are radically different from the experience of self when mentally submerged and engaged. We are much more than we seem, much less that we hoped we were.

The first thing to dawn on us as we wake up to our condition is that the difference between being awake and not being awake is so subtle that the two states are sometimes indistinguishable. Awake one minute, we are mentally engaged the next (asleep in Gurdjieff's terms) and oblivious to the fact that we are again submerged and *lost to self.* Particularly when thinking about being awake during our attempts to sustain the awake condition. In fact this is the mind's tricky response to the sensation of waking up – it is the mechanistic level of mind pulling us back into line. This is of course to raise the issue of our hardwired instinct for survival, an instinct closely aligned with ego in terms of self-preservation – we sense that to wake up in this fashion somehow threatens the self-orienting principle in psyche. We've survived extraordinarily well using the mind we've got, so why tamper with it? It's such a waste of time and energy trying to be awake in this extended sense; it disrupts mental coherence, produces unusual physical sensations and robs us of the ability to think. But that's not all. It also threatens the inner voice that helps hold our sense of personal identity in place. And so we give in, the pressure of our sensory systems and our cultural conditioning generally proving too strong to counteract.

There are of course compensations in failing in our attempts to stay awake and aware. As the mind moves towards the awake state, the state of our becoming more real to ourselves, the unconscious springs into action with what are often highly original insights into whatever had previously engaged the mind's attention. Out of nowhere they come, ideas pushing other ideas out of the way in a flurry we find difficult to ignore. If engaged in a project that requires fresh input, this freewheeling state of mind will prove very useful, but if intent on waking up as an act in itself, then it is no more than a distraction. This is of course the creative space where *flotillas of meaning come across the horizon of consciousness that should not be intercepted too soon,* but in this context it is a space superfluous to our needs. It does, however, reveal something important about the mind and its workings: a concerted effort to switch thought off can open us up to the experience of being intercepted by the sensation of significant meaning. Here then is the font of creativity sought by so many, the inspired space of a Coleridge or a Kekulé that with practice can be initiated at will. Disengagement, not engagement, is the secret of creative thought. We are at our creative best when mentally freewheeling.

Our unease with being ultra-aware of ourselves probably stems from the adolescent experience of becoming self-conscious – that is, ungainly and tongue-tied in our interactions with the world, and with the opposite sex. But this is to misunderstand what being fundamentally awake means as an experience. As we saw at 15.0 when considering Robert Forman's definition of a pure consciousness event, awareness of one's own awareness is only half of the proposition; the other half is that we are simultaneously aware of objects, thoughts, sensations or actions. It is not a matter of our being aware of ourselves in isolation; it is a matter of our being balanced on the knife's edge between awareness of self and what is observed. It is a subtle mental balancing act where both self and world are registering, but neither has usurped the conscious field. That is not self-consciousness as it is normally understood; it is an entirely new condition of mind that can be systematically developed. And neither is it "consciousness *of*" in the usual sense of awareness; it is "consciousness *as*", a form of awareness within which there is in fact no *content hook.* Thinking shudders to a halt in such a moment, as does identification with what is being observed. We are momentarily free of our submerged mental state and can, when we inadvertently slip out of it, re-establish it again when awake to what has happened.

The Generating of Mental Phenomena 17.3

The above observations return us to a problem that plagues contemplative and/or meditative experience in the major religious traditions, namely, visions that seem to confirm and support doctrinal formulas. As the saying goes: "If you meet the Buddha on the road, kill him." That is sound advice; it reminds us of Father Sylvan's injunction to chase Christ out of our minds until we are willing to pursue Christ into the core of being. As we saw at 7.0 in relation to Dionysius the Areopagite, the contemplative/meditator's job is to *penetrate the outward sheath to the core of the holy symbol.* Everything has to go, and that includes theological constructions attached to the living, breathing person that was Jesus.

Throughout Christianity's long history the Church has been ultra-careful in the way it handled mystic pronouncements, for these formulations of religious reality often tended to exceed the bounds of what the faithful had been taught to expect. There was sometimes a disturbing level of ambiguity in how mystic consciousness conceived God, and, more importantly, how Jesus the flesh and blood man related to that God. In this vein Meister Eckhart found himself accused of heresy, as did many another, and in our own time Bernadette Roberts has found herself similarly judged.

But there are of course those who do not rock the doctrinal boat, those whose visions confirm the expected doctrinal elements in visual or auditory form, devout souls who report exactly what the Church expects to hear from its cosmic travelers. So the question is this: What, in the final analysis, is the difference between this set of travelers and those whose reports cause consternation to Church authorities? Why the discrepancy? The answer isn't all that surprising; it depends on how, and in what, we invest the energy of attention. Thought, like everything else in existence, *is* energy. Thought drives the engine of the mind and helps sustains the illusion of personal identity through inner dialogue, rumination, memory replay and dominant methods of response. Direct one's thoughts in a particular direction and memory will respond with associations that correspond to our beliefs, hopes, needs and ambitions. If deeply religious in the Christian sense, we will reinforce our religious bent through reading and prayer, and if inclined towards contemplative prayer (inner silence) may even produce a visionary experience or two. Conversely, to penetrate beyond the safety barrier of belief is to experience phenomena that systematically unravel previously held religious convictions, for when the silence thickens and the ego's interfering fingers can no longer move, a quite different set of possibilities form on the horizon of consciousness. And so we have an Eckhart and a Roberts, contemplatives who pursued their faith into the depths of being and returned with, well, not quite what they either hoped for or expected. Going beyond the conscious mind's preoccupations they touched, through a spiraling inwardness, the core of their own psychophysical reality. Not many make such a daring journey; it takes a degree of tenacity and courage few of us are able to muster. For according to authoritative reports it entails a systematic dismantling of the ego and its bits, and that, as it begins to unfold, is enough to drive most explorers back into the safety zone of doctrinal certainty.

The Route of Philosophy 17.4

Given the obstacles lying between us and our psychophysical core, is it any wonder so few ever make the attempt? But reach it some do, and in doing so they help redefine whole areas of the mind presently under investigation. And no more so than the idea of consciousness itself, a concept now being carefully examined in both philosophy and psychology. Not so the word "conscious", however; we all seem to agree that when awake we are in fact conscious and not unconscious, for how else could we function? We talk and eat and do things and that signals that we are awake and not asleep. But of course it doesn't really; for as we discover through careful observation, our engagement with thought signals a self so busy in its submerged state that it loses all cognizance of its own immediate reality. It is, in a sense, asleep with its eyes wide open, and only occasional surfaces from its activity-filled slumber.

That philosophy is an alternative route to the contemplative's waking up to what waking up means would be refuted by some, but such a route does seem to exist. Philosophy, if it is fully engaged and has evolved a suitable language, cannot help but deal with the embeddedness of self in the world as an experience; but it seems to be only a certain kind of philosophical thinking that can function as a conduit for experiences generally considered to be religious in nature. We exist in time and space. The question is, to what extent do we exist in time and space?

George Steiner carefully defines our situation in his study of Martin Heidegger's philosophy, and the problem that arises in relation to philosophy when he says: "A philosophy that abstracts, that seeks to elevate itself above the everydayness of the everyday, is empty. It can tell us nothing of the meaning of being."[8] We have to excavate ourselves properly (Eckhart), and that requires a descent into being, an actualizing of what we are through an expansion of everyday awareness. Only a philosophy carrying a suitably developed language can assist us in this task, and that requires a language within which "being" as a question is made available to us beyond the sterilities of verbal abstraction. So in a sense we're back with poetry, to a form of language that transcends language, to a use of words so sensitively constructed they carry us into the very presence of ourselves as an experience. Sustain this question of questions over weeks, months or years, and the result will be a spiraling inwardness that gradually carries us far beyond language.

But what of the religiously-minded person who prays ardently and allows himself or herself to sink ecstatically towards the core of being? What of them? Why are their certainties, their intuitions, their visions and auditions thought by some to be problematical? Is it just a matter of the viewpoint held? Is the *via positiva* ultimately no different from the *via negativa?* The answer to this question carries us back to the manner in which we invest the energy of attention. Content-filled meditations are not just the other side of the contemplative coin as experienced by an Eckhart or a Roberts; they are often what allows the conscious mind *to continue in its submerged and engaged state* if the experience is a projection formed from religious need rather than an archetypal formation in its own right. Minds tethered emotionally and doctrinally to aspects of the fixed religious canon are apt to create their own experiences, the archetypal formations (images, sounds, etc) that preface *via negativa* experiences (over months and years) being experiences beyond the ego's ability to approach directly, or get hooked on. As intimated by Robert Forman, a kind of ritual circling is required, a non-looking looking that allows the looker to see without actually seeing. Attempt to look directly at an archetypal formation and it immediately vanishes – Hades (one's own limitless depth) cannot be looked at directly – the ego would disintegrate if that happened; it simply couldn't process the unimaginable volume of information available.

Archetypal formations are composed of energy belonging to the psychophysical system, an energy that either presents itself as an experience of one's own body in the sense of physiological processes *viewed from the inside,* or as encounters with psyche itself in terms of what drives the whole psychophysical vehicle. This is to say that what often passes for mystical experience is no more than a journeying into the body's networks that so astonishes the psychically anaesthetized ego that it misinterprets the experience as spiritual enlightenment. Alas, it is not; it is merely the psyche's extraordinary ability to view physicality from the inside rather than from the outside. Such experiences are mentioned in the world's spiritual literatures, and include experiences of the psychophysical energy sources located in the solar plexus, and in the head. These highly unusual experiences can herald the approach of a final stage in meditative/contemplative experience, the approach of the "still point" at the center of the affective system, but that need not be the case. The "still point" is not something one penetrates in the sense of a holy symbol; it is something that approaches of its own volition if the psychic means can be found to allow such a thing to happen. The way, as the Scriptures attest, is narrow, and few there are who find it.

The necessary escape velocity from belief-backed opinions is seldom reached. Why? Because a religiously conditioned mind in which questioning has been replaced with believing finds itself tethered to a mental stake where all it can do is mentally revolve around, rather than experientially resolve the contradictions confronting it. In the religiously convinced person's scheme all the major questions have already been dealt with, there is nothing left to do but say thanks to God and attempt to be good. And so this person travels, not into the question that being awake poses as an experience, but into ever more complex interactions with their already answered questions, projections of the ego that progressively strengthen the ego in its functioning. The reason for this is that the conscious mind abhors a vacuum; it panics when faced with too intense an internal silence. Shut off the noise of thought for even a few seconds and the mind will generate an endless stream of images and sensations attended by thought to counteract the situation – hence the difficulties faced early on in the meditative/contemplative state. It is a vicious circle. Silence is the ego's enemy; it robs it of the energy it requires to survive, and as we all know, survival of ourselves as a conscious being is our strongest instinct.

Feelings and Propositions 17.5

This returns us to Don Cupitt's assertion that mystical statements, by their very nature, lack propositional coherence, and that being the case the contemplative's descriptions of so-called transcendental states is without meaning or relevance. But he doesn't stop there. He also contends that feelings lack cognitive/propositional meaning, and that the early 20th century contention that they did was without substance.[9] In relation to feelings being used as propositional proofs to support doctrinal contentions, I fully agree with Cupitt. Such attempts are generally no more than affective delusions based on beliefs. They prove nothing except that the person involved is deeply convinced of certain religious ideas. In this sense what we're dealing with is aberrant emotion. The ecstasy experienced by the deeply religious personality has little to do with the contemplative space as it eventually forms; it has more to do with an ego intoxicated by religious ideas in which a huge emotional investment has been placed. As with empathy where feeling, and not emotion, dominates, (see reference note 7 this chapter) delicacy of feeling adds coherence to our responses, whereas emotional reactions cause us to progressively lose coherence.

In relation to the contemplative state, feelings assist us to lock onto the still point at the center of our affective system (Roberts), and can be likened to the maneuvering required by a space shuttle as it links up with a space station through the use of laser technology. Sensations of an extraordinarily delicate nature are in operation in such a moment, and without their delicacy the contemplative's journey into self could not take place, never mind develop in any coherent fashion. Nor would the tantalizing dimensions in any great work of art ever form. Without delicacy of feeling great poetry would not take shape, great fiction would never be written, or great paintings be painted. At our best, our deepest, our most telling, we are first and foremost creatures of feeling. Feelings are in themselves neither propositional nor coherent, but they do facilitate propositional coherence. To believe that propositional coherence arises as a result of language alone is to underestimate the complexity of our psychophysical system (see 15.1). It would be the equivalent of believing that language alone is writing this book and that my felt life has not in some sense contributed to the exercise. Robert Forman adds his own deep-space analogy (see 14.1) to the mix: "... mysticism is more like a space capsule than like a horse-drawn cart: pushed by the rocket of language, the capsule of experience is ultimately loosened from that which has pushed it, and becomes, as it were, weightless and afloat. The experience on the space capsule is no longer conditioned by its vehicle. It now results from other, novel factors."[10] Language is in this sense the computer program (Grotowski); strong subjectivity (see 12.1) *as* feeling is everything that we are (Roberts) brought to bear on the question of all questions. Or, as David Levin states in his essay 'Mudra as Thinking', "... feeling is our most tactful way into the opening depth of things.[11]

Further Methodology 17.6

There are two approaches to the meditative, contemplative state: the open-eyed approach and the closed-eyed approach. In the closed-eyed approach the mind quickly causes problems for itself due to its compulsion to fill in every waking minute with thought, rumination, analysis and memory. So also the open-eyed approach if attention is connected exclusively to sense of self or sense of world as "other". If it's an either/or situation, then we are at the mercy of the mind's tendency to automatically extrapolate through association. We are either "in here" and all wrapped up in self's needs, or "out there" and all wrapped up in the need to respond to event and happening. But not if we hold the mind at arm's length, so to speak. If we can balance ourselves on the knife's edge between the inner and the outer, between the seer and what is seen, between sense of self and sense of "other", then the mind's evaluations and projections lessen, and finally cease. This is more easily accomplished with the eyes open than with them closed, and the reason for this is that with our eyes open we are more firmly grounded in ourselves. With eyes closed we run the risk of thoughts and visual projections that can, as in dream or reverie, (see 5.1) grow associatively in response to the slightest hint of shape or meaning. With our eyes open there is less chance of being carried off into subtle forms of thought. It's not that the open-eyed approach is superior to the closed-eyed approach; it's just a better training ground. If you want to be a trapeze artist, you do not head immediately for the highest platform. It's also easier to spot what's going on – when you drift off into thought while walking, something will generally happen to make you aware of that fact. Monitor those moments of "coming to" over the course of an hour and you will quickly realize what I'm getting at.

But what does it feel like to be balanced between the outer and the inner? How does that work as an experience? What are the steps that have to be taken? Is the ability to *simultaneously hold presence of self and object of attention in one frame of mental reference* really as easy as blinking? Yes, it is, but it requires an intentional movement of attention between self and world (see 16.3) until the gulf between them, and our constant movement across that gulf, is fully appreciated. We shuffle unconsciously between inner and outer all day long, but have to consciously enact the process to understand it fully. And so a little perceptual game is necessary, a game of "in here" versus "out there", and through this game we awaken to what is going on in our unconscious conscious state. For that is what we are most of the time, unconscious while conscious.

Being in the World 17.7

We are not a mind and a body, we are simultaneously both, and these integrated factors constitute our *being in the world.* The problem is, we are seldom aware of our being in the world, only aware of the result of our being in the world. Even when concerned with self rather than world, our interaction with what passes for self (a hurtful feeling or a pain in the leg) is generally at the consciously unconscious level, not the fully conscious level. We are, in other words, all wrapped up in the experience of pain to the exclusion of sense of self as presence. We are, hard as it may be to accept, missing from the equation of our own pain just as we are missing from the myriad events and happenings we engage in moment by moment. Yes, the pain is felt, but we have become all pain in such a moment, just as we can become all book or all anything through identification. Identification is the problem; we are forever embedded in our identifications to the exclusion of self as a living presence. To wake up is to wake up out of this interactive dream and take charge, and this requires us to consciously move backwards and forwards between ourselves as subject, and the world as object, until the mechanism of exchange is thoroughly understood.

Another way of looking at this problem is to say that when we look at a car we become the car we're looking at. "Car" fills our mind to the exclusion of, say, the roast beef we had for lunch. Or we become all cat when fondling a cat. Or all mathematical problem when doing our income tax. Which confirms that thinking, too, can be identified with to the exclusion of sense of self. It's how we are, but it's not how we need constantly live. We can, and do, wake up out of this fog of identification at intervals, and if interested in making this happen, can, with a little practice, entice the awake state to form. But it takes patience, lots of patience.

Moving between ourselves as subject and the world as object requires us to momentarily withdraw attention from "out there" and place it "in here", and when "in here", do the opposite. And then do the opposite again and keep repeating the process until we become fully cognizant with how we slip from one mode to the other, how each experience eclipses the other. For you can't be both "out there" *and* "in here" simultaneously, can you? It's one thing or the other; at least that's how it seems. And when sense of the physical self has been separated out and understood, then comes the tricky business of sustaining sense of the physical self alongside our daily affairs through Ouspensky's trick of looking in two directions simultaneously. Particularly when in company. Or when washing the dishes. Or when involved in an argument. Or when boasting. Or when walking along a street or staring aimlessly out of a window. We'll dance backwards and forwards between self and object for a while, ricochet between them in an at-first jolting fashion, then, suddenly, we'll sense ourselves closing on our double target and everything will change. *Us* in existence as we sense ourselves looking. *Us* not in existence as we identify with the object under scrutiny and lose track of ourselves. *Us* in existence again as we stutter back into being aware of our physical presence alongside other or world. Then the dawning realization that something else is happening, that in attempting to do this impossible thing we have set in motion something beyond self as a physical sensation, as body "bodying", but as an arising or resurrection of Being. For as shown at 17.2, presence of self as being, when it emerges, is not a submerged or engaged form of recognition (it has no object); it is a pure consciousness event, and as such is without conscious content *in both directions.* To be or not to be is, as Shakespeare suggests, the "question", but it is not a question requiring an answer; more a question of what we are, or are not, in our essence.[12]

Benny Shanon neatly captures what is going on here when he tells us that, "as we draw to Cons5, at one end of the (consciousness) space, and to Cons1, at the other, the distinction between the regions diminish and become blurred. Specifically, at one end of the space consciousness is primitive and therefore not amenable to differentiation and distinction between experience and selfhood, whereas at the other end *it transcends such distinctions*." (Author's italics) And then comes the denouement: "Geometrically speaking," he says, searching his way into the experience where experience itself is transcended, "as one draws towards the two extremes, the distance between the lines marking the regions decreases and... converge to a point".[13] Shanon is unsure whether this geometrical point can ever finally be reached, whereas Bernadette Roberts attests to the fact that a remarkably similar sounding point (the still point at the center of the affective system) constitutes the entrance to an undifferentiated state beyond the reflexive mind and its wayward emotions. And so we double back to what was said about the still point approaching of its own volition, for this answers Shanon's astute question as to whether this geometrical balancing point in consciousness can be penetrated. It can't, but that point can envelope the watcher if the watcher has discovered how to watch without watching.

A Smoking Gun? 17.8

So is there a smoking gun behind all of this? Have we rediscovered an ancient teaching concerning the nature of the self safeguarded by early century Christian monks as Father Sylvan seems to suggest? Are we moving backwards rather than forwards in our explorations of what consciousness is, and is not? Or is it simply a matter of the human constitution being such that this kind of understanding is forever discoverable?

Given the information supplied by advanced Christian contemplatives such as Meister Eckhart, Bernadette Roberts and Father Sylvan, I think the latter rather than the former is the case. Having said that, however, there is no doubting that vital elements of this teaching have been passed on by experimentalists in just about every age, and in every culture. The evidence for a whole new level of mind being attainable is to be found in all the major religions, Christianity being no exception. But that does not mean that religion in general can claim copyright to that teaching, or any particular religion lay sole claim to that revelation. It was perhaps no more than the way human society evolved that caused things to turn out the way they did, the discoveries of naturally gifted individuals initiating an attempt by others to understand the outer reaches of thought and experience through reason alone. In saying this, it is not my intention to rob religion of its place in human affairs, or deny thinkers their right to think; it is to suggest that alongside any religious notion of reality there ought also to be a healthy and informed respect for the body's natural forces, the physical forces that underlie, support and augment our most sophisticated systems of reasoning, insight and creativity. Any attempt to sequester the great experiential truths of the contemplative life in doctrinaire religious formulas is, to my way of thinking, a mistake of major proportions; the attempt by some secular thinkers to render them inconsequential similarly shortsighted. Hence the tenor of this book with its mixture of history, philosophy, psychology, science and religious inquiry. There is, as far as I can see, no smoking gun as such, just the marvel of what we are in ourselves surfacing in spite of what sometimes seems every conceivable human attempt to derail the whole magnificent enterprise.

References & Notes

1: The Veil of Illusion

1) Cupitt, Don, *The Sea of Faith,* p 7.
2) Ibid, p 273.
3) Ibid, 9-10.
4) Berman, Morris, *Coming to Our Senses,* p 137.
5) Ibid, p 138.
6) Cupitt, Don, *The Sea of Faith,* p 271.
7) Berman, Morris, *Coming to Our Senses,* p 305.
8) Ibid, 307.
9) Roberts, Bernadette, *What is Self? A Study of the Spiritual Journey in Terms of Consciousness.* (Sentient Publications, LLC., 2005) p 54.
10) Berman, Morris, *Coming to Our Senses,* p 9.
11) Cupitt, *The Sea of Faith,* p 250.
12) Ibid.
14) Berman, Morris, *Coming to Our Senses,* p 306.
15) Lockhart, Douglas, *Jesus the Heretic,* p 10.
16) Walker, Kenneth, *A Study of Gurdjieff's Teachings,* p 12.
17) Berman, Morris, *Coming to Our Senses,* p 305. The German philosopher Martin Heidegger believed Western man had become so mechanical in his attitudes that he had forgotten what it felt like to exist as a human being. Reflection on existence as an experience in its own right had all but disappeared and been replaced with the metallic sheen of technological thinking. As a result we were becoming progressively more nihilistic in our attitudes.
18) Ibid, 306.
19) Moore, James, *Gurdjieff,* p 9.
20) Ibid, (flyleaf)
21) Pauwels, Louis, *Gurdjieff* (flyleaf)
22) Berman, Morris, *Coming to Our Senses,* p 138.

23) Ibid, 137.

24) Ibid, 79.

25) Furlong, Monica. (Quoted from memory; text not identified)

26) Steiner, George, *Martin Heidegger,* p 57

27) Claxton, Guy, *The Wayward Mind,* p 1-2. Claxton tells us that we are less in control of our minds than we would like to think. Being on automatic pilot is the least of our worries; there is also the little matter of dream, mood swings and creativity. Unsettled by such moments, we brush them off. In Claxton's words it is as if we are trying to domesticate the inherent wildness we sense in such moments, not to mention the guilt we may feel at owning a creative thought that has *appeared out of the blue.*

28) Ibid, p 282. In his paper "Mudra as Thinking", D.M. Levin captures this point beautifully when he says "... a free motility finds itself sedimented into habitualities; the archetypes, functioning primordially as corporeal schemata, are increasingly fixed into typical patterns of movement, habitual styles of gesturing and posturing, a familiar signature. [This is characteristic of an] inveterate tendency to become absorbed in an unnecessarily narrow, needlessly restricted world-field of purposive, and mostly self-centered action. There is no (felt) sense of the larger field, the open horizon, the background, and the ground underlying; no sense of a more pervasive and more universal field-continuum." This paper is to be found in *Heidegger and Asian Thought* edited by Graham Parkes, p 258.

29) Berman, Morris, *Coming to Our Senses,* p 181.

30) Neumann, Erich, *The Origins and History of Consciousness,* p 261-286.

31) Black, David, *The Ownership of Consciousness,* p 16. Emergence from the unconscious in the sense of developing a self-orienting principle in consciousness is, however, offset by the fact that we remain forever deeply attached to uncon-

scious processes without quite realizing that that is the case. In this sense we are not composed of two separate systems, but one psychophysical system, a unity that analytical psychology defines as the "self". There is, in this sense, unconscious purposivity.

32) Roberts, Bernadette, *What is Self? A Study of the Spiritual Journey in Terms of Consciousness* (Sentient Publications, LLC edition, 2005) p 49.

2: The Energy of Attention

1) Steiner, George, *Heidegger,* p 55.
2) Ibid. In this sense "questioning" is a religious experience; it introduces us to mental spaces and physical sensations that are often unfamiliar and challenging. To ask a "real" question necessitates that we ourselves become real.
3) Needleman, Jacob, *Lost Christianity* p 212. This extraordinary outburst by Father Sylvan alerts us to the dangers inherent in losing the ability to formulate proper questions because of fixed patterns of belief. Beliefs of a fixed nature undermine somatic-based sensitivity and replace it with conditioned emotional responses.
4) Roberts, Bernadette, *What is Self? A Study of the Spiritual Journey in Terms of Consciousness* (Sentient Publications, LLC edition, 2005, pp 99 & 101. Here Bernadette Roberts speaks of "grasping not-knowing as a way-of- knowing", as something Carl Jung never fathomed. She adds for good measure that "Psychological and spiritual freedom is the ability to live with not-knowing."
5) Needleman, Jacob, *Lost Christianity,* p 193.
6) Ibid, p 177.
7) Hick, John, *Evil and the God of Love,* p 215.
8) Needleman, Jacob, *Lost Christianity,* p 117.

3: Waking Up

1) *Journal of Consciousness Studies,* Vol 14, No. 3, March 2007.
2) Ibid, p 14.
3) *Lucid Dreams* by Celia Green, p 7.
4) Needleman, Jacob, *Lost Christianity,* p 217. Needleman's ongoing observation here that our inner life is composed mostly of outer events and happenings perhaps explains psychology's tentative conclusion that the self is little more than bundles of experience laid end to end. But is this altogether true? Is this not to ignore the unconscious level where experience is of a quite different caliber, where "bodying" is a vital part of comprehension through evaluative feeling?
5) Jung, Carl, *Man and His Symbols,* p 49.
6) Ibid, p 213. This anomaly is also noted by David Pole in *The Later Philosophy of Wittgenstein,* p 66.
7) Stephen's 2009 paper "Feelings are not Enough" is of interest here. Grant is of the opinion that feeling theorists go wrong in excluding cognitive processes from the ontology of emotion. Emotions include judgements about the world, and much else, we are told. It is, he says, "an indisputable feature of our emotions that they are "about the world, engagements in and with the world." Feelings can be thought of as "having intentionality when we see them registering representations of danger or offence." In this sense feeling "involves appraising or evaluating the object of our emotion." See "Journal of Consciousness Studies" Vol 16, No.4, 2009, pp 5-19.
8) Sylvan, Father, *Lost Christianity* by Jacob Needleman, p 213.

4: Beyond the Comfort Zone

1) Sylvan, Father, as cited in *Lost Christianity* by Jacob Needleman, p 87.

2) Graves, Robert & Joshua Podro, *The Nazarene Gospel Restored* (1953), p 6.
3) Eckhart, Meister, *A Modern Translation,* p 237. This is a powerful statement; it answers the question "What is will?" In Eckhart's sense of things, quality of will arises with quality of awareness – they can't be separated. Extend awareness and you extend will. Extend will through awareness and you further extend awareness. Awareness of the relationship between awareness and will changes the dynamic between self as a response mechanism and self as that which "sees" without hooks. It is in effect a contentless seeing, and as it develops it heralds the beginning of existential freedom.
4) Sylvan, Father, as cited in *Lost Christianity* by Jacob Needleman, p 95.
5) Ibid, p 191. This is a revolutionary statement. It tells us that ego and emotion endlessly sustain and support each another – hence the need to experientially tease them apart through acts of attentive self-presencing. To wake up to this is to catch sight of this relationship working itself out in our daily interactions with self, other or world.
6) Ibid, p 38.
7) Daniélou, Jean, Cardinal, cited from *Lost Christianity* by Jacob Needleman, p 51.
8) Neumann, Erich, Mystical Man, p 388.
9) Sylvan, Father, as cited by Jacob Needleman in *Lost Christianity,* p 210.
10) Ibid, p 394.
11) Ibid, p 384.
12) Sylvan, Father, as cited in *Lost Christianity* by Jacob Needleman, p 171.
13) Ibid, 119.
14) Ibid, p 168.
15) Ibid.

5: Depth

1) Cheyne, J.A., *The Ominous Numinous,* a paper in the *Journal of Consciousness Studies,* Vol 8, No. 5-7, 2001, p 148.
2) Ibid, p 134.
3) Hillman, James, *The Dream and the Underworld,* p 88.
4) Lockhart, Douglas, *Jesus the Heretic,* Chapter 16.
5) Hillman, James, *The Dream and the Underworld,* p 23.
6) Ibid, p 24. Here, once again, we are presented with the idea of mechanistic thinking allied to attitudes estranged from *sense of being,* plus the handy notion of "soul" as "depth" (bathun). Hillman also suggests that the descriptive terms such as Freud's "unconscious" and Bleuler's "depth psychology" reflect those very processes. It is, he says, "as if the archetypal material chooses its own descriptive terms as one aspect of its self-expression." In other words, the name chosen carries us towards the experience in itself. Which is to say that language can carry not just the idea of psychophysical depth, but can also function as an entry point into an experience of such depth. Language is therefore not as circumscribed as we may have thought. (See 14.4)
7) Ibid, p 28.
8) Ibid, p 35.
9) Ibid, p 16.
10) Jung, Carl, *Psychological Reflections* (1974), p 46.
11) Berman, Morris, *Coming to Our Senses,* p 76. There is a sense in which our self-conscious life is no more than a veneer – hence the frequency of "unity experiences" with nature, experiences where the self-other boundary lessens or disappears altogether.
12) Roberts, Bernadette, *What is Self? A Study of the Spiritual Journey in Terms of Consciousness.* (Sentient Publications, LLC, 2005, p 62.)
13) Ibid, p 154. Bernadette Roberts' view of Jesus is, however,

complex; it straddles points of view that at times appear to be contradictory. For instance, Part Three of her book, *What is Self?*, (see above for details) deals with what she terms the 'Eucharistic Christ' (p 136), and in spite of saying that Jesus did not conceive of himself as God, she nevertheless argues that the incarnation "has a dimension beyond that of the historical Christ who appeared in human form and consciousness." Human beings can experience what Christ manifested, but they are not that manifestation in their own right – that's the difference between the two. Prior to making this point Roberts' contemplative exposition is exemplary in its clarity, after this point, however, (p 204) it takes on a theological edge that many will find overly indebted to the Catholic scheme of spiritual reality. My own immediate reaction was to ask: How does Roberts differentiate between the historical Jesus and St. Paul's theological 'Christ'? If the Christ was made manifest by God, what exactly was the physical Jesus' relationship to this august figure? Roberts attempts to answer this question, but her answer becomes, for the first time, mired in what looks like theological sleight-of-hand. This is perhaps due to her background and training as a Carmelite, for in referring to the historical Jesus, she calls him the 'historical Christ', *not* the 'historical Jesus', and in doing so ignores Jesus the Jewish Messiah figure, his siblings (particularly James), and the dynastic background from which he sprang. 'Christ' is after all merely the Greek term for Messiah; it only becomes equated with divinity in Paul's theology, and that theology was radically different in conception from what was believed about Jesus by the early Jerusalem church of the apostles.

14) Funk, Robert, *Honest to Jesus,* p 20.

15) Wiles, Maurice, "Christianity Without Incarnation", an essay in *The Myth of God Incarnate,* edited by John Hick, p 2.

16) Ibid, p 9.

17) Ibid, p 3.
18) Young, Frances, "A Cloud of Witnesses", an essay in *The Myth of God Incarnate,* edited by John Hick, pp 15-16.
19) Ibid, p 45/ref 23.
20) Ibid, p 35.
21) Ibid, p 34.
22) Roberts, Bernadette, *The Experience of No-Self,* p 114.

6: The Deep End

1) Roberts, Bernadette, *The Experience of No-Self,* p 32 .
2) Ibid, p 107.
3) Ibid, p 181. At this point Roberts reveals herself to have experienced something beyond "fusion of opposites" and what she terms "the maintenance of a balance between the poles of difference and variation." The first part of this statement clearly differentiates what she has experienced from fusion experiences in the sense of *Participation Mystique,* and the second part helps define what is actually going on when a contemplative moves into the contemplative space. As can be seen at 16.3 in relation to the researches of the psychologist Robert Forman, and the observations of P.D. Ouspensky, such a balancing act may well constitute the springboard from out of which the no-self experience evolves, and Roberts confirms this point. This is made clear on page 175 of *The Experience of No-self* when she says: "Supposing that the fulcrum on which the continuum rests is the cognitive system, we can see that the process of integration is a balancing act wherein the ultimate goal is maintaining an equilibrium against all to the contrary." Optimum stability lies between the two systems; it is there that the contemplative gains maximum access to the still point. The balancing act is necessary, but it is superseded when the still point is penetrated.
4) Ibid, p 116. This is an interesting observation. It suggests

that Jesus had to do exactly what we in our own age are now trying to do in relation to Jesus himself: detect an underlying truth in Christianity that has become scrambled almost beyond recognition.

5) Ibid.
6) Ibid, p 112.
7) Ibid, p 104.
8) Ibid, p 61.
9) Ibid, p 174.
10) Ibid, p 173. Experiences of ecstasy and bliss may preface an eventual falling away of the self as Roberts describes, but if they continue, and intensify, they will most likely form a regression to the infantile state. In the first instance the self "falls away", in the second it disintegrates due to emotional intoxication.
11) Ibid, p 175.
12) Ibid, p 131.
13) Ibid.
14) Ibid, p 181.
15) Ibid, p 106.
16) Ibid, p 119.
17) Ibid, p 130-131.
18) Ibid, p 130.
19) Ibid.
20) Ibid, p 170. This is perhaps one of the most important observations made by Roberts concerning the nature of the self and the role of emotion. We do not *have* an affective life, she tells us, we *are* an affective life. Our feeling of separateness and interiority is *the effect of the entire affective network of the body registered cognitively*. True? Untrue? Father Sylvan seems to agree when he says, "Ego is the systematic affirmation of emotional reaction." (*Lost Christianity* p 191). The psychologist Jaak Panksepp (see 11.2) helps confirm this point when he says: "Every moment of our conscious lives is under-

girded by feelings, and... if the biological infrastructure of those intrinsic value-signaling systems were destroyed, one's sense of self would degrade."

21) Ibid, p 133. Christianity fully understands this point but has lost track of it. Putting an end to our "need to be forgiven" is perhaps our next greatest challenge.
22) Ibid.
23) Ibid, p 176. What a mysterious thing this "still point" is. Where is it? What is it? How do I find it? And what do I do when I do find it? Answer (1) It is the point where you become utterly still within yourself, and wait. (2) It is the point between *this* and *that*. (3) One does absolutely nothing.
24) Ibid, p 182. It is through an examination of the type of intelligence we have that we come to realize the nature of our problem. We are at the mercy of a cognitive system that can't stop doing what it is biologically predisposed to do: register the world through the senses and cause us to respond in such a manner as to safeguard ourselves as the perceiver. This system does not rest; it is constantly online.
25) Ibid, p 180.
26) Ibid, p 200.
27) Ibid. This is a contentious issue; it is a mixture of bad theology and distorted history that confounds attempts to unravel it. Suffice to say that if the history of the 1st-century is disentangled from its later theological overlay the character and intentions of the man Jesus fall into a quite different configuration.
28) Eckhart, Meister, *A Modern Translation*, p 248.
29) Ibid, p 252. Here again is confirmation of Bernadette Roberts' contention that self and the affective system are one and the same. God, Eckhart tells us, has no affective center, so if the affective center of a human being is brought to a "standstill", to use Roberts' term, then there is in essence no difference between the one and the other. This of course

suggests that God as a "being" is a mistaken concept. God is not some kind of super being beyond human conception; he is rather the equivalent of "being" or "is-ness" in the ontological sense. Hence the contemplative's journey into the center of "being", a journey that carries him/her firstly into a confrontation with the limited self and its emotionally based reactions, then towards the still point of being, then through the still point into a direct apprehension of being (is-ness) and the true nature of identity.

30) Armstrong, Karen, *A History of God,* p 256.
31) Roberts, Bernadette, *What is Self?,* p 127. Christians need not be alarmed at the idea of Christ being exploded. What we're dealing with here is a metaphor. It is our limited idea of truth that has to be exploded. What the conscious mind has built around Jesus must by its very nature be limited and misleading, so we have to make a descent into the self, into being, into our heart of hearts (the still point) to touch upon what he himself touched upon. This is what Father Sylvan means when he directs us to chase Christ out of our minds.
32) Ibid, p 126.
33) Needleman, Jacob, *Lost Christianity,* p 129.
34) Ibid, p 137.

7: Retreat to the Desert

1) Brown, Harold, O.J., *Heresies,* p 285-6.
2) Maycock, A.L., *The Inquisition,* p 63.
3) Plato, Stromateis i. 5. (29.1).
4) Heiler, Friedrich, "Contemplation in Christian Mysticism", an essay in *Spiritual Disciplines,* collected papers in the Eranos Yearbook, Bollingen Series XXX. 4. p 223, 1955.
5) Ibid, p 196.
6) Ibid, p 227.
7) *Britannica Encyclopedia,* 1956 edition, Vol 14, p 251.
8) Pagels, Elaine, *The Gnostic Gospels,* p 45.

9) Murk-Jansen, Saskia, Hadewijch and Eckhart, p 25.
10) Heiler, Friedrich, "Contemplation in Christian Mysticism", an essay in *Spiritual Disciplines,* collected papers in the Eranos Yearbook, Bollingen Series XXX. 4. p 224.
11) Bernard de Clairvaux, St., *Sermons on the Canticles,* LII, 2, 3 as cited by Friedrich Heiler in "Contemplation in Christian Mysticism", an essay in *Spiritual Disciplines,* collected papers in the Eranos Yearbook, Bollingen Series XXX. 4. p 222, 1955.
12) Heiler, Friedrich, "Contemplation in Christian Mysticism", an essay in *Spiritual Disciplines,* collected papers in the Eranos Yearbook, Bollingen Series XXX. 4. p 224, 1955.
13) Frend, W.H.C., *The Early Church,* p 188.
14) Ibid.
15) Ibid, p 192.
16) Ibid, p 194.
17) Ibid, p 195.
18) Ibid.
19) Pagels, Elaine, *The Gnostic Gospels,* Intro, p xxiii.
20) Ibid, p 179.
21) Armstrong, Karen, *A History of God,* p 114.
22) Genesis 28:12.
23) Ibid, 32-22.
24) Exodus 3: 2.
25) 1 Kings 19.
26) Isaiah 6.
27) Ezekiel 10.
28) Heiler, Friedrich, "Contemplation in Christian Mysticism", an essay in *Spiritual Disciplines,* collected papers in the Eranos Yearbook, Bollingen Series XXX. 4. pp 188-189, 1855.
29) Ibid, p 190.
30) Neumann, Erich, Mystical Man, p 386.

8: Gnosis

1) Sylvan, Father, *Lost Christianity* by Jacob Needleman p 139.
2) Ibid, p 211.
3) Ibid, p 209.
4) Ibid.
5) Romans 12: 2
6) Sylvan, Father, *Lost Christianity* by Jacob Needleman p 195.
7) Doresse, Jean, *The Secret Books of the Egyptian Gnostics,* p 48.
8) Ibid, p 36.
9) Ibid, p 50.
10) Petrement, Simone, *A Separate God,* p 356.
11) Mead, G.R.S., *Fragments of a Faith Forgotten,* p 14.
12) Ibid, p 29.
13) Doresse, Jean, *The Secret Books of the Egyptian Gnostics,* p 263.
14) Mead, G.R.S., *Fragments of a Faith Forgotten,* p 96.
15) Pagels, Elaine, *The Gnostic Gospels,* p 123.
16) Ibid, p 126.
17) Ibid, p 127.
18) Pagels, Elaine, *The Origin of Satan,* p 172.
19) Pagels, Elaine, *The Gnostic Gospels* pp 154-155.
20) Thomas, Gospel of, 37.20-35, in NHL, 119.
21) Ibid, 33.11-13, in NHL, 118
22) Silvanus, Teachings of, 88.24-92.12, in NHL 349-350.
23) Pagels, Elaine, *The Gnostic Gospels,* p 152.

9: Gathering Substance

1) Puech, Henri-Charles, "The Concept of Redemption in Manichaeism", papers from the Eranos Yearbook, Bollingen Series XXX, Vol 6 of *The Mystic Vision,* p 273.
2) Needleman, Jacob, *Lost Christianity,* pp 8-10. In reverse of Needleman's experience of being criticized by colleagues for taking Father Sylvan seriously, Morris Berman cites two cases in which he questioned the researches of colleagues because they contained no somatic content – that is, they

attempted to build complex theories on information that was purely statistical. Berman asks this question: "Who knows more about medieval sainthood – the historian who compiles data on age and nationality, or the one who goes to a monastery and sits in a cell for several months in complete silence?" *Coming to Our Senses,* pp 114-5.

3) Ibid, pp 87-88.
4) Ibid, pp 200-201.
5) Durant, Will, *Caesar and Christ,* p 606.
6) Petrement, Simone, *The Separate God,* p 478.
7) Kuhn, A.B., *Shadow of the Third Century,* p 283.
8) Epiphanius, Haer, 26. 3., as quoted by Hans Jonas in *The Gnostic Religion,* p 60. This idea of "gathering" bears a striking resemblance to Father Sylvan's notion of "energy accumulation", and may in fact be closely related. Jonas himself suspects that the metaphor being used has an inward aspect that goes beyond its cruder mythological meaning.
9) Ibid, Haer. 26. 13.
10) Jonas, Hans, *The Gnostic Religion,* p 60.
11) Petrement, Simone, *The Separate God,* p 137.
12) Ibid, p 151. This "unmixing" of spirit and matter may refer, in a veiled kind of way, to the process of dualistic balancing engaged in by the contemplative.
13) Porphyr, Ad Marcell, X, as quoted by Hans Jonas, *The Gnostic Religion,* p 61. The attempt to "gather in from the body all of its members" is clearly the contemplative's attempt to include sense of self alongside his/her ongoing perceptions of other and world, that is, rescue sense of self from the distracted condition in which it normally exists.
14) Jonas, Hans, *The Gnostic Religion,* p 62.
15) Puech, Henri-Charles, "The Concept of Redemption in Manichaeism", papers from the Eranos Yearbook, Bollingen Series XXX, Vol 6 of *The Mystic Vision,* p 284.

16) Ibid, p 273.
17) Ibid, p 278.
18) Ibid, p 281.
19) Ibid, pp 305-6.
20) Ibid, p 292.
21) Ibid, p 308.
22) Ibid, p 276.
23) Ibid, p 279.
24) Ibid, p 250.
25) Ibid, p 253.
26) Neumann, Erich, "Mystical Man", papers from the Eranos Yearbook, Bollingen Series XXX, Vol 6 of *The Mystic Vision,* p 377.
27) Jonas, Hans, *The Gnostic Religion,* p 95.
28) Ibid, p 95.
29) Ibid, p 69.
30) Secundinus, Epis. ad August., ed. Zycha, p 894, lines 21-22 as quoted by Henri-Charles Puech in "The Concept of Redemption in Manichaeism" papers from the Eranos Yearbook, Bollingen Series XXX Vol 6 of *The Mystic Vision,* p 291.
31) Puech, Henri-Charles, "The Concept of Redemption in Manichaeism", papers from the Eranos Yearbook, Bollingen Series XXX, Vol 6 of *The Mystic Vision,* p 299. To be "overpowered by the mixture" surely refers to identification with external events to the exclusion of self as presence.
32) Petrement, Simone, *The Separate God,* p 17.
33) Ibid, p 136.
34) Ibid, p 138.
35) Needleman, Jacob, *Lost Christianity,* pp 196-7.
36) Ibid.

10: To Be, or Not to Be

1) Roberts, Bernadette, *What is Self?* p 8.

2) Couliano, Ioan P., *The Tree of Gnosis,* pp 1-2.

3) Ibid.

4) Morin, Alain, *Journal of Consciousness Studies,* Vol 12, No 4/5, 2005.

5) Ibid, p 118. If Morin's observations are placed alongside those of Bernadette Robert, we end up with a self generated on two levels: (1) through emotional reactions, and (2) through internalized language responses. In this sense *all* internal articulations strengthen our concept of self; they need not actually concern the self at all. More often than not our internalized responses are emotionally based and purely fictional; that is, conducted with imagined persons with whom actual dialogues have not gone well. Rehearsal after the event is therefore the most common origin of "self-talk", although it can also serve the useful purpose of mental preparation. Whatever its form, "self-talk" creates the ongoing illusion of self-continuity, particularly when we question ourselves in relation to ideas or concepts. In such moments we talk to ourselves as if to a friend, but seldom reply in any coherent fashion. Nor do we have to, for it is at this point that unconscious realizations surface as conscious knowings.

6) Neumann, Erich, *The Origins and History of Consciousness,* pp 375-415.

7) Berman, Morris, *Coming to Our Senses,* p 343.

8) Ibid, p 344.

9) Roberts, Bernadette, *The Experience of No-Self,* p 156.

10) Needleman, Jacob, *Lost Christianity,* p 207.

11) Neumann, Erich, "Mystical Man", a paper from the Eranos Yearbook, *The Mystic Vision,* Bollingen Series XXX, Vol 6, p 397.

12) Ibid, p 399.

13) Ibid, p 410.
14) Needleman, Jacob, *Lost Christianity,* p 198. An interesting study in this connection is Julian Jaynes' *The Origin of Consciousness in the Breakdown of the Bicameral Mind.* Jaynes asks the big question: What is human consciousness, where did it come from, and what is its place in the material world? Answering these questions in a truly unique and thought-provoking manner, he suggests that ancient peoples from Mesopotamia to Peru could not "think" as we think today, and in this sense were not conscious as we are conscious. Unable to introspect, they hallucinated auditory responses and believed themselves to be communicating with divine beings. Jaynes' theory has been criticized over the years, but it is interesting to note how often it is now mentioned in psychological and philosophical studies. There is little doubt that conscious awareness emerged from unconscious processes; the question is: how and when?
15) Ibid, p 127. Jacob Needleman alerts us to the word *da'ath,* which is the Hebrew equivalent of *gnosis* in Greek. *Da'ath* is a form of knowledge that involves the whole person, not just the conscious mind. In Jewish tradition *da'ath* means divine omniscience, but when applied to a human being implies a knowing or awareness that infuses the whole human organism in the sense of a multi-faceted mind. Needleman pulls all of this into focus when he says, "*da'ath*... has its counterpart in the unfolding within man of the harmonizing power of consciousness, the growth of a new attention." (*Lost Christianity* p 127.)
16) Berman, Morris, *Coming to Our Senses,* p 158.
17) Needleman, Jacob, *Lost Christianity,* p 94.
18) Ibid.
19) Ibid, p 96. James Hillman's "truth *as* depth" definition applies here.
20) Roberts, Bernadette, *The Experience of No-Self,* p 157. See also

Tem Horwitz's essay "Reflections on my journey into non-being" as found in *Death and Philosophy* (p 10) edited by Jeff Malpas and Robert C. Solomon. In this essay Horwitz describes his experience after near physical death as being placed *squarely in the present*. When awake, he was "free of dreaming, wondering, speculating, fantasizing, analyzing." His thoughts "would rise up slowly and clearly. They would then dissolve into nothing. No residue. No Recycling. No tapes playing the same thoughts over and over. Initially there were abysses between thoughts. Vast empty spaces between thoughts. Peace." And later (p 11) "Having lost touch with the past, and not daydreaming into the future, I was lodged in the present. This present was peaceful, free from anxiety, free of discursive thinking, no tapes playing and replaying in my head."

21) Ibid, p 19.
22) Inge, W.R., *Mysticism in Religion,* p 199.
23) Neumann, Erich, "Mystical Man", a paper from the Eranos Yearbook, *The Mystic Vision,* Bollingen Series XXX, Vol 6, p 388.
24) Armstrong, Karen, *A History of God,* p 246.
25) Neumann, Erich, "Mystical Man", a paper from the Eranos Yearbook, *The Mystic Vision,* Bollingen Series XXX, Vol 6, p 397.
26) Forman, R.K.C., "What Does Mysticism Have to Teach Us About Consciousness", a paper in the *Journal of Consciousness Studies,* Vol 5, No 2, 1998.
27) Ouspensky, P.D., *Tertium Organum,* p 63.

11: The Underneath of Things

1) The likening of the unconscious to an iceberg was an image used by Gustav Fechner, Carl Jung and Sigmund Freud. Gustav Carl Carus also used this image, and compared the life of the psyche to that of a great, continuously circling

river illuminated in only one small area by the light of the sun. For Carus, the unconscious was the permanent infrastructure of consciousness itself, that which lay not only behind physiological functioning, but also behind imagination and perception.

2) Koestler, Arthur, *The Act of Creation*, p 190.
3) Ibid, p 166. The iceberg analogy is also used by cognitive unconscious advocates, but it has a quite different meaning from the one advanced here. The cognitive unconscious is seen to harbor all mental operations that structure and make conscious experience possible. This includes language, and is completely and irrevocably inaccessible to direct conscious control. In his 2008 paper, "The Dependence of Language on Consciousness" (Journal of Consciousness Studies, Volume 15, No. 6), Jordan Zlatev rejects this conception of the unconscious as both redundant and incoherent because it introduces a black box notion between neurobiological structures and processes on the one hand, and consciousness on the other. It is this conception of the unconscious, he argues, that first generation computationalist cognitive science thrived on, and it has influenced most second generation researchers to conceive embodied cognition as computational in origin. Hence the idea that it is only the tools of neuroscience that can unlock the secrets of the mind, all other approaches being considered inadequate. Zlatev's contention is that "consciousness is far from being the tip of an iceberg with respect to language, but rather constitutes its basis, i.e. *it is a necessary precondition for language.*"
4) Ibid.
5) Ibid, p 167.
6) Ibid, p 171.
7) Claxton, Guy, *The Wayward Mind*, p 222.
8) Jaynes, Julian, *The Origin of Consciousness in the Breakdown of the Bicameral Mind*, p 47.

9) Ibid, p 166. This should be kept in mind at 14.4 when dealing with Don Cupitt's claim that comprehension is bound to language
10) Jung, C.G., *The Integration of the Personality,* p 16.
11) Panksepp, Jaak, "The Periconscious Substrates of Consciousness: Affective States and the Evolutionary Origins of the Self", *Journal of Consciousness Studies,* Vol 5, No. 5/6, 1998, p 567. But there can also be a degrading of the self in terms of the rational ground we build for ourselves, a form of conscious reflection that systematically deprives us of feeling and sensibility – the body *as* 'truth' has been turned into a *body of truth* where the elemental field of being is all but ignored, or shunned. This also links us back to 6.4 and Bernadette Roberts' claim that self as an affectively governed system may only be temporary. At the same time, however, this system is said to constitute the ground of conscious functioning. We cannot have a knowing-self without a feeling-self, and vice versa. Why? Because it is the energy of the feeling center that fuels the reflexive mechanism of mind – without it we would have no sense of our own physical existence, and therefore no self-orientation in the world.
12) Claxton, Guy, *The Wayward Mind,* p 267.
13) Koestler, Arthur, *The Act of Creation,* p 13.
14) Hillman, James, *The Myth of Analysis,* p 31.
15) Butterworth, George (paper on Galen Strawson), *Journal of Consciousness Studies,* Vol 5, No. 2, 1998, p 132.
16) Thomson, Evan, *Journal of Consciousness Studies,* Vol 12, No 7, 2005, p 43.
17) Blackmore, Susan, *Journal of Consciousness Studies,* Vol 9, No 5/6, 2002, pp 17-28.
18) Ibid, p 19.
19) Ibid.
20) Ibid, p 27.

21) Ibid, p 19. Susan Blackmore observes that experimental scientists dislike "personal practice" in experimental situations. She, on the other hand, thinks it valuable: We "cannot avoid bringing implicit theories to bear on how we view our own experiences and what we say about them," p 23.
22) Malpas, Jeff, *Heidegger's Topology,* p 279.
23) Ibid, pp 290, 291.
24) Ibid, p 300.
25) Steiner, George, *Heidegger,* p 39.
26) Needleman, Jacob, *Lost Christianity,* pp 90, 91. The awakening or engendering of soul may be a simpler process than some philosophers think. Susan Blackmore's question "Am I conscious Now?" can be triggered through the simple process of nominating a physical object to act as a potential future trigger. For instance, I can decide that each time I see a BMW car on the street *I will come back to myself.* Any object can be chosen for this purpose, but it should be changed regularly to avoid habituation. This is of course no more than Eric Schwitzgebel's beeper experiment in a different form.
27) Koestler, Arthur, *The Act of Creation,* p 167.
28) Ibid, p 173.
29) Malpas, Jeff, *Heidegger's Topology,* p 182.
30) Jung, Carl, *Man and His Symbols,* p 84.
31) Keightley, Alan, *Wittgenstein, Grammar and God,* pp 64-5.
32) Hillman, James, *The Myth of Analysis,* p 13.
33) Roberts, Bernadette, *The Experience of No-Self,* p 182.

12: The Intermediate State

1) Sylvan, Father, *Lost Christianity* by Jacob Needleman, p 171.
2) Needleman, Jacob, *Lost Christianity,* p 69.
3) Ibid, p 152.
4) Ibid.
5) Pagels, Elaine, *The Gnostic Gospels,* p 162.
6) Ibid.

7) Needleman, Jacob, *Lost Christianity,* p 166.
8) Ibid, p 119.
9) Ibid, p 123.
10) Burns, Robert, (Poem not yet identified)
11) Needleman, Jacob, *Lost Christianity,* p 92.
12) Ibid, p 106.
13) Ibid, p 192.
14) Ibid, p 166.
15) Ibid, p 168.
16) Ibid.
17) Ibid, p 175. An excellent primer in what an after-death "self" or "entity" might be like is Corliss Lamont's *The Illusion of Immortality.* Surveying the chief religious conceptions of an afterlife from ancient times to the 20th century, he analyses these views in the light of modern science and philosophy, and furnishes us with what John Dewey calls "... an extraordinarily complete and well-informed discussion of the problem of continuing personal life after death."
18) Ibid, p 193.
19) Ibid, p 176.

13: Mount Purgatory

1) Sylvan, Father, *Lost Christianity* by Jacob Needleman, p 139.
2) Pagels, Elaine, *The Gnostic Gospels,* p 176.
3) Needleman, Jacob, *Lost Christianity,* pp 136-7.
4) Armstrong, Karen, *A History of God,* p 439.
5) Rahner, Hugo, "The Christian Mysteries and the Pagan Mysteries", an essay in *The Mysteries,* papers from the Eranos Yearbook, Bollingen Series XXX. 2. 1955.
6) Armstrong, Karen, *A History of God,* p 133.
7) Ibid, p 255.
8) Ibid, pp 116-117.
9) Needleman, Jacob, *Lost Christianity,* p 137. See also Joan Stambough's essay in *Heidegger and Asian Thought,* edited by

Graham Parkes (p 85), where Stambough notes that Heidegger's term 'releasement' (borrowed from Meister Eckhart as *Gelassenheit*) reflects the Stoic conception of *apatheia,* which he translates as "freedom from strong and turbulent emotions." Stambough further develops this point by saying that Heidegger characterized *Gelassenheit* as keeping oneself open, as waiting without an object in mind.

10) Ibid.
11) Armstrong, Karen, *A History of God,* p 134.
12) Rahner, Hugo, "The Christian Mysteries and the Pagan Mysteries", an essay from *The Mysteries,* papers from the Eranos Yearbook, Bollingen Series XXX. 2. 1955, p 57.
13) Needleman, Jacob, *Lost Christianity,* p 40.
14) Armstrong, Karen, *A History of God,* p 132.
15) Cowan, James, *Desert Fathers,* p 103.
16) Ibid, p 97.
17) Ibid, p 100.
18) Armstrong, Karen, *A History of God,* p 49.
19) Ibid, p 234.
20) Needleman, Jacob, *Lost Christianity,* p 87.
21) Ibid, p 96.
22) Rahner SJ, Karl, *Theological Investigations,* Vol 17, p 37.
23) Armstrong, Karen, *A History of God,* p 119.
24) Needleman, Jacob, *Lost Christianity,* p 174. According to Bernadette Roberts in *What is Self? A Study of the Spiritual Journey in Terms of Consciousness* (Sentient Publications LLC, 2005, p 169), salvation from sin was not the outcome of Christ's death on the cross. In her contemplative scheme of realization Christ saves us through our taking on his quality of consciousness. To follow Christ did not mean to put Christ on like a coat, it meant to have the same interior experiences, take on the same perspective and through that change in consciousness discover new forms of behavior.
25) Roberts, Bernadette, *The Experience of No-Self,* p 200.

26) Needleman, Jacob, *Lost Christianity,* p 196.
27) Ibid, p 197.
28) Eckhart, Meister, *A Modern Translation,* (New York: Harper Torchbooks. 1941, pp 231-32.
29) Needleman, Jacob, *Lost Christianity,* p 197.
30) Ibid.
31) Roberts, Bernadette, *The Experience of No-Self,* p 130.
32) Needleman, Jacob, *Lost Christianity,* p 138.
33) Ibid, p 137.
34) Ibid.
35) Basil, St, Epistle 234.1.
36) Armstrong, Karen, *A History of God,* p 255.
37) Cowan, James, *Desert Fathers,* p 101.

14: What Exactly is a Mystical Experience?

1) Cupitt, Don, *Mysticism after Modernity,* 1998, p 60.
2) Forman, R.K.C., "What Does Mysticism Have to Teach Us?" *Journal of Consciousness Studies,* Vol 5, No. 2, 1998, p188.
3) Underhill, Evelyn, *Mysticism,* Preface p vii.
4) Laski, Marghanita, *Ecstasy in Secular and Religious Experience,* p 254.
5) Ibid, p 133. In his paper "Mysticism, Language and the via negativa", Robert Forman acquaints us with "constructivist" and "decontextualist" theories of mystical experience, and slowly teases the problems in both approaches to the surface. But like Marghanita Laski, he tends to rest on the side of the decontextualists in that he dismisses the idea of all mystical experience being constructivist at base. It is, he writes, "not at all clear just how language and concepts are supposed to be involved in a mystical experience." Why does Forman think this? Because the mystic isn't supposed to be "seeing or smelling *any*thing". Where then is the purported intentional object? This seems correct, and one can add that the confusion arising at this point is due to

researchers failing to differentiate between *via positiva* and *via negativa* experiences. The latter are mystical, the former are more likely to spring from affective intoxication with religious beliefs. This does not mean that *via positiva* experiences cannot graduate to the *via negativa* level, but given the Christian faith's need to continually bolster its authority *as* a belief system, this graduation is more often than not unlikely.

6) Ibid, p 349. Here arises the problem of spiritual directors of traditional mold forcing *via negativa* experiences back into a *via positiva* framework. As seen at 14.3 in relation to R.C. Zaehner, this is to overlook the fact that the *negativa* experience is by its very nature an unhooking from images, sounds, smells, etc, and even a jettisoning of such phenomena altogether.
7) Forman, R.K.C., "Mysticism, Language & The Via Negativa", *Journal of Consciousness Studies,* Volume 1, No. 1, 1994, p 40.
8) Ibid.
9) Ibid.
10) Ibid, p 41.
11) Ibid, p 42.
12) Ibid, p 39.
13) Mangan, Bruce, "Language and Experience in the Cognitive Study of Mysticism" – *Commentary on Forman, Journal of Consciousness Studies,* Volume 1, No. 2, 1994, p 250.
14) Ibid.
15) Kotoh, Tetsuaki, "Language and Silence" in *Heidegger and Asian Thought* edited by Graham Parkes, p 203.
16) Cupitt, Don, *Mysticism after Modernity,* 1998, p 41. In his research paper, "Mudra and Thinking", David M. Levin catches the reductionist flavor of Don Cupitt's thinking when he says "Traditional Western metaphysics would assert that our motility and gesturing (*legein*) depend upon, and are in need of, a 'rational' grounding (*logos*). But the concept of this 'rational' grounding is the historical product of a reflection

depriving itself of feeling and sensibility, a reflection that, in reaching the historical stage of formal metaphysics, has virtually lost all touch with the bodily truth of its original and elemental field of being." This paper is to be found in *Heidegger and Asian Thought,* edited by Graham Parkes, p 255.

17) Ibid, p 38.
18) Hunt, H., "The Truth Value of Mystical Experience", *Journal of Consciousness Studies,* Vol 13, No. 12, 2006, p 28.
19) Needleman, Jacob, *Lost Christianity,* 1990, p 51.
20) Hunt, H., "The Truth Value of Mystical Experience", *Journal of Consciousness Studies,* Vol 13, No. 12, 2006, p 30.
21) Ibid, pp 30-31.
22) Ibid, p 31.
23) Laski, Marghanita, *Ecstasy in Secular and Religious Experience,* p 252. The idea of "induced ecstatic experience" may have more than one meaning; it could also refer to experiences induced as a result of the belief system we happen to carry, not just 'techniques' used to gain entry to ecstatic states. This fact has been conveniently overlooked by ardent believers in the stock Jesus story.
24) Ibid.
25) Ibid, p 123.
26) Ibid.
27) Ibid, p 131. In *Wittgenstein, Grammar and God,* p 99-101, Alan Keightley hits on this question from a slightly different angle. He suggests that Albert Camus' Sisyphus "symbolizes a secular response to contingency which is very similar to [Professor D.Z.] Phillips' [Christian] believer... Camus' 'divinity' lurks on the beaches of Algiers and is connected with the light of his native land... Phillips' 'divinity' hails from Palestine and is related to the suffering of the Jews and particularly to one Jew, Jesus of Nazareth. Thus the vocabulary and concepts which both Camus and Phillips use to

express their commitment will clearly be different. Yet is this a reason for putting their positions into logically different categories(?)" This is to say that "the distinctive characteristics of religious belief can be closely paralleled by the 'eternal' view of a man [Camus's] who vigorously held that Christianity was an illusion." Touching on the problem of language use, he then says, "Phillips uses terms like 'God', 'grace', 'sacrifice', etc., and Camus uses 'unconquerable summer,' 'fate', 'the given', etc. The difference is in the language they use. The term 'God' has a very wide religious usage and the phrase 'unconquerable summer' is presumably private to Camus. Nevertheless, they both perform the same expressive function."

28) Underhill, Evelyn, *Mysticism,* Preface p ix. Having made this point, however, it should be pointed out that Bernadette Roberts sees quite a difference between, say, the Hindu conception of the Absolute and the Christian conception of God. There is, she contends, a fundamental difference in relation to the Hindu or Christian contemplative's experience of this ultimate divine principle. But this has to do with the contemplative's interpretation of what she/he may have experienced, not with what was experienced in itself. As Roberts' experience of God or the Absolute is by far radically different from what Christian contemplatives have described historically (Meister Eckhart accepted), this does not disallow Laski's claim that they may in fact be fundamentally the same experience. The reason for this discrepancy may well be the same as that separating Roberts' experience of the divine from that of her peers both now and in the past. Whether Hindu, Buddhist or Christian, there is probably a tendency, when back in the ordinary conscious realm of experience, to conform to and confirm what is expected according to the spiritual canon one has been brought up with. This would result in thinking one's spiritual journey

had reached its zenith when it in fact had not. (See *What is Self?*, Sentient Publications, LLC., 2005, p 90.)

29) Cupitt, Don, *Mysticism after Modernity*, 1998, p 62.
30) Woods, Richard, "Mysticism and Social Action: The Mystic's Calling, Development and Social Activity", *Journal of Consciousness Studies*, Vol 3, No. 2, 1996, p 158.
31) Cupitt, Don, *Mysticism after Modernity*, 1998, p 61.
32) Ibid. Don Cupitt would probably find Eckhart's "I pray God to quit me of God", or his "God is love because he is above love and affection" (see 6.6) non-propositional and therefore nonsensical, but such statements can in fact be unpacked quite easily when you understand what not having an affective center means experientially. Bernadette Roberts is again specific: "The contemplative is more at home with not-knowing than he is with knowing." She adds interestingly: "Jung never grasped not-knowing as a way-of-knowing. Instead he was totally taken up with knowing; indeed, this is his Gnosticism." (*What is Self?*, Sentient Publications, LLC, 2005, p 99.)
33) Shanon, Benny, "A Psychological Theory of Consciousness", *Journal of Consciousness Studies*, Volume 15, No. 5, 2008, p 42.
34) Grotowski, Jerzy, "A Kind of Volcano", an essay in *Gurdjieff*, edited by Jacob Needleman and George Baker, p 90.
35) Cupitt, Don, *Mysticism after Modernity*, 1998, p 61. And again it is Morris Berman who comes to our assistance in *Coming to Our Senses*, p 122, where he says, "In the last analysis *mentalities* remains abstract, preserving the psychic distance so central to modern cognition. Mind and body, fact and value, still wind up on opposite sides of the fence… The history of *mentalities* reflects the great divide set up by the Scientific Revolution, and it in fact understands this. To remedy the situation, however, it goes on a journey that is ultimately baroque and convoluted.... That is to say, it attempts to recover the body by making a journey within the

mind… This peek-a-boo structure – itself a variant on the theme of psychic distance – has finally emerged as the real structure of modern cognition, and so long as the subjective experience of the body and the emotional life is excluded from historical understanding we shall continue to go round in circles.

36) Zlatev, Jordan, *Dependence of Language on Consciousness,* p 38. As noted at reference 16 above, David M. Levin perceives traditional Western philosophy as having so grounded its thinking in the 'rational' that it has ended up deprived of the ability to bring 'feeling' (the 'felt sense' of one's existence) to bear on the same questions. He later expands on this point (page 256 of *Heidegger and Asian Thought* edited by Graham Parkes) by suggesting that this very different method of reflection consists of a *permeating of the body* through a more thoughtful awareness, a recollection of the presence of Being, a re-membering of Being that allows us to perceive reality touched by a pre-conceptual, pre-ontological understanding of our mortal being.

37) Claxton, Guy, *The Wayward Mind,* p 307.

38) Ibid, p 357.

39) Berman, Morris, *Coming to Our Senses,* p 118-9. Bernadette Roberts is in agreement with Berman. The "real drama, change and struggle of transformation takes place in the feeling-self. The deepest feeling-self IS the experience of life, being, existence…" (*What is Self?,* Sentient Publications LLC, 2005, p 89.)

40) Jung, Carl, *Man and His Symbols,* p 66. Bernadette Roberts also touches on this problem. She states that *all* consciousness is self-consciousness, not just the conscious level. Awareness OF penetrates to the unconscious level of consciousness. Consciousness is all of a piece; it is we who, in our search for conscious clarity, break it into BEFORE and AFTER realms of experience. What Roberts seems to be

saying is that we cannot have a knowing self (an awareness OF self) without a feeling self, or a feeling self without a knowing self. They go hand in hand. Each sustains the other and could not exist without the other. Proof of this lies in our experience of our own individual lives moment by moment – reflexive mind is seamlessly embedded in our experience of being an alive being and cannot be detached from it. We are simultaneously dual and non-dual beings. (*What is Self?* (Sentient Publications edition, 2005 p 59.)

41) Davies, Paul, *The Mind of God,* p 16. Another approach to this question is to be found in M.L. von Franz's essay "The Process of Individuation", where she remarks on the frequency with which the symbol of the Self is often an object of inorganic matter. There is, she suggests, an unknown relationship between what we call the unconscious psyche and what we call matter... "it may prove to be that 'psyche' and 'matter' are actually the same phenomenon". *Man and His Symbols,* p 226.

42) *Nietzsche, Basic Writings of,* ed. Walter Kaufmann, Random House, New York, 1968, pp 933-95. In relation to Wolfgang Pauli, M.L. von Franz reports in "Science and the Unconscious", her concluding essay in *Man and His Symbols,* p 181, that Pauli believed we should "parallel our investigation of outer objects with a psychological investigation of the *inner origins* of our scientific concepts." As this should include unconscious as well as conscious influences in our perceptions of world, self and other, Niels Bohr's theory of complementarity is perhaps even more complex than first deduced.

43) Franz, M.L., "The Process of Individuation", an essay in *Man and His Symbols,* conceived and edited by Carl Jung, p 253.

44) Abram, David, *The Spell of the Sensuous,* p 56.

45) Ibid, pp 74-75.

46) Lancaster, Brian, "New Lamps for Old: psychology and the

13th century flowering of mysticism", *Transpersonal Psychology Review,* 2001, Vol 5, pp 3-14. In recent research done by Guy Claxton and Paul Howard-Jones at Bristol University, what are termed 'uncreative' people can be teased out of their rigid mental frame of mind and into a creative one with relative ease. See *The Wayward Mind,* pp 267-268.

47) Steiner, George, *Heidegger,* 1992, p 46.

48) Ibid, p 47. See also Otto Poggeler's description of a conversation Heidegger had with a Japanese guest where he described his own thinking as "a trace on the way" (*Wegspur*) – traces that *directed his thinking into the realm of its source.* This 'thinking' is obviously not verbal rumination, but in the delicate sense meant by the poet Rilke in his essay on Hölderlin's poem "Brot und Wein" where Hölderlin speaks of "the trace of the gods who have disappeared". For Poggeler this translates as: "Being becomes a trace of the Holy, the Holy the trace of the Godhead." And again, "Being as trace is for Heidegger voice and counsel (*Zuspruch*), but not in such a way that the one speaking hears his own voice... but in such a way that the counsel withdraws into the unspoken." Bernadette Roberts could not have put it better. Poggeler's essay – "West-East Dialogue" – is to be found in *Heidegger and Asian Thought,* edited by Graham Parkes, p 70.

49) Malpas, Jeff, *Heidegger's Topology, Being, Place, World,* 2006, pp 35-36.

50) Ibid, p 36.

51) For Heidegger, thinking necessarily moves towards a destination of which it has no foreknowledge. In this sense the nebulous form of language used by Heidegger is, as J.L. Mehta suggests in "Heidegger and Vedanta", "not a confusion but part of the stringency or rigor (which is something quite different from 'exactness,' as Heidegger

points out) necessitated by this path of thinking itself." This essay is to be found in *Heidegger and Asian Thought,* ed. Graham Parkes, p 31-35.

52) Poggeler, Otto, "West-East Dialogue", as found in *Heidegger and Asian Thought,* ed. Graham Parkes, p 68.

53) Keightley, Alan, Wittgenstein, Grammar and God, p 29.

54) Ibid.

55) Shanon, Benny, "A Psychological Theory of Consciousness", *Journal of Consciousness Studies,* Volume 15, No. 5, 2008, p 37.

56) Zlatev, Jordan, "Dialectics of Consciousness and Language", *Journal of Consciousness Studies,* Volume 15, No. 6, 2008, p 8. There is no doubting the importance of language; the self talks to the self and by doing so reinforces its selfness. But as Zlatev shows in his paper, to adopt the extreme position that it is language alone that brings about the illusion of having qualitative experience (D. Dennett, 1991 and E. Macphail, 1998) is perhaps to go too far. J Searle agrees with Dennett that there is nothing but the biological organism at base, but he follows with the observation that consciousness is equally basic to the biological organism, having intrinsic intentionality. This suggests that language inherits its intentionality in a derived manner. (*Mind, Language & Society: Philosophy in the Real World,* Weidenfeld and Nicolson, London, 1999.)

57) Kotoh, Tetsuaki, "Language of Silence", as found in *Heidegger and Asian Thought,* edited by Graham Parkes, pp 201-211. Kotoh further suggests that Heidegger's "echo of silence" is heard and followed within "the silence of stillness", a choice of words that merges with Bernadette Roberts' *still point at the center of the affective system.* In Kotoh's terms it is not a matter of "organizing a chaotic world into an already acquired system of meaning", it is a matter of realizing that philosophical thinking does not need to "consider language as ultimate and regulate everything in accordance with language."

58) Shanon, Benny, "A Psychological Theory of Consciousness", *Journal of Consciousness Studies,* Volume 15, No. 5, 2008, p 9. This reading of things contradicts Heidegger's notion that all consciousness is consciousness *of* something, that there is no such thing as a worldless subject. But if that were truly the case, then his replacing of the Aristotelian "now" with "presence" would cease to hold and fall back into *a string of nows* governed by time and cognitions *of.* But as he himself indicates, there is "room" for man and Being to be "appropriated" to each other, and that seems to disallow the idea that *all* cognitive operations are meta-mentations – that is, productions of mind inspected further through reflection (Cons 3).
59) Roberts, Bernadette, *What is Self? A Study of the Spiritual Journey in Terms of Consciousness.* (Sentient Publications, LLC, 2005) p 54.
60) Shanon, Benny, "A Psychological Theory of Consciousness", *Journal of Consciousness Studies,* Volume 15, No. 5, 2008, p 22.
61) Ibid, 28.
62) Ibid, p 33. Shanon's is perhaps the most important psychological contribution to the subject of transcendence I've come across of late; it moves dexterously into Bernadette Roberts' territory and leaves the reader with a useful conception of what the transcendent levels are *as* experiential categories.
63) William, Archbishop Rowan, *Lost Icons,* p 180. Quote referred to is from *Inwardness and Existence. Subjectivity in/and Hegel, Heidegger, Marx and Freud,* by Walter Davies, p 104.

15: Back to Bernadette

1) Roberts, Bernadette, *What is Self?*, p 4.
2) Ibid, pp 4-6.
3) Forman, R.K., "What Does Mysticism Have to Teach Us About Consciousness?", *Journal of Consciousness Studies,* Vol 5, No. 2, 1998, p185.

4) Ibid. See also Joan Stambaugh's research paper "Heidegger, Taoism, and Metaphysics", as found in *Heidegger and Asian Thought,* edited by Graham Parkes, p 86. According to Stambough, Heidegger characterized *Gelassenheit* (releasement) as a kind of waiting without expectation. Waiting in this sense has no object, it is contentless, yet not pointless; it is closer to keeping oneself open without having anything definite in mind. In this sense *Gelassenheit* means to "stop doing all the things we constantly do."
5) Ibid, p 186.
6) Ibid.
7) Claxton, Guy, *The Wayward Mind,* p 152. See also Joan Stambough's essay, "Heidegger, Taoism and Metaphysics", as found in *Heidegger and Asian Thought,* edited by Graham Parkes, p 85. Here there is a tantalizing similarity between what Guy Claxton and Robert Forman are trying to articulate about non-thinking thinking and Heidegger's description of a form of thinking that is not representational. In Heidegger's scheme this form of thinking is a *waiting* with no object in mind, an *openness* devoid of mental *doing*. In this sense Heidegger's term *Gelassenheit* (releasement)is taken by Stambough to mean "to stop doing all the things we constantly do." Then comes an interesting correlation: "Anyone familiar with any kind of meditation will recognize what Heidegger is trying to deal with here," (p 87.) And so we come back to 'waiting', to a 'doing' that is not a doing of anything, to an attentive, intensive form of concentration (*Andenken*) likened by Stambough to "non-willing willing" as found in the teachings of the Buddhist thinker Dogen.
8) Ibid, p 150.
9) Ibid, pp 127-8.
10) Forman, R.K., "What Does Mysticism Have to Teach Us About Consciousness?", *Journal of Consciousness Studies,* Vol 5, No 2, 1998, p 200. William James suggested that the idea

of the unconscious could be compared to the "field" concept in physics. So could it be that as particles appear in a certain order in a magnetic field that psychological content may also pattern itself within the unconscious field? This question was posed by M.L. von Franz, one of Carl Jung's associates.

11) Roberts, Bernadette, *What is Self?*, p 4.
12) Ibid.
13) Ibid, p 7.
14) Claxton, Guy, *The Wayward Mind*, p 193.
15) Ibid, p 203.
16) Ibid, p 257.
17) Ibid, p 262.
18) Kotoh, Tetsuaki, "Language and Silence", from *Heidegger and Asian Thought* edited by Graham Parkes, p 202.
19) Roberts, Bernadette, *What is Self?*, p 7.
20) Ibid, pp 10-11. An interesting slant on the question of unity in consciousness is to be found in Jeff Malpas' 1999 paper, *Constituting the Mind: Kant, Davidson and the Unity of Consciousness.* Malpas pushes beyond the idea that self-reflexivity alone underlies such a unity, and suggests, via Kant, that knowledge is composed of judgments, and that judgments that properly give rise to knowledge are always synthetic, that is, essentially dependent on the connecting up or synthesis of representations. In the absence of such connections such states of mind could be said to have no content at all.
21) Ibid, p 11.
22) Roberts, Bernadette, *What is Self?*, p 66.
23) Shanon, Benny, "A Psychological Theory of Consciousness", *Journal of Consciousness Studies,* Volume 15, No. 5, p 35. As noted in Chapter 14, Benny Shanon's breakdown of consciousness levels and states affords us a glimpse of mental processes seldom detected by regular researchers, and in this instance the observation made by Shanon is

particularly telling in relation to Roberts' description of an affective still point in consciousness. He tells us that as we draw towards Cons4 "the distinction between the regions diminish and become blurred. Specifically, at one end of the space consciousness is primitive (Cons1) and therefore not amenable to differentiation and distinction between experience and selfhood, whereas at the other end (Cons5) it transcends such distinctions. Geometrically speaking, as one draws towards the two extremes, the distance between the lines marking the region decreases and that in the limit they converge to a point… "

24) Merton, Thomas, *Zen and the Birds of Appetite,* pp 4-5, as quoted by Jacob Needleman in *Lost Christianity,* p 114.
25) Ibid, *Zen and the Birds of Appetite,* p 38, as quoted by Jacob Needleman in *Lost Christianity,* p 114.
26) Roberts, Bernadette, *What is Self?,* Introduction p x.

16: Dying Like a Dirty Dog

1) Grotowski, Jerzy, "A Kind of Volcano", an essay in *Gurdjieff,* edited by Jacob Needleman and George Baker, p 90.
2) Don Cupitt rejects the idea of subjective self-reflectivity as being in any way valuable in terms of meaning; that was a hope sandwiched between the early seventeenth and the early twentieth centuries that bore no useful fruit. Arguments from religious experience were of no consequences then, and equally of no consequence now. True as this observation is on many levels (trying to prove the existence of God or some implicit moral order cannot be done by way of subjective experience), Cupitt's argument weakens when he automatically equates mystical experience with religious beliefs and pronounces mystical experience subjectively invalid because of that supposed relationship. At the *via positiva* level of mystical experience, emotional intoxication can seem to verify religious beliefs for the

experiencer, but at the *via negativa* levels the very opposite is true as Harold O.J. Brown attests in the introductory quote at 7.0. When *via negativa* mysticism begins to gain ground in the full-blown sense it unravels rather than confirms religious beliefs. This is perhaps why Cupitt is later forced to interpret the tendency of experienced mystics to question belief forms as a species of political subversion. (*Mysticism after Modernity* pp 35-61.)

3) Ibid, p 93.
4) Claxton, Guy, *The Heart of Buddhism,* p 127.
5) Needleman, Jacob, "Gurdjieff, or the Metaphysics of Energy", an essay in *Gurdjieff,* edited by Jacob Needleman and George Baker, pp 83-84. The question of conscience is a difficult one for Christians, indeed for anyone. The modern, democratic idea of conscience is that we each, ultimately, have the right to decide what is right and what is wrong for ourselves. This is a "rights of the individual" argument that has taken hold in our time, but it may be mistaken in its basic premise. Not in the Catholic sense of a willful ignoring of established doctrine for selfish purposes (the use of contraceptive devices is, for the Catholic hierarchy, a major sin), but in the sense of our becoming aware of how we overlook our own habituated foibles. We are adept at side-stepping our own weaknesses, yet do manage to glimpse them from time to time. It's a matter of awareness levels. Caught mostly in submerged and engaged thought as we are, our capacity for self-reflection is impaired. In this sense, and in this sense alone, is our ability to view and correct our own behavior through conscience not as robust as we might think.
6) Needleman, Jacob, *Lost Christianity,* p 212.
7) Williams, Archbishop Rowan, *Lost Icons,* pp 183-4.
8) Needleman, Jacob, "Gurdjieff, or the Metaphysics of Energy," an essay in *Gurdjieff,* edited by Jacob Needleman and George Baker, p 80.

9) Sylvan, Father, as cited in *Lost Christianity* by Jacob Needleman, p 194.
10) Ibid.
11) Ibid, p 193.
12) Needleman, Jacob, "Gurdjieff, or the Metaphysics of Energy," an essay in *Gurdjieff,* edited by Jacob Needleman and George Baker, Intro, p ix.
13) Walker, Kenneth, *Venture with Ideas,* Intro, p 10.
14) Roberts, Bernadette, *What is Self? A Study of the Spiritual Journey in Terms of Consciousness.* (Sentient Publications, LLC edition, 2005, pp 165-6.) Roberts makes an extraordinary statement in this section of her book. She accuses God of overstepping himself and pushing her human limits at age nine too far. She then caps this statement with the following observation: The result… left me with the decided intuition that God's work in this human form [herself] was actually a piece of research, or that God was testing to see just how far he could stretch the human limits – possibly with the idea of refashioning them." One makes of this what one will.
15) Ouspensky, P.D., *In Search of the Miraculous,* p 119.
16) Forman, Robert K., "What Does Mysticism Have to Teach us?", a research paper in the *Journal of Consciousness Studies,* Vol 5, No. 2, 1998, p 186.
17) Mehta, J.L., "Heidegger and Vedanta", p 32. As found in *Heidegger and Asian Thought,* ed. Graham Parkes.
18) Ouspensky, P.D., *In Search of the Miraculous,* p 119.

17: "In the Blink of an Eye"

1) Choisnel, Jacques, "An Unfinished Creation", as quoted in *Gurdjieff* by Jacob Needleman, p 203.
2) Origen, *Homelies sur les nombres,* XXIV.2. In relation to the question of systems of ethics mentioned in this paragraph, I should draw attention to one notable exception, that of Warwick Fox's book *A Theory of General Ethics: Human*

Relationships, Nature, and the Built Environment, MIT Press, USA, 2006. This is a sensitive evaluation of the ethical problems we face in relation to empathy that deserves close attention.

3) James, the Epistle of, 1: 24. Additional texts to consult on these important issues are Robert Eisenman's *James the Brother of Jesus,* and Jeffrey Butz's *The Brother of Jesus.* (See Select Bibliography)
4) Forget, Alain, *How To Get Out Of This World Alive.*
5) Hence the idea of God as an "entity" and Jesus the "man" *as* God. Useful as these anthropomorphic ideas were in the early centuries, however, they later became an impediment due to the literalist tendency to construct out of them highly elaborate theological schemes. Hillman's suggestion that we *imaginatively* replace our psychological complexes with the Greek gods is of course an altogether different proposition – it may even be fun to perceive our psychic "bits" in this way.
6) Forget, Alain, *How To Get Out Of This World Alive,* p 61.
7) In his paper "Empathy Needs a Face", Jonathan Cole notes that in terms of simple definitions "empathy" and "sympathy" are closely related, but are not identical. Supplying us with a definition that must surely remind us of the differentiation made between "emotion" and "feeling" at 3.4, he says, "Sympathy involves an identification and similarity of feeling with another. Empathy, though a closer and more intimate process, does not necessarily involve such an emotional correspondence, though it usually does." What interests me about this definition is its recognition that empathy does not necessarily involve emotion. In this deeper sense empathy equals *evaluative feeling;* it may contain emotion, but that does not make it superficial in character. Nor does it empty it of feeling, for feeling need not have wayward emotional content. (*Journal of Consciousness Studies,* Vol. 8, No. 5-7, 2001.)

8) Steiner, George, *Heidegger,* p 83.
9) Cupitt, Don, *Mysticism after Modernity,* p 36.
10) Forman, R.C., "Mysticism, Language & The Via Negativa", a paper in the *Journal of Consciousness Studies,* Vol. 1, No. 1, 1994.
11) Levin, David M., "Mudra as Thinking", as found in *Heidegger and Asian Thought,* edited by Graham Parkes, p 252. See also Morris Berman's *Coming to Our Senses* (p 59) where he suggests that the medieval practice of self-flagellation may represent not merely an attempt to degrade the body, but also a way of feeling the body that had been desensitized.
12) Martin Heidegger sometimes describes Being as a 'look' (Blick), and as an 'insight' (Einblick) into that which is. This is not intellectual insight in the sense of the mind lighting up with conscious understanding, it is more an intimation or hint of the Holy in the sense of our becoming open to what is – it is what the poet Rainer Maria Rilke means in *The Notebooks of Malte Laurids Brigge* when he speaks of *learning to see.*
13) Shanon, Benny, "A Psychological Theory of Consciousness", *Journal of Consciousness Studies,* Volume 15, No. 5, 2008, p 35.

Select Bibliography

Abrams, David, *The Spell of the Sensuous,* Vintage Books, New York, 1997.

Angus, S, *The Mystery Religions and Christianity: A Study in the Religious Background of Early Christianity,* John Murray, London, (reprint) 1925.

Armstrong, Karen, *A History of God,* Mandarin, 1994.

The First Christian: St. Paul's Impact on Christianity, Pan, London, 1983.

The Battle for God: Fundamentalism in Judaism, Christianity and Islam, Harper Collins, 2001.

Bachelard, Gaston, *The Poetics of Reverie,* Beacon Press, Boston, 1960.

Bainton, Roland, H., *Early Christianity,* Van Nostrand Reinhold Company, New York, 1960.

Bancroft, Anne, *The Luminous Vision; Six Medieval Mystics & Their Teachings,* George Allen & Unwin, London, 1982.

Bernard de Clairvaux, St., *The Influence of,* Anglican Essays with an introduction by Jean Leclercq OSB,

Fairacres Publication No. 60, 1976.

Bernard de Clairvaux, St., *Sermons on the Canticles,* L11, 2, 3 as cited by Friedrich Heiler in "Contemplation in Christian Mysticism", an essay in *Spiritual Disciplines,* collected papers in the Eranos Yearbook, Bollingen Series XXX.

Berman, Morris, *Coming to Our Senses,* Bantam Books, New York, 1990.

Bettenson, Henry, *The Early Church Fathers,* Oxford University Press, 1991.

Black, D.M., The Ownership of Consciousness, *Journal of Consciousness Studies,* Volume 15, No. 7, 2008.

Blackmore, Susan, *Journal of Consciousness Studies,* Vol 9, No 5/6, 2002.

Consciousness: An Introduction, Hodder & Stoughton, UK, 2003.

Bredero, Adriaan H., *Bernard of Clairvaux: Between Cult and History,* William B. Eerdmans Publishing Company, Grand Rapids, Michigan, 1996.

Brenneman, James E., *Canons in Conflict: Negotiating Texts in True and False Prophesy,* Oxford University Press, New York, 1997.

Britannica Encyclopedia, 1956 edition, Vol. 14.

Brook, Peter, *The Empty Space,* Penguin Books, 1972.

Bultmann, Rudolf, *Primitive Christianity in its Contemporary Setting,* Collins, The Fontana Library, 1960.

Butterworth, George, *Journal of Consciousness Studies* Vol 5, No. 2, 1998.

Butterfield, Herbert, *Christianity and History,* G. Bell & Sons, London, 1950.

Butz, Jeffrey, J., *The Brother of Jesus and The Lost Teachings of Christianity,* Inner Traditions, Rochester, Vermont, 2005.

Cameron, Ron, Editor, *The Other Gospels: Non-Canonical Gospel Texts,* Lutterworth Press, Cambridge,1982.

Cheyne, J.A., "The Ominous Numinous", *Journal of Consciousness Studies,* Vol 8, No. 5-7, 2001.

Choisnel, Jacques, *An Unfinished Creation,* as quoted in *Gurdjieff,* edited by Jacob Needleman and George Baker, Continuum, New York, 1996.

Churton, Tobias, *The Gnostics,* Weidenfeld and Nicolson in association with Channel Four Television Company Ltd, and Border Television plc, 1987.

Claxton, Guy, *The Heart of Buddhism,* Aquarian/Thorsons, London, 1990.

The Wayward Mind, ABACUS, 2005.

Couliano, Ioan P. *The Tree of Gnosis, Mythology from Early Christianity to Modern Nihilism,* Harper SanFrancisco, 1992.

Cowan, James, *Desert Father/A Journey in the Wilderness with Saint Anthony,* New Seeds Books, Boston, 2006.

Corbin, Henry, *The Man of Light in Iranian Sufism,* translated from the French by Nancy Pearson for Shambhala, Boulder, Colorado, 1978.

Corliss Lamont, Wisdom Library, A Division of Philosophical Library, New York, (3rd edition) 1959.

Cross, Lawrence, *Eastern Christianity: The Byzantine Tradition,* E.J. Dwyer, Australia, 1988.

Cupitt, Don, *The Sea of Faith/Christianity in Change,* British Broadcasting Corporation, 1984.

"The Christ of Christendom", an essay in *The Myth of God Incarnate* edited by John Hick, SCM Press, Ltd., 1977.

Mysticism after Modernity, Blackwell Publishers, Oxford, 1998.

The Debate About Christ, SCM Press, Ltd., 1979.

Dallmayr, Fred, *The Other Heidegger,* Cornell University, New York, 1993.

Davies, Oliver, *God Within: The Mystical Tradition of Northern Europe,* Darton, Longman & Todd, London, 1988.

Davies, Paul, *The Mind of God,* Simon & Schuster, London, 1992.

Davies, Walter, *Inwardness and Existence. Subjectivity in/and Hegel, Heidegger, Marx and Freud,* Madison, Wisconsin, 1989.

Davies, W.D., *Paul and Rabbinic Judaism,* SPCK, London, 1948.

De Rosa, Peter, *Vicars of Christ: The Dark Side of the Papacy,* Corgi Books, London, 1988.

Dennett, D., *Consciousness Explained,* Little Brown, Boston, MA, 1991.

Donald, Merlin, *Origins of the Modern Mind: Three Stages in the Evolution of Culture and Cognition,* Harvard University Press, Cambridge, Massachusetts, 1991.

Doresse, Jean, *The Secret Books of the Egyptian Gnostics: An Introduction to the Gnostic Coptic manuscripts discovered at Chenoboskion,* 1960.

Durant, Will, *Caesar and Christ,* Simon and Schuster, New York, 1944.

Eckhart, Meister, *A Modern Translation* by Raymond B. Blakney, Harper & Brothers, Publishers, New York, 1957.

Teacher and Preacher, edited by Bernard McGinn, Paulist Press, New York, 1986.

Fernandez-Armesto, Filipe & Derek Wilson, *Reformations: A Radical Interpretation of Christianity and the World 1500-2000,* Scribner, 1996.

Ferre, N.F.S., *Reason in Religion,* Nelson's Library of Theology, Thomas Nelson & Sons, ltd., 1963.

Findlay, J.N., *Ascent to the Absolute,* George Allen & Unwin, London 1979.

Forget, Alain, *How To Get Out Of This World Alive: A Practical Philosophy Toward Consciousness,* Published by Alain Forget, 2006.

Ehrman, Bart D., *Lost Christianities: The Battles for Scripture and the Faith we Never Knew About,* Oxford University Press, 2003. Also: *The Orthodox Corruption of Scripture: The Effect of Early Christological Controversies on the Text of the New Testament,* Oxford University Press, 1993.

Eisenman, Robert, *James the Brother of Jesus,* Faber and Faber, London, 1997.

Forman, R.K.C., "What Does Mysticism Have to Teach Us About Consciousness?", *Journal of Consciousness Studies,* Vol 5, No 2, 1998.

Also: *The Problem of Pure Consciousness: Mysticism and Philosophy,* New York & Oxford: Oxford University Press, 1990.

Fox, Warwick, *A Theory of General Ethics: Human Relationships, Nature, and the Built Environment,* MIT Press, USA, 2006.

Frend, W.H.C., *The Early Church,* Fortress Press, Philadelphia, 1985.

Funk, Robert, *Honest to Jesus,* Hodder & Stoughton, 1996.

Gackenbach, Jayne, An internet discussion between Gackenbach (*Lucidity Letter* Editor) and Professor Charles Tart examining similarities between *Dream Lucidity, Witnessing and Gurdjieffian Self- Remembering.*

Geering, Lloyd, *Christianity Without God,* Polebridge Press, Santa

Rosa CA, 2002.

Geivett, R. Douglas, *Evil and the Evidence for God: The Challenge of John Hick's Theodicy,* Temple University Press, Philadelphia, 1995.

Grant, Patrick, *A Dazzling Darkness: An Anthology of Western Mysticism,* William B. Eerdmans Publishing Company, 1985.

Graves, Robert & Joseph Podro, *The Nazarene Gospel Restored,* publisher not known, 1953.

Green, Celia, *Lucid Dreams,* Hamish Hamilton, London, 1968.

Grotowski, Jerzy, "A Kind of Volcano", an essay in *Gurdjieff,* edited by Jacob Needleman and George Baker, Continuum, New York, 1996.

Gurdjieff, G.I., *Meetings with Remarkable Men,* Routledge & Kegan Paul, London, 1963.

Harrison, Ted, *Stigmata: A Medieval Mystery in a Modern Age,* Penguin Books, 1994.

Heidegger, Martin, *Towards the Definition of Philosophy,* Continuum, 2000.

Heidegger, Martin, *On Time and Being,* translated by Joan Stambaugh, Harper & Row, USA, 1972.

Hick, John, *Evil and the God of Love,* Macmillan, London 1985.

Hillman, James, *The Dream and the Underworld,* Perennial Library, Harper & Row, New York, 1979.

Studies in Jungian Thought, Harper Colophon, 1972.

Inter Views, Conversations with Laura Pozzo on *Psychotherapy, Biography, Love, Soul, Dreams, Work, Imagination, and the State of the Culture,* Harper Colophon Books, 1984.

Insearch: Psychology and Religion, Spring Publications, Ins., Dallas, Texas, 1984.

Heiler, Friedrich, "Contemplation in Christian Mysticism", an essay in *Spiritual Disciplines,* collected papers in the Eranos Yearbook, Bollingen Series XXX.

Hunt, H., "The Truth Value of Mystical Experience", *Journal of Consciousness Studies,* Vol 13, No. 12, 2006.

Inge, W.R., *Mysticism in Religion,* Rider & Company, 1969.

Jaynes, Julian, *The Origin of Consciousness in the Breakdown of the Bicameral Mind,* Houghton Mifflin Company, Boston, 1976.

Jensen, Dr. Peter, *The Future of Jesus,* Boyer Lectures, ABC Books, 2005.

Johnson, Paul, *A History of Christianity,* Penguin Books, London, 1976.

Jonas, Hans, *The Gnostic Religion: The Message of the Alien God and the Beginnings of Christianity,* 2nd Edition, Beacon Press, Boston, 1963.

Jung, Carl, *Psychological Reflections, A New Anthology of His Writings 1905-1961,* Selected and edited by Jolande Jacobi in collaboration with R.F.C. Hull, Routledge & Kegan Paul, *reprint 1974.*

Aion/Researches into the Phenomenology of the Self, 2nd Edition, *Man and His Symbols,* Conceived and Edited by Carl Jung, Picador, 1978.

Bollingen Series XX, Princeton University Press, 1979.

Katz, Steven (ed.), *Mysticism and Philosophical Analysis,* New York, Oxford University Press, 1978.

Kee, Alistair, *The Way of Transcendence,* Pelican Books, 1971.

Keightley, Alan, *Wittgenstein, Grammar and God,* Epworth Press, London, 1976.

Kelly, Edward F. & Kelly, Emily Williams, *Irreducible Mind, Towards a Psychology for the 21st Century,* Rowman & Littlefield Publishers, Inc, USA.

King, Charles William, *Gnostics & Their Remains,* Wizards Bookshelf, Minneapolic, 1973.

Kingsland, William, *The Gnosis or Ancient Wisdom in the Christian Scriptures,* George Allen & Unwin, (2nd impression) 1954.

Kuhn, A.B., *Shadow of the Third Century,* The Theosophical Publishing House, Wheaton, Ill., USA, 1949.

Koestler, Arthur, *The Act of Creation,* Hutchinson, London, 1964.

Janus: A Summing Up, Hutchinson, London, 1978.

Laski, Marghanita, *Ecstasy in Secular and Religious Experience,* Jeremy P. Tarcher, Inc., Los Angeles, 1961.

Layten, Bentley, *The Gnostic Scriptures,* Doubleday, New York, 1987.

Levison, Rev. N., *The Jewish Background of Christianity,* T & T Clarke, Edinburgh, 1932.

Lockhart, Douglas, *Jesus the Heretic,* Element Books, Wiltshire, England, 1997.

The Dark Side of God, Element Books, Wiltshire, England, 1999.

Mangan, Bruce, Language and Experience in the Cognitive Study of Mysticism: Commentary on R.K. Forman, *Journal of Consciousness Studies, Volume 1, No. 2, 1994.*

Maccoby, Hyam, *The Mythmaker: Paul and the Invention of Christianity,* Weidenfeld & Nicolson, London, 1986.

Mack, Burton, *The Lost Gospel: The Book of "Q" & Christian Origins,* Harper, SanFrancisco, 1993.

Malpas, Jeff, *Heidegger's Topology: Being, Place, World,* MIT Press, Cambridge, Massachusetts, 2006. Solomon, Routledge, 1998.

Constituting the Mind: Kant, Davidson and the Unity of Consciousness, International Journal of Philosophical Studies, Volume 7, No. 1.

Maycock, A.L., *The Inquisition,* Constable & Company, Ltd., (2nd edition) 1928.

McGinn, Bernard, *The Foundation of Mysticism: Origins to the Fifth Century,* Vol. 1 of *The presence of God: a history of Western Christian mysticism,* London, SCM Press, 1992.

Meister Eckhart, Teacher and Preacher, edited by Bernard McGinn, Paulist Press, New York, 1986.

Mead, G.R.S., *Fragments of a Faith Forgotten,* University Books, New York, 1960.

Moore, James, *Gurdjieff, The Anatomy of a Myth: A Biography,* Element Books, Shaftesbury, 1991.London,

Morin, Alain, *Journal of Consciousness Studies,* Vol 12, No 4/5, 2005.

Murk-Jansen, Saskia, "Hadewijch and Eckhart", a paper on

Meister Eckhart and the Beguine Mystics, edited by Bernard McGinn, Continuum, New York, 1994.

Musurillo, Herbert A., *The Fathers of the Primitive Church,* Mentor-Omega Books, UDA, 1966.

Needleman, Jacob, editor, *Lost Christianity,* Element Books, Wiltshire 1990.

The Inner Journey/Views from the Gurdjieff Work, Morning Light Press, 2008.

Needleman, Jacob & George Baker, editors, *Gurdjieff/Essays and Reflections on the Man and his Teaching,* Continuum, New York, 1996.

Neumann, Erich, *The Origins of Consciousness,* Bollingen Series, XLII, Routledge & Kegan Paul, 1973.

"Mystical Man", a paper from the Eranos Yearbook, *The Mystic Vision,* Bollingen Series XXX, Vol. 6, Princeton University Press, 1968.

Ouspensky, P.D., *Tertium Organum: A Key to the Enigma of the World,* Routledge & Kegan Paul, London, 1957.

Conscience/The Search for Truth, Routledge & Kegan Paul, London, 1979.

In Search of the Miraculous: Fragments of an Unknown Teaching, Harcourt, Brace & Company, 1949.

The Fourth Way: A Record of Talks and Answers to Questions based on the Teaching of G.I. Gurdjieff, Routledge & Kegan Paul, London, 1957.

Pagels, Elaine, *The Gnostic Gospels,* Vintage Press, New York, 1981.

Beyond Belief/The Secret Gospel of Thomas, Random House, New York, 2005.

Panksepp, Jaak, "The Periconscious Substrates of Consciousness: Affective States and the Evolutionary Origins of the Self", *Journal of Consciousness Studies,* Vol 5, No. 5/6, 1998, p 567.

Parkes, Graham, editor, *Heidegger and Asian Thought,* University of Hawaii Press, Honolulu, 1990.

Pauwels, Louis, *Gurdjieff,* Times Press, Ltd., Isle of Man, 1964.

Petrement, Simone, A *Separate God: The Origin and Teachings of Gnosticism,* originally published as *le Dieu separe: les origunes du gnostisisme* by Les Editions du Cerf, Paris, 1984, and translated by Carol Harrison for Harper SanFrancisco, 1990.

Plotinus: *Key Writings,* Commentary by Elmer O'Brien, A Mentor Book, New American Library, 1964.

Pole, David, *The Later Philosophy of Wittgenstein,* University of London, The Athlone Press, 1958.

Price, H.H., *Belief,* George Allen & Unwin, London, 1969.

Puech, Henri-Charles, "The Concept of Redemption in Manichaeism", papers from the Eranos Yearbook, Bollingen Series XXX, Vol 6 of *The Mystic Vision.*

Rahner, Hugo, "The Christian Mysteries and the Pagan", paper from *The Mysteries,* the Eranos Yearbook, Bollingen Series XXX, 2, 1955.

Rahner SJ, Karl, *Theological Investigations: Jesus, Man and the Church,* Vol 17, Darton Longman & Todd, London, 1981.

Ranke-Heinemann, Uta, *Eunuchs for Heaven: The Catholic Church and Sexuality,* Andre Deutsch, London, 1990.

Rilke, Rainer Maria, *The Notebook of Malte Laurids Brigge,* Oxford University Press, 1984.

Roberts, Bernadette, *The Experience of No-Self,* Shambhala, Boston, 1984.

What is Self?, DeVorss & Company, Distributors, Marina Del Rey, CA, 1989.

Also *What is Self?,* Sentient Publications, LLC, 2005. 1113 Spruce Street, Boulder, CO 80302. www.sentientpublications.com

Robinson, John A., *Exploration into God,* SCM Press, Ltd., London, 1967.

Russell, Bertrand, *A Free Man's Worship,* Unwin Paperbacks, 1976.

Sanders, E.P., *The Historical Figure of Jesus,* Penguin Books, London, 1993.

Sartre, Jean-Paul, *The Transcendence of the Ego: An Existentialist*

Theory of Consciousness, The Noonday Press, a division of Farrar, Straus and Giroux, New York, 1973.

Schonfield, Hugh, *The Pentecost Revolution,* Element Books, UK, 1985.

Those Incredible Christians, Element Books, 1985.

The Passover Plot, Element Books, 1985.

Schumann, Friederich K., *Kerygma and Myth,* edited by Hans Werner Bartsch, and translated by Reginald H. Fuller, SPCK, London, 1960.

Schwitzgebel, Eric, *Journal of Consciousness Studies:* Vol 14, No. 3, March 2007.

Shanon, Benny, "A Psychological Theory of Consciousness", *Journal of Consciousness Studies,* Vol 15, No. 5, 2008.

"Ideas and Reflections Associated with Ayahuasca Visions", *Bulletin of the Multidisciplinary Association for Psychedelic Studies,* 1998.

The Antipodes of the Mind, Charting the Phenomenology of the Ayahuasca Experience, Oxford University Press, 2002.

Searle, J., *Mind, Language & Society: Philosophy in the Real World,* Weidenfeld and Nicolson, London, 1999.

Sheehan, Thomas, *The First Coming,* Random House, New York, 1986.

Shermer, Michael, *How We Believe: Science, Skepticism and the Search for God* (2nd edition) A.W.H. Freeman/Owl Books, 2000.

Simpson, David, Irony, Dissociation and the Self, *Journal of Consciousness Studies,* Vol 15, No. 6, 008.

Smith, D. Moody, *Johannine Christianity: Essays on its Setting, Sources and Theology,* T & T Clark Ltd., Edinburgh, 1987.

Smith, Jody Brant, *The Image of Guadalupe: Myth or Miracle,* Souvenir Press, 1983.

Spong, John Shelby, *Why Christianity Must Change or Die,* Harper, SanFrancisco, 1998.

Staal, Frits, *Exploring Mysticism,* Penguin Books, 1975.

Steiner, George, *Heidegger,* Fontana Press, London, 1992.

Real Presences: Is There Anything in What We Say?, Faber and Faber, London, 1989.

Stoyanov, Yuri, *The Hidden Tradition in Europe: The Secret History of Medieval Christian Heresy,* Arkana/Penguin Books, 1994.

Tabor, James D., *The Jesus Dynasty,* Harper Element, London, 2006.

Tart, Charles, *Waking Up,* Element Books, 1988.

Thiede, Carsten Peter & D'Ancona, Matthew, *The Jesus Papyrus,* Weidenfeld & Nicolson, London, 1996.

Thomson, Evan, "Primates, Monks, and the Mind: The Case of Empathy", *Journal of Consciousness Studies,* Vol 12, No 7, 2005.

Thomas, *The Gospel According to,* edited by Raghavan Iyer, Concord Grove Press, 1983.

Trethowen, Lloyd, *Mysticism & Theology: And Essay in Christian Metaphysics,* Geoffrey Chapman, Publisher, 1975

Underhill, Evelyn, *Mysticism,* Bracken Books, London, 1995.

Vleeschauwer, Herman-J, de, *The Development of Kantian Thought/The History of a Doctrine,* translated by A.R.C. Duncan, Thomas Nelson & Sons Ltd., 1962.

Walker, Benjamin, *Gnosticism: Its History and Influence,* Crucible, 1989.

Walker, Kenneth, *A Study of Gurdjieff's Teachings,* Jonathan Cape, London, 1957.

Venture with Ideas, Luzac Oriental, London, 1995.

Walker, Thomas, *The Teaching of Jesus and the Jewish Teaching of His Age,* George Allen & Unwin, London, (reprint), 1924.

Webb, James, *The Harmonious Circle: An Exploration of the Lives and Work of G.I. Gurdjieff, P.D. Ouspensky and Others,* Thames and Hudson,1980.

Weiss, Johannes, *Earliest Christianity,* Vol 2, Harper Torchbooks, New York, 1965.

Westman, H., *The Springs of Creativity,* Routledge & Kegan Paul, London, 1961.

West, Morris, *A View from the Ridge: The Testimony of a Twentieth-Century Christian,* HarperCollins, 1996.

Wiles, Maurice, "Christianity Without Incarnation", an essay in *The Myth of God Incarnate,* edited by John Hick, CSM Press, Ltd., 1977.

Williams, N. P., *The Ideas of the Fall and of Original Sin,* Bampton Lectures, 1924.

Williams, Archbishop Rowan, *Lost Icons,* T & T Clark. A Continuum Imprint, London 2003.

Woods, Richard, "Mysticism and Social Action: The Mystic's Calling, Development and Social Activity", *Journal of Consciousness Studies,* Vol 3, No. 2, 1996.

Young, Frances, "A Cloud of Witnesses", an essay in *The Myth of God Incarnate,* edited by John Hick, CSM Press, Ltd, 1977.

Zaehner, R.C., *Mysticism, Sacred and Profane: An Inquiry into Some Varieties of Praeter-Natural Experience,* Oxford, Clarendon Press, 1957.

Zlatev, Jordan, "The Dialectics of Consciousness and Language", *Journal of Consciousness Studies,* Vol 15, No. 6, 2008. "The Dependence of Language on Consciousness" (as above).

About The Author

The author of GOING BEYOND THE JESUS STORY is presently an Honorary Research Associate of the University of Tasmania's School of Philosophy, and an Associate Member of the Westar Institute in the USA. During the seventies he spent three years on the Central Committee of the Association for Humanistic Psychology in London, and taught part-time at the Franklin School of Contemporary Studies. The Westar Institute is composed of some two-hundred international New Testament scholars whose declared aim is religious literacy, and this affords him cutting-edge familiarity with the many problems that have surfaced in this thorny area of debate and argument. The Franklin School was similarly involved, being an experimental school set up in '74 to teach and do research in psychology, history, religion and philosophy. The author's teaching endeavors there were under the supervision of a leading UK scientist and philosopher doing research in consciousness, awareness, and pain management. This work entailed the development of experimental techniques in relaxation, meditation and biofeedback procedures, and was done in conjunction with researchers at London's Bart's hospital. For further information please go to www.douglaslockhart.com.

BOOKS

O is a symbol of the world, of oneness and unity. In different cultures it also means the "eye," symbolizing knowledge and insight. We aim to publish books that are accessible, constructive and that challenge accepted opinion, both that of academia and the "moral majority."

Our books are available in all good English language bookstores worldwide. If you don't see the book on the shelves ask the bookstore to order it for you, quoting the ISBN number and title. Alternatively you can order online (all major online retail sites carry our titles) or contact the distributor in the relevant country, listed on the copyright page.

See our website **www.o-books.net** for a full list of over 500 titles, growing by 100 a year.

And tune in to myspiritradio.com for our book review radio show, hosted by June-Elleni Laine, where you can listen to the authors discussing their books.

MySpiritRadio